Fearless

Books by Michele Evans

Michele Evans' Recipes for Beautiful Soup
Michele Evans' All-Poultry Cookbook
Michele Evans' Easy Seafood Recipes
Michele Evans' Recipes You Can Afford
The Salad Book
The Slow Crock Cookbook
American Cuisine Minceur
Fearless Cooking for Men

Cooking for One

Michele Evans

 Simon and Schuster / New York

For Tully, again

Copyright © 1980 by Michele Evans
All rights reserved
including the right of reproduction
in whole or in part in any form
Published by Simon and Schuster
A Division of Gulf & Western Corporation
Simon & Schuster Building
Rockefeller Center
1230 Avenue of the Americas
New York, New York 10020

SIMON AND SCHUSTER and
colophon are trademarks
of Simon & Schuster

Designed by Jeanne Joudry
Manufactured in the United States of America
Printed and Bound by Fairfield Graphics, Inc.

1 2 3 4 5 6 7 8 9 10

Library of Congress Cataloging in Publication Data
Evans, Michele.
Fearless cooking for one.

Includes index.
1.   Cookery.   I.   Title.
TX652.E92   641.5′61   80-265
ISBN 0-671-24416-7

Acknowledgments

I wish to thank the following family members, friends, and acquaintances, who generously shared for this volume their own special recipes, views, and experiences on the subject of cooking for one. They join me in the conviction that eating well when alone is essential to good health, happiness, and well-being.

Helen Abbott, Valerie Anderson, Susan Angel, Melissa Avildsen, Harry Baron, Andrew Bergman, Patricia Brill, John Bunge, Madame Claire, Marian Faux, Cecilia Goodman, Jeff Greenfield, Sheilah Rae Gross, Elouise A. Hetherly, Vera Kock, Suzanne Evans Levi, Ross and Julie McClennan, Elizabeth Ann McGinn, Constance M. Madina, Vance Muse, Marion and Esther Newberg, Angela Pagliaroli, Betty Pappas, Frank Perdue, Tully Plesser, Mario Puzo, Martin Rapp, Roger of Harry's Bar in Venice, Joy Rossi, Sandra Stewart, Sabine Sugarman, Cristin Torbert, Ann Urban, Maria Urtubey, Joseph Wechsberg, and George Willig.

Contents

INTRODUCTION

1. THE FUNDAMENTALS OF COOKING
   FOR ONE   17
   Cooking Equipment, 18
   The Basic Larder, 22
   Four Ingredients That Should Always Be Fresh, 25
   Marketing for One, 25
   Cooking Tips and Reminders, 27
   *The Merits of Leftovers Once You Have Changed the Name
        to Extras*, 28
   Storage Information, 29
   Serving Suggestions, 31
   A Glossary of Important Cooking Terms, 32
   Measurements, 38
   Rules for Cooking and Eating Alone, 39

2. STARTERS   41
   Appetizers and First Courses, 42
   Quick and Easy Appetizers and First Courses, 55

Contents

Spreads, Dips, and Croutons, 58
Soups, 62

3. EGGS   69
Your Own Basket of Egg Dishes, 70
Fifteen Omelet Recipes, 77
Quiches, 84

4. SALADS   87
Tossed and Mixed Green Salads, 88
Vegetable Salads, 94
Poultry, Rice, Seafood, and Beef Salads, 98
Dressings, 106

5. FOURTEEN PASTA DISHES   113

6. GLORIOUS BLACK BEAN DAYS   127

7. BIRDS   133
Fourteen Chicken Breast Entrées, 134
Chicken Legs, Thighs, and Wings, 150
The Whole Chicken (or Half), 159
One Dozen Cornish Game Hens, 161
Duck, 174
Turkey Breast, 176

8. MEATS   179
A Roundup of Beef Dishes, 180
Favorite Ground-Beef Recipes, 186
One Dozen Hamburgers, 189
Easy Veal for One, 197
Great Lamb Solos, 203
Singular Pork and Ham, 210

9. SEAFOOD   221
    Fish, 222
    One Dozen Shrimp Recipes, 234
    Crabmeat, Scallops, Mussels, Soft-shell Crabs,
        and Lobster, 246

10. MEAL-IN-ONE DISHES   257
    Hearty Soups, 258
    Stews, a Ragout, Chilies, and a Casserole, 267
    Sandwiches, 273
    Rice Dishes, Crepes, and Pizzas, 282
    Specialties, 288

11. FRESH SEASONAL VEGETABLES, A–Z   299

12. FOR POTATO EATERS   317

13. STOCKS, SAUCES, AND BUTTERS   331
    Stocks, 332
    Hot and Cold Sauces, 336
    Butters, 340
    Crème Fraîche, 342
    Mustards, 343
    Seasoned Salt, 344

14. DESSERTS   345
    Thirteen Fruit Desserts, 346
    Other Favorite Delicious Desserts, 352

15. SPIRITED DRINKS   369
    Alcoholic, 370
    Nonalcoholic, 374

    INDEX   377

Introduction

Cooking for one is a celebration of privacy. Consider the advantages of the situation: we single diners eat what we like, where we want, at whatever hour suits our schedule, dressed as we please, accompanied by Bach or the Bee Gees, by candlelight, sunlight, or the glow of television.

The solo cook is the producer, creator, performer, director, and audience. Cooking for one is the culinary equivalent of such exhilarating singular experiences as painting, reading, writing, skiing, jogging, surfing, flying, bicycling, swimming, or playing a musical instrument, but it is a most misunderstood occasion.

One evening at a dinner party, a man who has been married most of his adult life learned that I was completing a volume on cooking for one. He asked me directly, "Isn't the whole idea of dining something to share with family and friends? Eating alone is—well, a lonely affair. I'd rather skip a meal completely than eat alone."

Those who share this man's view often do so more from conditioning than from actual experience.

It is remarkable how loneliness disappears when we cook for ourselves. Anticipating a delicious dinner and cooking it feels good. We cook to make others happy, so why not make the effort for ourselves? Living alone and not cooking nourishing meals is personal neglect.

Nearly 16 million of us live alone. We account for nearly a quarter of all the households in America. In the past seven years our numbers have grown by 60 percent.

Impressed with these figures, manufacturers are offering new lines of mini cooking appliances for single households, and food companies are preparing single-serving convenience foods, from soups to desserts.

Whether single or part of a large family, all adults eat alone some of the time because of varied work or social schedules. According to "The National Cooking Survey," conducted by Consensus, Inc., in 1979:

> Three out of four American adults prepare and serve a meal just for themselves from time to time, and 44 million people in the United States cook and dine alone at least once daily. When we include those who cook for one once a week or more frequently, the proportions increase to 45% of all adult men vs. 54% of women, 64% of persons under 30 years of age vs. 58% of persons 60 and older, and 50% of white-collar-job holders vs. 57% of blue-collar workers.

Jeff Greenfield, in his highly praised book *Television, The First Fifty Years*, states, "If there is one consistently dishonest element in every situation comedy—no matter how realistic, how bold, how relevant or controversial it may be, it is that no one in a situation comedy is isolated, alone, atomized. The trend of living alone is becoming a national fact."

In the March 1978 issue of *Gourmet* magazine, Joseph Wechsberg wrote on Kafer, one of Munich's best restaurants and Germany's largest party-catering service:

> Not long ago a rich man in Munich—a devoted Kafer customer—asked Gerd Kafer to arrange his fiftieth birthday party. "A party of one," says Kafer. "He wanted to spend the day alone at his beautiful villa—no wife, no children, no friends, no business associates. He happens to be happily married, and his wife understood. Heaven bless her. The family moved out of the house, and we took over. The customer had given us

carte blanche. Two liveried butlers were installed, and they were there from morning to midnight. It was the king-for-a-day fantasy. We arranged a fine, light lunch of things he enjoyed the most, each dish served by the butlers. A string trio performed discreetly in an adjoining room—Mozart and Champagne. Later in the afternoon, tea and drinks. Then there was a lovely dinner, followed by a theatrical performance. A light midnight supper completed the day, and the butlers left. The next day he called me and said he would never forget his birthday.*

Mr. Kafer's story is probably the ultimate example of elegance and dignity in the single dining experience.

When people who don't often dine alone have the occasion to do so, they tend to feast on huge quantities of foods they like. I certainly had that urge when, in my early teens, I was left on my own for the first time.

My parents went away for a weekend, leaving me in charge of the meals I would be eating. Knowing my interest in food and my love for cooking, they left convinced I would dine well. They gave me too much credit. My secret treats at that time were celery stuffed with cream cheese, baked macaroni and cheese, fresh plums, and crullers from a local bakery. I bought an enormous supply of the ingredients needed for my favorite foods, plus half a dozen crullers, and ate with abandon. I remained ill through Tuesday of the following week, but I learned one important lesson of solitary dining: moderation, moderation, moderation.

We have heard tales of similar eating rampages of single cooks—whether they consume entire bags of popcorn with a pint of ice cream or go on binges of eating the same dish for weeks at a time.

It's not just the spirit that makes dining alone successful. Menu planning, small-portion shopping, proper-sized cooking equipment, and timing are all vital to the single cook's success. Happily, there are many foods that lend themselves to single servings. Concentrate on those and save the roast suckling pig for family or guests.

This collection of recipes is not limited to the obvious standard

---

* Reprinted by permission of Joseph Wechsberg and *Gourmet*.

dishes for one: a mixed salad, a small broiled steak, and a commercial frozen dessert. The dishes range from Mixed Vegetable Terrine to Sautéed Chicken Breast with Walnuts and Sesame Oil to an individual Chocolate Soufflé. They are an accumulation of varied and interesting recipes for single cooks at all levels of expertise.

The recipes and sentiments on the subject of cooking for one contributed by numerous relatives, friends, and acquaintances will inspire, enlighten, encourage, and satisfy individual cooks of either sex, of all ages, married or single.

Fearless cooking for one means more than the courage to dine alone; it means enjoying the pleasure of your own company.

Michele Evans

I think this is the most extraordinary collection of talent, of human knowledge, that has ever been gathered at the White House—with the possible exception of when Thomas Jefferson dined alone.

    —JOHN F. KENNEDY at a White House dinner
    honoring Nobel Prize winners
    in 1961

1. The Fundamentals of Cooking for One

Cooking Equipment

Good-quality cooking equipment is essential to good cooking. Slicing a tomato with a dull knife is a frustrating experience. My grandmother, Eva Lowe, used to say, "A sharp knife is handy as a pocket." Cooking equipment for one is basically the same as that required in any household: a vegetable peeler, a four-sided grater, wooden spoons, wire whisks, etc., but some of the pots, pans, and baking dishes should be smaller in size. Proper-sized pans insure more precise cooking and eliminate burning.

Because so many individuals are cooking for themselves today, manufacturers are coming out with numerous gadgets specially designed for the single cook, such as the tea-for-one machine, the single hot dog steamer, the single hamburger cooker, junior-sized pizza makers, and mini deep-fryers, to name a few. Some of these devices are helpful, but I see them mostly as needless expenses that take up valuable kitchen space. Why buy a specially designed tiny deep-fryer when a heavy, high-sided 3-quart saucepan will accomplish the same job? The saucepan, moreover, can be used for many other purposes as well—for instance, to make soups and sauces and to cook vegetables. Furthermore, most of the new appliances are electric and there are already too many electric cords consuming energy in the kitchen.

Any kitchen will work better if the cooking utensils and equipment are well organized. Instead of keeping whisks, spatulas, slotted spoons, and strainers in various drawers according to size, put them into a 6-inch-high widemouthed crock or jar near the work area. Opening and closing drawers takes time, and if your fingers are wet or covered with food, it can be messy. Also, try hanging racks or a pegboard with hooks to hold utensils and equipment; your tools will be within easy reach and you will have an attractive decor.

Whether you have your pots and pans in open view or stored in kitchen cabinets, a pantry, or the oven drawer, keep them in good condition by thoroughly cleaning them after each use.

The quality of pots and pans is more important than most people appreciate. A heavy aluminum skillet that costs $20 may seem expensive when a thin aluminum pan can be had for $6, but the heavy skillet will last for years if you take care of it, and food will cook much more evenly in it than in the cheap pan.

I prefer carbon-steel knives because they are easy to sharpen and do a great job. Scrub and dry them thoroughly after each use or they will rust. Never put carbon-steel knives in the dishwasher. Store your knives in a wooden knife rack, on a magnetic holder, or in any easily accessible place where they are protected. If you prefer an exposed magnetic holder, be sure it's situated out of the reach of children and pets.

I enjoy collecting cooking equipment, especially when I'm traveling, but space in my kitchen is very limited. Therefore, I don't often use my butter churn, my celery vase, or my English cheese scoop when I'm cooking for myself. Like most treasures, they must be stored. Actually, a relatively small amount of kitchen equipment suffices for efficient cooking. Below are listed those items I consider basic, plus others that could be added to increase efficiency, but they would be luxuries.

SMALL EQUIPMENT

Bottle opener
Can opener
Chopping board (hard wood or plastic, 16 × 18 inches)
Colander
Corkscrew

Grapefruit knife
Four-sided grater
Ice cream scoop
Set of 4 dry measuring cups
2-cup liquid measuring cup
Set of 4 measuring spoons
Set of mixing bowls
Pastry brush
Pepper mill
Rolling pin
Flour sifter
Metal spatula
Rubber spatula
Slotted spoon
Wooden spoons (2)
Strainers (small and medium-sized)
Tongs
Vegetable peeler
Wire whisks (small and medium-sized)

OPTIONAL IMPLEMENTS

Balloon whisk
Cleaver
Food mill
Funnel
Garlic press
Kitchen shears
Ladle
Meat pounder
Melon-ball cutter

POTS, PANS, AND BAKING DISHES

1½-quart saucepan with lid
2½-quart saucepan with lid
5-quart Dutch oven or pot with lid

2-quart double boiler
6-to-8-inch omelet pan (nonstick or French steel)
9-inch straight-sided skillet with lid
10-to-12-inch straight-sided skillet with lid
2 individual ramekins or au gratin dishes (round or oval)
8-by-12-inch baking dish
Small broiling pan
12-by-16-inch roasting pan
3¾-by-7½-inch bread or meat-loaf pan or terrine
Individual soufflé dish (1½-cup capacity)
Custard cups (2)
Individual tart pans (2)
12-by-16-inch baking sheet
1-quart casserole dish with lid
2½-quart casserole dish with lid

KNIVES

Stainless-steel or carbon-steel blades
Small, sharp-pointed paring knife
6-to-8-inch slicing knife
10-to-12-inch chef's or chopping knife
Steel to sharpen knives or the small Zip Zap
Chef's fork

OPTIONAL ELECTRICAL APPLIANCES

Blender
Can opener
Food processor
Mixer
Toaster
Coffeepot

The Basic Larder

Since appetites are often difficult to predict, having a well-stocked larder will enable you to prepare any number of dishes on short notice.

Store supplies in small quantities and replace items when necessary. This may take a little time, but it will save money in the long run. It will also save space. Instead of buying a 10-pound bag of potatoes, buy 1 or 2 pounds at a time.

Keep herbs and spices in tightly sealed containers away from the heat.

Store all dairy products and perishable ingredients (fish, meat, vegetables, and fruits) in the refrigerator, and cover refrigerated ingredients so that they will not absorb unwanted odors or flavors.

This suggested basic larder should be altered according to individual tastes. Don't buy capers if you don't like them.

HERBS AND SPICES

Basil
Bay leaves
Cayenne pepper
Celery seeds
Chili powder
Cinnamon
Coriander
Cumin
Curry powder
Hot pepper flakes
Mint
Dry mustard
Oregano
Nutmeg (whole)
Paprika

Peppercorns
Rosemary
Sage
Seasoned salt
Salt
Tarragon
Thyme
Turmeric

DAIRY PRODUCTS

Butter or margarine
Eggs
Milk
Parmesan cheese
Yogurt

MISCELLANEOUS INGREDIENTS

Baking powder
Baking soda
Bread crumbs (plain and seasoned)
Capers
Chili sauce
Cornstarch
Crackers
Flour (all-purpose)
Gelatin (plain)
Gherkins
Honey
Horseradish
Ketchup
Mayonnaise
Mustard (Dijon-style)
Pasta
Rice (long-grain)
Soy sauce

Sugar
Tabasco sauce
Vanilla extract
Vegetable oil
Vinegar (white and red-wine)
White wine or dry vermouth
Worcestershire sauce

CANNED PRODUCTS

Anchovies
Beef and chicken broth
Coffee
Tea
Tomato paste
Tomato sauce
Tomatoes (whole)
Tuna fish

FRESH FOODS

Garlic
Lemons
Onions
Parsley
Potatoes
Shallots

KITCHEN SUPPLIES

Aluminum foil
Plastic containers of varying sizes for freezing foods, including an
    ice-cube tray with removable individual sections
Plastic wrap
String
Toothpicks
Waxed paper

Four Ingredients That Should Always Be Fresh

Dishes prepared with fresh ingredients are always superior to dishes containing frozen, freeze-dried, dried, or canned products. Unfortunately, fresh foods aren't always available, but there are four ingredients that are abundant everywhere and that greatly improve cooking: onions, garlic, parsley, and whole peppercorns.

Never use onion or garlic salt or powder, dried parsley flakes, or preground pepper. It may cost a few more pennies to keep the fresh ingredients in supply, but the gain in quality is well worth it. The pepper mill is one of the most important implements in the kitchen. Its size and shape are unimportant, as long as it grinds the pepper. If you do a great deal of cooking, a small electric coffee grinder is an excellent pepper mill. In my kitchen, a Turkish brass coffee mill serves as both pepper mill and souvenir of happy spice shopping in Istanbul's Egyptian Bazaar.

Marketing for One

The major shopping guideline for the single cook is to buy top quality in small quantities. This procedure will eliminate waste and repetition of dishes made with the same food and will save money. Sale items in large quantities will spoil before the single cook can use them up, so they're no bargain. Even if the food can be frozen, remember that freezer space is limited and that fresh food is better in taste and quality than frozen food.

Individual eating habits and appetite must be considered. If you squeeze fresh oranges for juice every day, buy oranges in quantity. However, if you decide to make a recipe that includes an apple, but you don't eat raw apples often, buy only one.

Shopping for one is easier in cities than in small towns, because there are large concentrations of single people, and therefore many supermarkets package single portions of meat, vegetables, and fruit.

In rural and suburban areas, small-quantity shopping can prove troublesome. For instance, pork chops may be available only in twelve-chop packages. Be fearless and ask the butcher to break up the package or to cut you one or two chops. I've never had a butcher refuse to do this, but if yours does, shop elsewhere.

Small private butcher shops will usually give you the exact amount you require, but their prices are generally high. It helps to know your butcher and to order from him in advance if possible.

There will be times when you can find the food you need only in a large quantity. The remainder you will have to store. How you store it is crucial. See the section on storage information below.

Many food manufacturers, aware of the increasing number of single cooks, have begun packaging products in smaller quantities. The government has also begun to take an interest in small-quantity shoppers. In 1976 the New York State Department of Agriculture and Markets issued a regulation relating to the sale of small quantities of prepackaged fresh fruits and vegetables for sale in retail markets, which reads in part: "When varieties or grades of fresh fruits or vegetables are not available in unpackaged form and the same are being offered for sale at retail in packaged form, upon customer request a package of fresh fruit or vegetables of the same variety and grade being offered shall be opened to provide any small quantity of fresh fruits or vegetables which the customer desires."

In shopping for one, follow these simple suggestions:

1. A well-balanced diet takes a little planning. With nutrition in mind, try to have at least one food a day from each of these food groups: dairy products, whole-grain products, vegetables or fruits, and meat or seafood.

2. Keep an ongoing list of the food and kitchen supplies you need and add to the list as soon as you run out of an item.

3. Plan menus seasonally for fresh fruits and vegetables. You'll get better-flavored products for less money when the products are available in abundance.

4. Try not to shop when you're hungry. You'll probably end up buying more food than you need.

5. Check grocery store advertisements for sale items.

6. Don't be too rigid in menu planning. If you have lamb on your menu but the spareribs look better at the market, buy the ribs. Compromise should take place when you buy the food, not when you eat it. (If your larder is well stocked, you'll have the ingredients on hand for the barbecue sauce.) The same procedure for buying what is freshest and best applies to seafood, fresh vegetables, fruit, and bread.

7. Never buy poor-quality food, damaged food, dented cans, or overripe vegetables or fruit.

8. Buy small-sized produce items: small heads of lettuce, small cabbages, small onions, etc. Small sizes will most often be called for in recipes for one.

9. Buy whole nuts and whole pieces of cheese, for they have longer shelf life. Chopped nuts become stale faster than whole nuts, and cheese dries out fast once it has been shredded or sliced.

10. Frozen food packages that are swollen may have thawed and been refrozen, so avoid buying them.

Cooking Tips and Reminders

1. Before beginning to cook, read each recipe thoroughly so that you can assemble ingredients, cooking utensils and equipment, and, if necessary, preheat the oven.

2. Determine how much time is needed for every dish in the meal and cook dishes in order, starting with the one requiring the longest cooking time. This is not as difficult as many cooks think, particularly since many dishes can be prepared in advance, or while longer-cooking dishes are on the stove.

3. For more interesting menus, vary cooking methods in a single meal and during the week.

4. Consider presentation in every meal so that dishes are not all one color or texture.

5. To create interesting variations while economizing, use extras from previously cooked dishes.

6. In cooking for one, precise timing and the use of exact portions in individual recipes are vital to the success of every dish. Don't add more of an ingredient because you like it, or use less because it's not your favorite.

7. Follow each recipe suggestion as to what size pot, pan, or baking dish you should use. Cooking a casserole for one in a 5-quart pot will spread the liquid out over too large an area and burn it. It will also dry out the casserole.

8. When a recipe says, "Season with salt and pepper to taste," add seasoning sparingly. More salt or pepper can always be added, but overseasoning usually cannot be undone.

9. For recipes to turn out well, each direction must be followed carefully. If a crushed clove of garlic is listed, don't simply cut one in half; the flavor will be different. If shredded cheese is called for, don't slice it instead.

10. Generally, avoid making substitutions in recipes. If shallots are required, but you only have scallions on hand, you may use the scallions cut as directed in the recipe. But if a recipe calls for apple slices, don't substitute applesauce. Find an apple or make a different dish.

11. Put away ingredients and wash utensils, bowls, and pots as they are used, if time permits. Organization in a kitchen saves time and effort.

12. Try not to taste too often while you're cooking. You can end up eating your dinner standing at the stove.

The Merits of Leftovers Once You Have Changed the Name to Extras

Leftover is an unappetizing word, especially when it refers to food. It connotes a scrap, remnant, surplus, or unwanted remainder. If a restaurant listed Leftover Lamb Stew on its menu, it's doubtful that there would be many orders for the dish, although the taste of lamb stew actually improves after 24 hours.

In cooking for one, you will often have leftovers, but only on this page and in the index will the word *leftovers* appear in this book. I am replacing it with *extras,* because *extras* has the sound of a bonus, which leftovers frequently are. Extras can save you time and money, no inconsequential feat today.

Throughout the book, after individual recipes that result in extras, I add a section called Extras Suggestions. For example, after Broiled Flank Steak with Mustard Pepper Crust, you will find this note:

> EXTRAS SUGGESTIONS: The remaining uncooked half of the flank steak can be wrapped and frozen or used the next day in the recipe for Stir-fried Chinese Beef with Black Bean Sauce. Any extra cooked steak will make an elegant Cold Beef Vinaigrette or a Sliced Steak Sandwich. (See index for recipes.)

Storage Information

Efficient storage of both fresh products and extras from cooked meals contributes to better-quality food that lasts longer.

The refrigerator and freezer are the most important storage spaces we have. Air circulation in the refrigerator causes food to dry, so most foods should be covered to retain moisture as well as to prevent transference of aromas and flavors. However, fruits and certain vegetables like tomatoes and unhusked corn decay quickly in moist surroundings, so store them as far away from the coldest part of the refrigerator as possible and do not crowd them.

Potatoes and onions survive longer in a dry, cool place where air can freely circulate around them at about 60°F.

Cheese should be wrapped tightly so that it won't dry out. The opposite is true of meat, which should be loosely wrapped so that it has breathing space. Cook refrigerated whole cuts of meat within 2 or 3 days of purchase. Cook ground meat, fish, and seafood within 1 or 2 days of purchase. They should be wrapped and stored near the coldest part of the refrigerator.

Never put hot food in the refrigerator. Cool cooked food to room temperature, then cover and refrigerate it.

Chicken and duck should be loosely wrapped, stored in the coldest part of the refrigerator, and used within 2 days of purchase.

To keep eggs from drying out, store them in the carton they come in or in a covered container.

Dairy products (milk, cream, sour cream, butter or margarine, buttermilk, and yogurt) must be covered tightly and kept refrigerated. Nonfat dry milk needs no refrigeration; store it in a cool, dry place, well sealed. After you add water to it, however, it must be refrigerated and treated as regular milk.

Flour, sugar, baking powder, baking soda, and cornstarch should be kept in tightly covered containers at room temperature. Herbs and spices should be stored in small quantities in tightly covered containers at room temperature, away from the heat of the stove or sunlight.

Vegetable, peanut, and olive oil need no refrigeration if bought in small quantities and used within 2 weeks. Keep extra oil refrigerated.

Bread will resist mold longer if refrigerated. Wrapped well and frozen, it will keep for a month or two.

Nuts should be placed in a tightly covered container and refrigerated. If canned, nuts can be stored at room temperature until the can is opened, but then they must be refrigerated or they will quickly become rancid, especially chopped nuts.

Condiments such as mustard, mayonnaise, ketchup, Worcestershire sauce, Tabasco sauce, preserves, jellies, chutney, pickles, relishes, and olives should be refrigerated after they are opened. Seal containers tightly.

Dry beans, lentils, and peas will keep for months stored separately in tightly covered containers in a cool, dry area.

Canned foods should be stored at room temperature away from the heat of the stove and sunlight. After opening a can, remove the contents and store them in a tightly covered container in the refrigerator. (Never buy swollen or dented cans.)

Buy coffee and tea in small quantities and store them in tightly covered containers at room temperature. An opened can of ground coffee may be refrigerated, but it isn't necessary if you use it within a short period of time.

Freezer space for one person is usually limited to the freezing compartment of a refrigerator, so be judicious in selecting the foods you store there. Don't let your freezer turn into Fibber McGee's closet.

Freezer temperature should be at 0°F or lower.

Label freezer food packages not easily identifiable, including the date frozen, and use earliest dated packages first.

Do not freeze fresh fruits and vegetables without at least partially cooking them.

Freeze foods in small quantities for convenience in single servings and for quick thawing time.

Wrap food well in moistureproof paper before freezing.

Frozen foods keep for varying lengths of time. At proper freezer temperature, fish, seafood, pork, ground meat, and cooked meat dishes should be used within 3 months; the sooner the better. Other uncooked meats and chicken keep for 5 to 6 months. Cooked vegetables and fruits keep 7 to 8 months. Butter should be used within 1 month, as should ice creams and sherbets.

Frozen food should remain in the refrigerator or at room temperature for thawing, and it should be cooked immediately after it is thawed.

Serving Suggestions

On a trip through southern Italy, I once saw a fisherman eating his lunch on a tiny table set on the deck of his small boat. He was the picture of contentment, complete with wine bottle, dishes, and silverware, oblivious to everything but his food.

Even with only your own tastes to satisfy, however, cooking and dining alone require a few more decisions than just what to serve. Consider how much time you have to prepare and eat your meal, what you will be eating, where you will be most comfortable, and whether you would like to punctuate your meal with music, a book, or the luxury of silence.

The kitchen table or counter top may be all right for a quick, easy menu, but if you have time and are in the right mood, the occasion of dining deserves a more pleasant setting: candlelight, flowers on the table, and your best linen, china, silver, and crystal. Whether the tone is one of elegance or simplicity, always treat yourself to a proper table setting, the right selection of glassware and utensils, and the most comfortable chair you can find.

Alternate the places where you dine. A tray in bed or in front of the fireplace may be a pleasant change. If you have a sunny terrace or a patio, have at least an occasional alfresco meal, served on a colorful blanket or tablecloth or from a picnic basket. There is something about sitting on pillows on the floor with a meal spread out on a low table that brings out the best in Oriental or Middle Eastern foods, and football fans often get more out of their long Sunday afternoon luncheon scrimmages if they eat off a small serving table in front of the television set.

Lighting needn't be overly dramatic, but just remember that improper lighting will change the look and appeal of whatever you are eating. Make sure you can see your food.

Always dress for dinner, not in a long gown or in black tie necessarily, but in whatever clothes fit your mood. I always change clothes before cooking a dinner for myself, regardless of what I've been wearing all day; anything to make the meal comfortable and, sometimes, a little special.

A Glossary of Important Cooking Terms*

There are many special terms used in cookbooks, and though most of them will be familiar to you, some you may be unsure of, and others

* Glossary and Measurements reprinted from *Fearless Cooking for Men* by permission of Warner Books.

you will not know at all. In order to be a successful cook, it is important to understand exactly what the words in a recipe mean. A few of the terms are self-explanatory; for example, to brush something means to apply an ingredient such as butter or egg yolk to it with a pastry brush. Other terms must be learned. In cooking, for instance, to score something has nothing to do with the playing field. It means to make shallow slits or gashes with a knife or fork in the outer surface of the food.

When you first look over a recipe, if there are any new or unfamiliar terms in it, refer to this glossary to learn exactly what is to be done, *before you begin to prepare the dish.*

I've included the most essential terms and have tried to keep the explanations short and to the point so that you can learn what you need to know quickly and proceed to the cooking well advised.

Al dente—An Italian phrase which means "to the tooth," used to describe pasta that is cooked only to the point of offering the slightest resistance when bitten into.

Aspic—A jellylike substance made with the juices of meat or vegetables with gelatin added, then chilled.

Au gratin—Cooked with crumbs or grated cheese (or both) on top of the dish, the top then browned in the oven or under the broiler.

Au jus—Served with natural juices or gravy, often of beef.

Bake—To cook in an oven by dry, steady heat. Cooking meat by this method is called roasting.

Baste—With a large spoon or pastry brush, moisten food with liquid such as sauce, marinade, butter, or oil during cooking in order to prevent drying out or burning and to add flavor.

Batter—A slightly thickened liquid mixture, such as crepe batter, that can be poured.

Beat—To mix by rapidly stirring by hand or electric mixer.

Blanch—To cook a food briefly in boiling water, in order to remove excess fat in the case of bacon, or to loosen skin from such foods as tomatoes or nuts.

Blend—To combine ingredients evenly, usually with a spoon, in a circular motion.

Boil—To cook liquid until bubbles break on the surface. Water boils at 212°F at sea level.

Bouquet garni—Herbs in a little bag made of cheesecloth. The bag is used to add flavoring to a dish while it's cooking and is discarded when done.

Braise—To brown in a small amount of fat, then cook slowly in a small amount of liquid in a covered pan.

Bread—To coat food with dried bread crumbs in order to form a crisp crust on food that is to be baked or fried.

Broil—To cook under or over direct heat.

Brown—To cook food until it actually turns brown in color either in the oven, under a broiler, or on top of a stove in a pan with a little fat. Browning meat seals in the flavor and makes it appealing to the eye.

Brush—To coat food with fat, egg, or liquid with a pastry brush.

Caramelize—To heat sugar until melted and browned or to coat food with sugar that has browned by this process.

Casserole—A deep, heavy dish with a tight-fitting lid, in which food is baked and served.

Chill—To cool food in a refrigerator until cold but not frozen.

Chop—To cut food into small pieces. Chopped food pieces are larger than minced food pieces.

Clarify—To clear greaseless stock by adding egg whites and shells and simmering for several minutes. The stock is then skimmed and strained. Butter can also be clarified by melting slowly over heat. Milk solids sink to bottom, leaving clear yellow clarified butter. This liquid butter is poured off and used to cook with. Clarified butter burns less quickly than regular butter. It can be refrigerated in a jar with a tight-fitting lid for a few weeks.

Coat—To roll or sprinkle food with a layer of another food such as bread crumbs or mayonnaise.

Cream—To mix a single ingredient or more to a creamy consistency.

Crisp—To wash lettuce or any other vegetable in cold water in order to firm it, or to cook in any manner until food is cooked but still crunchy.

Croutons—Small pieces of bread (sliced or cubed) either fried or toasted until crisp.

Cube—To cut food into uniform cube shapes of small size.

Deep-fry—To cook food totally immersed in hot fat.

Dice—To cut food into small cubes or squares. Diced food pieces are smaller than cubed food pieces.

Dissolve—To mix a dry ingredient with liquid.

Dredge—To coat food with flour, cornmeal, bread crumbs, sugar, or some other ingredient.

Drippings—The fat expelled from meat while roasting or frying.

Fillet—A piece of meat or fish from which all the bones have been removed.

Flake—To break apart a food such as fish with the gentle use of a fork so that it resembles flakes.

Fold in—To blend one mixture with another with a spoon or spatula in a folding motion. The movement is from the bottom up and over ingredients and repeated.

Fry—To cook food in hot fat. Fried food can be cooked immersed in fat or only partly covered.

Garnish—A decoration of some colorful food added to a prepared dish to enhance its appearance.

Glaze—To coat or cover food with a glossy coat called a glaze by covering it with icing, aspic, syrup, or sauce.

Grate—To rub a food over a grater so that it is reduced to tiny particles or thin shreds.

Grease—To lightly coat a surface with butter or oil.

Grill—To cook under or over direct heat.

Grind—To reduce food to a powdery consistency such as that of coffee, pepper, or flour, or to pass it through a meat grinder.

Julienne—To cut food such as carrots, potatoes, or cheese into thin, even strips.

Knead—To repeatedly press, pull, and fold dough into a smooth mass with hands on a flat, lightly floured surface.

Lard—To insert fat into flesh of meat with a special needle to make meat juicier.

Legumes—French for vegetables, including beans, peas, and lentils.

Marinate—To allow a food to rest in a mixture to season and sometimes tenderize it.

Melt—To heat butter or other food and reduce it to a liquid state.

Mince—To cut pieces of food into very small bits.

Pan-broil—To cook in an uncovered skillet over direct heat.

Pan-fry—To cook in a small amount of fat in a skillet.

Parboil—To boil a food until partially cooked. Cooking is then completed by some other method.

Pare—To peel outer skin with peeler or sharp knife.

Peel—To remove outer skin or layer of a food by using sharp knife. If thin-skinned fruits or vegetables, such as peaches or tomatoes, are immersed in boiling water for 8 seconds, their skins will easily be removed with the help of a small pointed knife.

Pinch—Approximately ⅛ of a teaspoon. Usually referring to salt, sugar, nutmeg, etc. Something that can be held between the forefinger and thumb.

Pit—To remove seed from food.

Poach—To simmer food gently in hot liquid.

Preheat—To allow oven (or pan) to reach exact temperature required to cook dish before putting dish in the oven.

Puree—To reduce food to a smooth mixture by use of a sieve, food mill, electric blender, or food processor.

Reduce—To evaporate a liquid by boiling.

Render—To melt solid fat, usually animal fat, such as chicken fat, lard, or suet, by cooking slowly. Also called "to try out."

Roast—To cook food (especially meat) by dry heat in oven or on a spit over heat.

Sauté—To cook a food in a small amount of fat over direct heat in skillet or other pan.

Scald—To heat liquid to the point just before it boils.

Scallop—Layers of food baked with or without sauce in a casserole usually covered with bread crumbs. Also thinly sliced meat, such as veal or lobster.

Score—To make shallow slits or gashes with knife or fork through outer surface of a food (usually fat of roast, etc.).

Sear—To brown meat quickly in a pan over intense heat.

Season—To add flavor to a food by the addition of salt, pepper, or other seasoning, herb, or spice.

Shred—To tear or cut food into thin strips or pieces.

Shuck—To remove covering of food such as the husk of corn or shells of clams or oysters.

Sift—To put dry ingredients through a fine sieve.

Simmer—To cook food gently in liquid just below boiling point.

Skewer—A thin metal or wooden pin on which food is secured and cooked.

Skim—To remove fat or particles from surface of a liquid with spoon, ladle, or skimmer (shallow, perforated disk with long handle). To remove cream from milk.

Sliver—A thin shred of food.

Sponge—A batter made with yeast.

Steam—To cook food by direct steam on a rack placed in deep container holding small amount of boiling water.

Steep—To let substance such as tea stand in a liquid, usually hot water.

Stir—To mix 2 or more ingredients in circular motion with spoon.

Stock—A liquid in which food has cooked.

Tenderize—To soften tough fibers of meat by pounding with an implement resembling a gavel designed for this purpose. Meat can also be tenderized by marination.

Terrine—A baking dish with lid for making pâtés. Usually made of earthenware.

Thicken—To make substance (usually a sauce) become thick by the use of thickening agents such as arrowroot, cornstarch, or eggs, or by cooking food longer to cause evaporation and therefore thickening a sauce or gravy.

Toast—To brown or make crisp.

Truss—To secure legs and wings of poultry or game with a string so that meat will cook more evenly.

Try out—To melt animal fat. Also called render.

Whip—To beat mixture by hand with whisk or electric beater, incorporating air into mixture and increasing its volume.

Measurements

Correct measurements are as basic and necessary to good cooking as quality ingredients are. Fortunately, there are only a few measurements you will need to learn for cooking. The ones listed below are actually liquid measurements, but they also apply to dry ingredients in this cookbook, as in most others. Pints and quarts are used only for fluids. You will need 2 types of measuring cups—dry and liquid. A set of 4 dry measuring cups consists of a ¼-cup, a ⅓-cup, a ½-cup, and a 1-cup. Use these cups to measure exactly a dry ingredient, such as flour or sugar, by filling the cup to the top and then smoothing the top of the ingredient flat with the back of a knife. The liquid cup, which should be a 2-cup size, looks like a pitcher and is marked so that you can pour the required liquid in to the proper measuring mark. You will also need to own a set of measuring spoons: a ¼-teaspoon, a ½-teaspoon, a 1-teaspoon, and a 1-tablespoon.

1 teaspoon	=	⅓ tablespoon
1 tablespoon	=	3 teaspoons
4 tablespoons	=	¼ cup
1 fluid ounce	=	2 tablespoons
1 cup	=	½ pint or 8 fluid ounces
2 cups	=	1 pint
1 quart	=	2 pints
1 gallon	=	4 quarts

OVEN TEMPERATURES IN CENTIGRADE AND FAHRENHEIT

C	F	C	F
100°	= 212°	205°	= 400°
121	= 250	218	= 425
135	= 275	246	= 475
163	= 325	260	= 500
177	= 350	288	= 550

OVEN TEMPERATURE CHART

Very slow	250°F	Moderately hot	375°F
Slow	300°F	Hot	400°F
Moderately slow	325°F	Very hot	450° to 500°F
Moderate	350°F	Broil	500° and over

Rules for Cooking and Eating Alone

DOS

Keep a shopping list of the ingredients you need.

Plan well-balanced menus.

Experiment with new foods and dishes to improve your cooking techniques and skills.

Take the time to shop for quality food.

Get to know your various local food merchants—those who sell meat, produce, fish, etc.

Organize your equipment and ingredients before you begin to cook.

Follow recipe directions closely.

Select where and how you want to set your table before you prepare the meal.

Allow yourself as much time as you would take to have a leisurely meal in a fine restaurant.

Store extra food properly to maintain its quality.

DON'TS

Don't take the easy way out, by eating quick junk foods.

Don't eat standing up.

Don't talk on the telephone during your meal.

Don't get carried away at the stove and eat your entire meal right out of the pots and pans.

Don't rush the preparation or eating of your meal.

Don't cook the same foods day after day.

Don't cook or eat too much.

Don't put off cleaning up the kitchen. Nothing will spoil your enjoyment of dining alone more than awakening to an uncleared table and a sink full of dirty dishes.

2. Starters

Appetizers and First Courses

There is always a tendency to prepare too much food when one is eating alone. In general, if you let your appetite be your guide, each course can end up being a meal in itself. For that reason I don't recommend starting with both an appetizer and a first course or soup. That's just too much food.

Appetizers and first courses should be carefully prepared overtures to a meal. It's too easy to open a bag of potato chips or fill a bowl with peanuts. We may all enjoy these tasty foods, but they are fattening and not very imaginative. I always think of them as airline food, and I know when I'm eating them that I'm not eating very well.

Even the simplest crudities, like raw carrots, cauliflower, or zucchini with a good dip, are far more interesting and nutritious. And a well-made fish or seafood appetizer, pâté, or au gratin dish can be the high point of a meal.

When planning a meal, consider the size of the appetizer or first course; the larger the starter, the smaller the main course should be, and vice versa.

ONION AND ANCHOVY CANAPÉS

3 anchovy fillets, mashed with a fork
¼ teaspoon Dijon-style mustard
2 slices white bread
Mayonnaise (see index for recipe)
1 onion 1½ inches in diameter, very thinly sliced
Olive oil
Freshly ground pepper

Mix the mashed anchovies with the mustard. Trim the crusts from the bread and cut each slice into 4 rounds, using a 1½-inch cookie cutter or the lid of a jar. Spread each round with mayonnaise, then with the anchovy and mustard mixture. Top each with an onion slice. Brush each with olive oil and sprinkle with freshly ground pepper. Place the canapés under a heated broiler until the onion slices sizzle and turn golden.

HAM-FILLED BISCUITS

On Kentucky Derby Day, delectable ham-filled biscuits are traditionally served at breakfasts and luncheons all over Louisville. They are a perfect proof of how delicious simplicity in food can be.

2 hot biscuits
Butter
4 ¼-inch-thick slices cooked smoked ham

Separate the hot biscuits and spread them generously with butter. Place 2 slices of ham on each biscuit bottom and replace the tops.

CHICKEN LIVER PÂTÉ

Chicken liver pâté is a two-meal dish. It provides an appetizer one evening and an open-faced Danish-style sandwich for lunch or dinner the following day. It will keep for 3 days.

    ½ pound chicken livers, with the tough tissue removed
    ¼ cup melted chicken fat or butter
    Salt and freshly ground pepper to taste
    2 tablespoons minced scallions
    Pinch of ground cloves
    Pinch of ground nutmeg
    1 teaspoon Dijon-style mustard
    2 tablespoons Cognac or sherry
    1 tablespoon fresh chopped parsley

In a small saucepan, simmer the livers in just enough water to cover them for about 15 minutes. Drain well and puree in a blender with all the remaining ingredients except the parsley (or force the livers through a food mill and mix in remaining ingredients by hand). Turn the pâté into a small glass bowl or crock, sprinkle with the parsley, and cover. Refrigerate for a few hours before serving.

   Serve half of the recipe as an appetizer with Fried Butter Croutons or Pain Grillé. (See index for recipes.)

EXTRAS SUGGESTIONS: Spread the remaining pâté on pumpernickel and top with thin slices of raw mushrooms and red onion rings.

MELON CUBES WRAPPED IN CHEESE AND PROSCIUTTO

8 1-inch cubes cantaloupe or honeydew melon
4 thin slices Bel Paese cheese
4 thin slices prosciutto

Place one slice of cheese on top of each slice of prosciutto. Cut each combined slice in half lengthwise. Wrap one strip around each melon cube and secure it with a toothpick.

ENGLISH-STYLE CUCUMBER TEA SANDWICH

English afternoon tea appeals to me as a civilized custom. Of course, a cucumber sandwich can be eaten as an appetizer or as a light snack anytime.

2 thin slices firm white bread, such as Pepperidge Farm
1 teaspoon Herb Butter, at room temperature (see index for recipe)
1½ teaspoons Mayonnaise (see index for recipe)
8 very thin slices peeled cucumber
Salt and freshly ground white or black pepper to taste

Place the bread under a baking sheet and press down moderately hard. The bread should be half its original thickness. Trim off the crusts. Spread butter on one slice and mayonnaise on the other. Arrange the cucumber slices on the buttered slice. Sprinkle them with the salt and pepper. Top them with the slice spread with mayonnaise. Cut the sandwich in half, forming two rectangles.

FRESH CRISP VEGETABLES WITH GREEN MAYONNAISE

2 stalks fennel or celery
3 cherry tomatoes
2 cucumber sticks
2 cauliflower florets
2 red or green pepper rings
1 scallion
(Or any combination of fresh raw vegetables)

Green Mayonnaise:

¼ cup Mayonnaise (see index for recipe)
2 tablespoons fresh chopped parsley
½ teaspoon basil
½ teaspoon tarragon
1 teaspoon lemon juice
Freshly ground pepper to taste

Arrange the vegetables on an individual salad plate. Combine the green mayonnaise ingredients in a blender or by hand in a bowl and serve it with the vegetables. (This sauce will be better if it is made in advance and refrigerated for several hours.)

BOILED ARTICHOKE WITH HERBED PEPPER SOUR CREAM SAUCE

1 teaspoon salt
1 large artichoke

Herbed Pepper Sour Cream Sauce:

¼ cup sour cream
1 tablespoon fresh chopped parsley
½ teaspoon tarragon
¼ teaspoon basil
¼ teaspoon oregano
1 teaspoon vinegar
½ teaspoon freshly ground pepper
Salt to taste

Bring 2 quarts of water to a boil in a 3-quart saucepan. Add the salt. Cut off the stem end and ½ inch of the top of the artichoke. Cut off the sharp point of each leaf with a scissors. Place the artichoke in boiling water stem end down and simmer over medium-low heat for 40 minutes or until tender. Turn the artichoke after 30 minutes' cooking time. The artichoke is done when the sharp point of a knife inserts easily into the stem end. Drain it well by resting it stem end up in a wire rack or on paper towels. Combine the sauce ingredients and serve the sauce in a small, shallow bowl.

The artichoke may be eaten at room temperature or well chilled.

CLAMS OREGANATO

6 fresh cherrystone clams, shucked
1½ tablespoons diced green pepper
1½ tablespoons minced roasted red pepper
1 tablespoon minced onion
1 clove garlic, minced
½ teaspoon oregano
1 teaspoon fresh chopped parsley
Salt and freshly ground pepper to taste
2 tablespoons seasoned bread crumbs
2 tablespoons butter

Chop the clams and save the liquid. Put the clams with their liquid in a bowl with the green pepper, red pepper, onion, garlic, oregano, and parsley. Sprinkle the mixture lightly with salt and pepper and combine it well. Spoon equal amounts into 3 clam shells. Sprinkle the mixture with bread crumbs and dot it with butter. Place the shells on a baking sheet under the heated broiler for 4 or 5 minutes until the mixture sizzles.

CREAMED MUSHROOMS ON FRIED TOAST

2 tablespoons butter
5 fresh mushrooms, sliced
Salt and freshly ground pepper
½ cup heavy cream
1 slice firm white bread
3 tablespoons vegetable oil
1 tablespoon Cognac or other brandy
1 teaspoon fresh chopped parsley

Heat the butter in a 9-inch skillet and sauté the mushrooms for 4 minutes over medium-high heat, stirring often. Season with salt and pepper. Remove from heat. Place the heavy cream in a small saucepan and bring it to a boil over medium-high heat. Cook for about 3 minutes, stirring with a wire whisk occasionally until thickened. Meanwhile, trim the crusts from the bread. Heat the oil in the cleaned 9-inch skillet. Fry the bread until it is golden on both sides. Drain the bread on paper towels. Add the Cognac to the cream and cook, stirring, for 1 minute. Add the sautéed mushrooms to the sauce. Spoon the mixture over the fried toast and sprinkle it with the parsley.

CURLY SHRIMP WITH LEMON CAPER SAUCE

3 large shrimp, shelled and deveined
1½ tablespoons butter
1 teaspoon lemon juice
1 teaspoon fresh chopped parsley
3 tablespoons heavy cream
2 teaspoons capers
Salt and freshly ground pepper to taste

Cut each shrimp into 3 strips lengthwise. Heat the butter in a 9-inch skillet and sauté the shrimp for 3 or 4 minutes over medium-high heat, stirring. Remove the shrimp with a slotted spoon. Add the lemon juice, parsley, and heavy cream to the skillet and bring to a boil, stirring. Cook over high heat for 3 minutes. Add the capers and return the shrimp to the pan. Toss and season with salt and pepper.

Serve on toast points.

SHRIMP WRAPPED WITH SNOW PEA PODS

6 fresh snow pea pods
6 small shrimp, shelled, deveined, and boiled
Soy sauce

Drop the snow pea pods into boiling water and remove them in 30 seconds. Drain them and pat them dry. Wrap one snow pea pod around each shrimp and secure with a toothpick. Sprinkle lightly with soy sauce.

Serve with Curried Lemon Mayonnaise. (See index for recipe.)

SAUTÉED TINY SMOKED SAUSAGES WITH MUSTARD

2 teaspoons butter
5 tiny smoked sausages
Dijon-style mustard

Heat the butter in a 9-inch skillet. Sauté the sausages until they are browned.

Serve them with the mustard.

TOMATO MOLD WITH VEGETABLES AND FRESH BASIL

1½ teaspoons plain gelatin
1 5½-ounce can tomato juice
1 tablespoon lemon juice
1 teaspoon Worcestershire sauce
¼ cup chopped raw cauliflower
1 scallion, thinly sliced
2 tablespoons diced green pepper
Salt and freshly ground pepper to taste
2 or 3 large fresh basil leaves

In a cup, soften the gelatin with 1½ tablespoons of cold water. Heat the tomato juice in a small saucepan. Remove from heat. Stir in the softened gelatin. Continue stirring until the gelatin dissolves. Pour the mixture into a bowl and stir in the remaining ingredients through salt and pepper. Pour this mixture into a 1½- to 2-cup mold and refrigerate it for several hours until it is set. Unmold it by dipping the mold into hot water up to the rim for 5 seconds. Invert the mold onto the fresh basil leaves on a plate.

MIXED VEGETABLE TERRINE

1 tablespoon plain gelatin
1½ cups canned clear chicken consommé
1 cup blanched diced carrots
¼ cup blanched diced cauliflower
2 tablespoons cooked green peas
1 tablespoon dry sherry
1 tablespoon fresh chopped parsley

Soften the gelatin in 3 tablespoons of cold water. Meanwhile, heat the consommé in a small saucepan until it is hot but not boiling. Remove the pan from the heat. Stir in the softened gelatin and stir until the gelatin dissolves. Add the remaining ingredients. Pour the mixture into a 1½-to-2-cup mold. Refrigerate it until it sets. Unmold it by dipping the mold in hot water up to the rim for 5 seconds. Invert the mold onto a plate.

Serve with Green Mayonnaise. (See index for recipe.)

NOTE: Other blanched or cooked vegetables in the same quantities can be substituted for the vegetables in this recipe.

HONEYDEW MELON WITH CURRIED SHRIMP, WALNUTS, AND APPLES

4 medium cooked shrimp, chopped
2 tablespoons chopped walnuts
½ apple, cored and sliced
2 tablespoons Mayonnaise (see index for recipe)
1 tablespoon heavy cream
1 teaspoon lemon juice
½ teaspoon curry powder
½ teaspoon sugar (optional)
2 tablespoons chopped chutney
¼ honeydew melon, seeded, peeled, and thinly sliced

Combine the shrimp, walnuts, and apple slices in a bowl. In a smaller bowl, mix together the mayonnaise, heavy cream, lemon juice, curry powder, sugar, and chutney. Pour this mixture over the shrimp mixture and blend. Arrange the melon slices on a plate and spoon the mixture over them.

CELERY ROOT RÉMOULADE

Celery root, or celeriac, is one of the dishes I love to prepare for myself. If there is any left, which is seldom, it tastes better after several days in the refrigerator. If you are unfamiliar with celery root, ask your greengrocer to save one for you when he receives a supply. The subtle flavor is well worth getting acquainted with, especially on a warm summer day.

1 tablespoon fresh lemon juice
1 medium celery root

Mustard Sauce:

5 tablespoons olive oil
1 tablespoon red wine vinegar
2 tablespoons Dijon-style mustard
¼ teaspoon salt
¼ teaspoon freshly ground pepper

Pour 3 cups of water and the lemon juice into a medium-sized sauce-pan and bring to a boil. Peel and quarter the celery root. Cut it into ¼-inch slices and add it to the boiling water. Cook for 2 minutes. Drain immediately in a colander. In a bowl, mix the sauce ingredients with a whisk. Cut the celery root into thin julienne strips and add it to the sauce in the bowl. Toss. Cover and refrigerate for several hours or overnight.

Serve on crisp lettuce leaves as a first course or a light luncheon.

GUACAMOLE

1 small ripe avocado or ½ medium avocado
1 small clove garlic, crushed
1 tablespoon minced onion
1 small tomato, peeled, seeded, and finely diced
    (see instructions below)
1 teaspoon lemon juice
Dash of Tabasco
Salt and freshly ground pepper to taste

Mash the avocado with a fork until it is very smooth. In a bowl, mix the avocado with the remaining ingredients. Cover and refrigerate for 1 hour before serving.

Excellent served as a first course with Fried Plantains. (See index for recipe.)

EXTRAS SUGGESTIONS: If you are left with half an avocado, brush its cut surface with 1 teaspoon of lemon juice, cover, and refrigerate. The following day pour 2 tablespoons of Vinaigrette Sauce (see index for recipe) into the avocado well and serve it for lunch or as a first course. Or peel and cut the avocado into slices and add it to a mixed salad.

HOW TO PEEL AND SEED A FRESH TOMATO

Bring 3 inches of water in a saucepan to a rolling boil. Immerse the tomato in the boiling water for 8 seconds. Remove it with a slotted spoon. Peel off the skin with the aid of a small, sharp, pointed knife.

Cut the tomato in half crosswise. Place one half of it in the palm of your hand and gently squeeze out the seeds. Use a demitasse spoon or your finger to get out any hard-to-remove seeds. Repeat with the other half.

MARINATED MUSSELS

1 dozen mussels
½ cup dry white wine or vermouth
1 clove garlic, peeled and halved
¼ cup olive oil
1 tablespoon lemon juice
½ teaspoon grated lemon rind
1 clove garlic, chopped
1 tablespoon fresh chopped parsley
Dash of cayenne pepper
Salt and freshly ground pepper to taste
2 tablespoons finely chopped pimiento

Scrub the mussel shells with a stiff brush and pull off any beard. Wash them under cold running water. Bring 1 cup of water and the dry white wine to a boil with the halved garlic in a large saucepan. Add the cleaned mussels, cover, and cook for about 6 minutes, until shells open. (Discard any mussels that don't open.) Drain the mussels and put them in a dish to cool. Combine the remaining ingredients except for the pimiento in a blender and puree until smooth. Pour the mixture into a small bowl and add the pimiento. Taste for seasoning. Remove the shells from the mussels and discard them. Arrange the mussels on a plate and spoon the sauce over them. Cover and refrigerate for at least 1 hour before serving.

FRIED SESAME CHICKEN BREAST BITES

1 medium chicken breast, skinned and boned
Salt and freshly ground pepper to taste
½ cup flour
1 egg yolk
⅓ cup water
¼ teaspoon salt and freshly ground pepper
½ cup seasoned bread crumbs
1 tablespoon sesame seeds
Vegetable oil
Soy sauce

Cut the boned chicken breast into bite-sized pieces and season it with salt and pepper. Combine the flour, egg yolk, water, salt, and pepper. Dip each piece of chicken in the flour mixture and then roll it in combined bread crumbs and sesame seeds. Heat ½ inch of oil in a medium-sized skillet and fry the chicken pieces until they are golden on all sides. Drain the chicken on absorbent paper. Sprinkle it lightly with the soy sauce.

Serve the chicken on shredded lettuce.

Quick and Easy Appetizers and First Courses

Our busy schedules often limit the time we have to prepare good starters. Here are several suggestions for using prepared foods and improving them greatly by means of simple additions.

Herring in Cream Sauce with Mustard and Capers

Combine 4 ounces of herring in cream sauce with 1 teaspoon of Dijon-style mustard and 1 tablespoon of capers. Serve it on a bed of crisp lettuce leaves with buttered toast.

Caponata

Combine a small can of caponata with 1 heaping tablespoon of diced cucumber, 1 small sliced scallion, ⅓ cup of white meat of tuna or chicken, 1 teaspoon of vinegar, and 1 tablespoon of toasted pine nuts.

Sardines with Red Onion Rings and Bacon

Drain a small can of boneless, skinless sardines and place the sardines on a slice of buttered pumpernickel. Top with thinly sliced red onion rings and 2 pieces of crisp cooked bacon.

Italian Chicken Salad Cocktail

Combine 3½ ounces of canned boneless chicken with 2 tablespoons of mayonnaise, 1 teaspoon of Dijon-style mustard, 1 tablespoon of capers, 2 tablespoons of chopped black olives, 1 tablespoon of minced onion, and ½ teaspoon of Worcestershire sauce. Serve the mixture on a bed of shredded lettuce.

Ham and Bread Stick Rolls

Spread 3 sesame-seed bread sticks with butter and wrap each in 1 thin slice of ham.

Brioche Filled with Sour Cream and Black Lumpfish Caviar

Cut off the top third of a brioche. Cut out center of bottom two-thirds of brioche. Spoon combined ¼ cup of sour cream, 2 teaspoons of finely chopped onion, and 1 teaspoon of lemon juice over the center. Top with 2 tablespoons of black lumpfish caviar and place the brioche top on the caviar.

Marinated Mushrooms

Empty a small jar of marinated mushrooms into a bowl. Mix in 1 tablespoon of chopped pickle, 1 tablespoon of minced pimiento, 1 small minced scallion, and ¼ teaspoon of freshly ground pepper. Cut a small French roll in half and remove the center bread. Fill the roll with the mushroom mixture, and cover with top of roll.

Marinated Artichoke Hearts in Curry Sauce

Empty a small jar of marinated artichoke hearts into a bowl. Remove the artichokes and cut them into small pieces. Spoon combined ¼ cup of sour cream, 2 tablespoons of the marinade liquid and spices, 1 small chopped tomato, ½ teaspoon of curry powder, and 1 teaspoon of lemon juice over the chopped artichoke hearts and stir well. Serve the mixture on toasted French bread.

Spreads, Dips, and Croutons

PEPPER CREAM CHEESE AND RED SALMON CAVIAR

> Vegetable oil
> 3 ⅓-inch-thick slices French bread
> ¼ cup cream cheese, at room temperature
> ½ teaspoon fresh lemon juice
> ½ teaspoon freshly ground pepper
> 2 tablespoons red salmon caviar

Cover the bottom of a 9-inch skillet with the oil. Sauté the bread slices until they are golden on each side. Drain the bread on absorbent paper and allow it to cool for 5 minutes. Mix together the cream cheese, lemon juice, and pepper. Spread the mixture on the bread slices and top it with equal amounts of caviar.

PIMIENTO CHEESE AND BACON SPREAD

> 3 tablespoons cream cheese, at room temperature
> 1 tablespoon finely chopped pimiento
> 2 crisp cooked bacon strips, crumbled
> ½ teaspoon minced onion
> Freshly ground black pepper

Mix the ingredients well and spread the mixture on Fried Butter Croutons (see recipe on opposite page) or any toasted bread.

PEACH-FLAVORED CREAM CHEESE

¼ cup cream cheese, at room temperature
1 tablespoon finely chopped fresh ripe peach

Combine the ingredients, cover, and refrigerate for several hours or overnight before using. Spread on Fried Butter Croutons or Pain Grillé. (See recipes below.)

ORANGE-FLAVORED CREAM CHEESE

¼ cup cream cheese, at room temperature
1 teaspoon grated orange rind

Combine the ingredients, cover, and refrigerate for several hours or overnight before using. Spread on Fried Butter Croutons or Pain Grillé. (See following recipes.)

FRIED BUTTER CROUTONS

A canapé base can be made of a variety of breads, pastries, or crackers, but fried butter croutons combine crisp texture with a nut-buttery flavor that complements almost any topping.

3 tablespoons Clarified Butter (see index for recipe)
4 ¼-inch-thick slices of French bread

Melt the butter in a 9-inch skillet. Lightly brown the bread slices on each side over medium-high heat. Drain the slices on absorbent paper.

These delicious morsels, whole or cubed, also serve as attractive garnishes to soups, stews, and egg dishes.

PAIN GRILLÉ

Pain grillé is French for grilled bread. In France it is presented in varying sizes and thicknesses, some grilled over charcoal, others simply toasted under a broiler. Both are glorious.

In Monte Carlo, right on the French border, there are several restaurants specializing in pain grillé. Some chefs slice giant round-shaped loaves of French bread (*boules*) into 1-inch-thick pieces and serve the hot, crisp, charcoal-grilled slices with creamy whipped butter. There is never any need to order a first course in these restaurants.

Elsewhere in France pain grillé is most often made from thin bread loaves (*ficelles*), which are toasted under the broiler on both sides to a nutty brown color.

Treating yourself to a loaf of fresh French bread to make pain grillé for one may seem like an extravagance, but it isn't if the remaining bread is used to make sandwiches, French toast, or bread crumbs. And, of course, the extra bread can be effectively frozen.

If there is a good French bakery near you, buy the bread, or if time permits, make several loaves of French Bread from the recipe in this book. (See index for recipe.) Use the bread as needed and freeze the rest.

3 ½-inch slices fresh French bread

Grill the bread under a hot broiler until it is lightly browned on both sides. Pain grillé can be served with pâtés and other first courses or with fish soups, but it is also delicious as an accompaniment to any salad or meal.

Suggested Canapés

The following combinations are some suggested toppings for Fried Butter Croutons or Pain Grillé. (See index for recipes marked *.)

Curried Deviled-Egg Salad* and bacon
Roast beef and sliced cornichon
Scrambled egg with herbs topped with sautéed mushroom slices
Creamy Horseradish Dressing* with baby shrimp
Sautéed Tiny Smoked Sausages with Mustard*
Brie and capers
Orange-Flavored Cream Cheese* topped with sliced pickled beet
Peach-Flavored Cream Cheese* topped with baked or boiled ham
Curried Lemon Mayonnaise* and cooked sliced chicken
Red Pepper Mustard* topped with sardine pieces
Green Mayonnaise* with julienne strips of cucumber
Garlic Butter,* a fresh basil leaf, and a tomato slice topped with a
     few drops of olive oil and freshly ground pepper
Curried Tuna Salad* with toasted sesame seeds
Sour cream mixed with fresh snipped chives, topped with black
     caviar
Pimiento Cheese and Bacon Spread*

SAUTÉED BREAD CRUMBS

     3 tablespoons butter
     ¼ cup fresh bread crumbs made from firm white bread

Heat the butter until the foaming subsides. Add the bread crumbs
and cook, stirring, until they are golden brown. Remove them from
the pan immediately with a spatula.

     Use sautéed bread crumbs as a garnish or over hot cooked vegeta-
bles, salads, or chops and steaks.

FRIED CREPES WITH HONEY BUTTER

> 2 tablespoons butter, softened
> 1½ teaspoons honey
> Vegetable oil
> 2 Basic Crepes (see index for recipe)

Combine the butter and honey and refrigerate them until you are ready to serve. Pour ½ inch of oil into a 9-inch skillet and heat it. Fry the crepes, one at a time, until they are lightly browned on one side and then on the other. Drain the crepes on absorbent paper and serve them with the honey butter.

Soups

COLD CUCUMBER AND YOGURT SOUP

> ¾ cup plain yogurt
> ½ cup shredded cucumber, peeled and seeded
> ¼ cup cold club soda
> 1 teaspoon fresh lemon juice
> 1 teaspoon fresh chopped mint leaves or ¼ teaspoon dried mint
>   leaves
> Salt and freshly ground pepper to taste
> 4 crumbled walnuts
> 1 tablespoon golden raisins (optional)

Combine the ingredients and refrigerate the soup for at least 1 hour. Stir the soup before serving.
   Serve it with toasted pita bread.

ARTICHOKE SOUP

1¼ cups Chicken Broth (see index for recipe)
1 scallion, thinly sliced
1 teaspoon fresh lemon juice
3 cooked artichoke hearts (fresh, frozen, or canned—in that
    order of preference)
Salt and freshly ground pepper to taste
2 tablespoons heavy cream

In a saucepan bring the chicken broth, the scallion, and the lemon juice to a boil. Immediately reduce heat and simmer for 10 minutes. Cut the artichoke hearts into bite-sized pieces. Add them to the pan. Season with salt and pepper. Stir in the heavy cream. Bring to the boil, stirring until the soup thickens slightly.

FRESH GREEN PEA SOUP

2 teaspoons butter
2 tablespoons chopped onion
1½ cups Chicken Broth (see index for recipe)
½ cup shelled fresh peas
1 small carrot, peeled and diced
⅛ teaspoon oregano
Salt and freshly ground pepper to taste

Melt the butter in a 1-quart saucepan. Sauté the onion for 3 minutes, stirring often. Add the broth, peas, carrot, and oregano. Bring to the boil, then reduce heat and simmer for 15 minutes or until the peas are tender. Puree the soup in a blender. Season it with salt and pepper to taste.

FRESH GREENS SOUP

1¼ cups Chicken Broth (see index for recipe)
½ cup cooked fresh spinach, well drained and finely chopped
¼ cup finely chopped watercress
1 teaspoon fresh chopped chives
1 teaspoon fresh lemon juice
1 scallion, thinly sliced
Salt and freshly ground pepper to taste

Bring the broth to a boil in a small saucepan. Add the spinach, watercress, chives, lemon juice, and scallion. When the broth boils again, reduce the heat and simmer for 10 minutes. Puree the ingredients in a blender or force them through a food mill. Return the soup to the pan and heat it to the boil. Season with salt and pepper. Garnish with Fried Butter Croutons. (See index for recipe.)

FRESH HOT TOMATO AND ONION SOUP

1 tablespoon butter
1 tablespoon olive or vegetable oil
½ cup chopped onion
1 small clove garlic, crushed
1 cup chopped tomato, fresh or canned (if fresh, peel)
½ teaspoon basil
Salt and freshly ground pepper to taste
1¼ cups Chicken Broth (see index for recipe)
2 dashes of Tabasco sauce
Grated Parmesan cheese
Fresh chopped parsley
1 tablespoon chopped red onion (optional)

Heat the butter and oil in a saucepan. Sauté the onions and garlic for 5 minutes, stirring. Add the tomato, basil, salt, and pepper and simmer for 8 minutes. Pour in the broth and bring to a boil; then reduce heat and simmer for 10 minutes. Add the Tabasco. Puree the mixture in a blender or force it through a food mill. Strain it and heat it in a clean saucepan. Taste for seasoning. Garnish with the Parmesan cheese, parsley, and onion.

QUICK BLACK BEAN SOUP

Most canned foods, with the exception of tomatoes, tomato sauce, and tuna, are robbed of flavor. Most canned vegetables are practically inedible, but beans, black beans in particular, are hearty and stand up well under canning. This easy recipe attests to that.

1 tablespoon olive or vegetable oil
1 small clove garlic, crushed
1 tablespoon chopped onion
1 tablespoon chopped green pepper
1 cup canned black beans
¾ cup Chicken Broth (see index for recipe)
1 tablespoon dry sherry
⅛ teaspoon cumin
1 bay leaf
Freshly ground pepper to taste

Heat the oil in a 2-quart saucepan. Sauté the garlic and onion with the green pepper for 5 minutes, stirring over medium heat. Add the remaining ingredients and bring to the boil. Immediately reduce heat and simmer for 20 minutes. Check seasoning.

RED LENTIL, RED PEPPER, AND TOMATO SOUP

Red, or Egyptian, lentils are about half the size of regular brown lentils. The salmon-colored lentils are subtle in flavor and cook quickly. Long an admirer of red lentils, I keep a glass jar in the kitchen pantry at all times. They keep indefinitely and can be found in food shops specializing in dried beans, peas, and lentils.

2 tablespoons butter
2 tablespoons finely chopped onion
¼ cup finely chopped red pepper
1 tablespoon fresh chopped parsley
⅓ cup red lentils
½ cup Chicken Stock (see index for recipe)
¾ cup tomato juice
1 teaspoon lemon juice
Salt and freshly ground pepper to taste

Heat the butter in a medium saucepan until the foaming subsides. Sauté the onion and red pepper for 4 minutes, stirring often. Add the remaining ingredients and bring to a boil; then reduce heat and simmer for 20 minutes. Taste for seasoning.

Garnish with crisp, cooked, crumbled bacon or Fried Butter Croutons. (See index for recipe.)

EXTRAS SUGGESTIONS: The extra red pepper can be added to any salad or can be used in Zucchini and Red Pepper Sauté. (See index for recipe.)

SENEGALESE SOUP

  3 tablespoons butter
  2 tablespoons finely chopped onion
  2 tablespoons finely chopped celery
  1 scant tablespoon flour
  ½ teaspoon curry powder or to taste
  1 cup heated Chicken Stock (see index for recipe)
  Salt and freshly ground pepper
  ½ cup heavy cream
  ½ cup cubed cooked chicken

Heat the butter in a small saucepan. Sauté the onion and celery over medium heat for 5 minutes. Stir in the flour and curry powder. Cook for 2 minutes, stirring. Slowly pour in the heated chicken stock and keep stirring until the mixture thickens. Season with salt and pepper. Add the cream and chicken. Cook for 5 minutes. This soup may be served hot or well chilled.

3. Eggs

Your Own Basket of Egg Dishes

Eggs provide endless possibilities in cooking for one because they are conveniently portion-controlled by nature. They supply valuable protein and are excellent for dieting. To minimize calories, boil them in the shell, poach them, or fry them without fat in a nonstick pan.

Compared to other protein-rich foods, eggs are inexpensive. Brown eggs cost even less than white eggs, but they taste the same on the plate.

Although eggs mean breakfast to most Americans, they are also superb for lunch, dinner, or a midnight supper.

Eggs can be fried, baked, boiled, poached, or coddled. They can be served in the shell or on toast—sunny-side up or scrambled, in an omelet, a soufflé, a quiche, or a frittata, in a salad, or as a garnish for hot or cold meat or fish. If any food can be called a Renaissance food, surely the egg deserves the honor.

VALERIE ANDERSON'S SCOTCH EGGS

Valerie Anderson manages the New York office of a British chemical company. Although she is from Cheshire, England, not Scotland, Scotch eggs were a regular dish in the Anderson household. Valerie likes to mix cuisines and has added Italian and Chinese ingredients to the old family recipe. She says, "I never make just one or two Scotch eggs; they are too good. I make four: two as a meal for me and two for extras, which can be reheated in the oven at 300°F for 20 minutes and served sliced on buttered toast later. I have also taken them to the office for lunch."

4 eggs
8 ounces sausage meat
½ teaspoon marjoram
Pinch of crushed red pepper flakes
2 teaspoons Hoisin sauce
1 finely chopped scallion
⅓ cup flour seasoned with salt and pepper
2 eggs, beaten
½ cup Italian-style seasoned bread crumbs
2 cups vegetable oil
½ teaspoon sesame oil

Hard-boil the eggs. Meanwhile, mix the sausage meat with the marjoram, red pepper flakes, Hoisin sauce, and chopped scallion. When the eggs are shelled and cool, dip them in the seasoned flour; then cover them thickly and evenly with the sausage-meat mixture. Then coat them with the beaten egg and cover them with bread crumbs. Heat the vegetable and sesame oils in a skillet just large enough to hold the eggs comfortably. Fry the eggs in hot, but not smoking, oil until the meat is cooked and crisp on the outside. Remove the eggs and drain them on absorbent paper.

Halve two of the eggs lengthwise and serve them on a bed of fresh basil, decorated with tomato slices. Cover and refrigerate the remaining eggs for the next day. Do not freeze them.

POACHED EGGS

2 fresh large eggs
1 teaspoon white vinegar

Fill a 10- to 12-inch skillet with 1½ inches of water and bring it to a boil. Reduce heat to the lowest simmer possible. Break one egg into a saucer and slip it into the water. Repeat with the second egg, keeping eggs as far apart as possible. Cook the eggs for about 4 minutes, until the whites are firm but the yolks are still soft. Lift the eggs out of the water with a slotted spoon or a slotted spatula. Drain them on paper towels. Trim off the egg white evenly with a small sharp knife and serve the eggs immediately.

Poached eggs can also be made in advance. Cook them according to the above directions for 4 minutes or until they are set. Remove and trim. Carefully transfer them with a slotted spoon to a bowl of cold water. If you are not using them within the hour, refrigerate them. (Eggs will keep overnight.) Either drain them and use them cold, or reheat them by immersing them, one at a time with a slotted spoon, in hot, but not boiling, water for 1 minute and then drain.

Poached eggs can be served on plain buttered toast, toasted English muffins, or virtually any bread. Probably the most famous poached eggs dish is Eggs Benedict, which consists of toasted English muffins topped with slices of grilled ham, poached eggs, and Hollandaise Sauce. Poached eggs are also excellent served on top of a hamburger or in rich Beef Broth. (See index for recipes.)

PRINCE CHARLES'S SCRAMBLED EGGS
    WITH SMOKED SALMON

A *Time* magazine cover story on Prince Charles of England revealed that when dining alone he prefers light meals; a particular favorite dish mentioned in the piece was scrambled eggs with smoked salmon.

The following recipe is guaranteed to make the single diner feel like royalty.

3 eggs
1 tablespoon heavy cream
Salt and freshly ground pepper to taste
1 tablespoon butter
¼ cup smoked salmon, cut into small pieces

In a bowl beat the eggs and heavy cream lightly and season them with salt and pepper. Heat the butter in a 9-inch skillet. When the foaming of the butter subsides, add the egg mixture and cook over medium heat for 15 seconds, stirring with a tablespoon. Scatter the salmon over the eggs and stir until the eggs are cooked to the desired consistency.

Serve them with buttered toast points, a green salad, and a glass of chilled white wine.

EGG BAKED IN CREAM

½ teaspoon butter
3 tablespoons heavy cream
1 large egg
Salt and freshly ground pepper to taste

Grease an individual ramekin or baking cup, no more than 3 inches in diameter, with the butter. Pour 1 tablespoon of the heavy cream into the dish. Break the egg into the center of the dish. Cover it with the remaining cream. Place the dish in a small baking pan with enough water in it to come halfway up the side of the dish. Cook in a preheated 375°F oven for 8 minutes or until the egg is just set and soft inside. Season it with the salt and pepper.

CECILIA GOODMAN'S SUNDAY SCRAMBLED EGGS

   3 eggs
   2 tablespoons heavy cream
   1 tablespoon cream cheese, at room temperature
   2 tablespoons butter
   4 fresh mushrooms, thinly sliced
   2 cooked link sausages, crumbled
   Salt and freshly ground pepper
   ½ teaspoon freshly chopped chives

Mix the eggs, cream, and cream cheese in a blender or beat them vigorously with a whisk. Melt 1 tablespoon of the butter in a skillet and sauté the mushrooms for 3 minutes, stirring. Add the remaining butter. When it is melted, pour in the egg mixture and sprinkle it with the sausage and salt and pepper to taste. (Because sausage already contains a goodly amount of salt, use the salt sparingly.) Cook the eggs over medium heat, turning them with a tablespoon until they are cooked to the desired consistency. Sprinkle them with chives.

FRENCH TOAST

French toast served with maple syrup or fruit preserves along with crisp cooked bacon, sausages, or grilled ham has long been a tradition in my family. Although my sister and I always considered it a breakfast or luncheon treat, it is a satisfying meal at any hour of the day. The secret to making good French toast is in the bread. Challah and French sourdough bread make the best French toast. Firm white or whole wheat bread is also good.

> 2 eggs, beaten
> Salt and freshly ground pepper to taste
> 3 1-inch slices of challah, French sourdough, or other bread
> 1½ tablespoons Clarified Butter (see index for recipe)

Beat the eggs in a shallow bowl. Season them with salt and pepper. Soak the bread in the eggs, coating each side evenly for 10 seconds. Heat the butter in a 12-inch skillet (nonstick, if possible), and fry the bread until it is golden brown on one side. Then turn it with a spatula and brown it on the other side.

Serve it immediately with maple syrup or preserves, or sprinkle confectioners' sugar over the top.

VANCE MUSE'S HUEVOS RANCHEROS

Vance Muse is the author of *Don't Buy a Car Made on Monday*. He says, "The breakfast I make most every weekend, as a transplanted Texan, is *huevos rancheros*, or ranch eggs; a simple, eye-opening Tex-Mex dish that assumes rare poignancy when cooking for oneself in New York City." Here are Vance's careful directions.

¾ cup pinto beans for *frijoles*
1 tablespoon picante sauce (commercial brand)
2 tablespoons chopped onions
Butter
2 fresh eggs
4 tortillas
Taco sauce (commercial brand)
Freshly ground black pepper

"Have *frijoles* on hand, which you make by mixing about ¾ cup of cooked and seasoned pintos with about a tablespoon of picante sauce in a blender. (Canned *frijoles*, or refried beans, will do in a pinch.) While the *frijoles* are heating with the chopped onions in a small, lightly oiled skillet, select a Freddie Fender album and put on the stereo. Return to kitchen, and gently crack the eggs into a moderately hot buttered skillet to prepare them 'over.' Remove the *frijoles* when they're warm (don't let them dry out) and spoon them onto your plate. Heat a few tortillas in the skillet or on a griddle—do this with haste, and don't let the tortillas burn. Place eggs on top of *frijoles*, dash on a bit of taco sauce (watch out—it's hot), and pepper the whole creation. Treat the tortillas as you would biscuits; you may roll them around the *frijoles* and eggs, or butter them as a side dish.

"Nice complements: tomato slices, jalapeño peppers, cheeses. And, of course, coffee."

Fifteen Omelet Recipes

As a breakfast, lunch, dinner, or late-night supper, an omelet is especially well suited to the solo cook's repertoire. Omelets are quickly prepared, nourishing, inexpensive, and, if made properly, delicious.

Almost any food can be added to enhance an omelet, but watch out for ingredients like eggplant or tomatoes, which produce a lot of moisture and therefore require special attention. An omelet is a great way to use extras from previously cooked meat, seafood, and vegetable dishes.

This section's omelet recipes should spark the creation of your own omelet formulas with the ingredients that you like best.

For the cholesterol-conscious, this section has a cholesterol-free omelet made with egg whites, and a low-cholesterol omelet made with 1 egg yolk and 3 egg whites.

BASIC OMELET

> 1 tablespoon butter
> 3 eggs, beaten
> Salt and freshly ground pepper
> ½ teaspoon fresh chopped parsley

Heat the butter in a 7- to 8-inch omelet pan. When the foaming of the butter subsides, add the eggs, after you have seasoned them with salt and pepper. Immediately stir the eggs with a fork in a full circular motion, picking up the eggs from the bottom of the pan. This procedure cooks eggs evenly. When the eggs begin to set, smooth them over the entire surface of the pan with the back of a tablespoon. Tilt the pan slightly and gradually begin turning the omelet over and over on itself from the elevated side until it is rolled into the bottom corner of the pan. Turn it out onto a warmed plate. Sprinkle it with parsley.

Twelve Omelet Variations

Crouton, Prosciutto, and Parmesan Cheese

> 2 or 3 thin slices prosciutto or boiled ham, chopped
> 1 tablespoon fresh grated Parmesan cheese
> ¼ cup crisp Fried Butter Croutons (see index for recipe)

Stir the prosciutto and cheese into the basic omelet mixture and cook until the eggs begin to set. Sprinkle the croutons over the surface of the eggs. Tilt the pan and begin folding the omelet over, inch by inch, covering the croutons. Turn it out onto a warmed plate.

Aux Fines Herbes

> 1 teaspoon fresh chopped parsley
> 1 teaspoon fresh chopped tarragon or ¼ teaspoon dried tarragon
> 1 teaspoon fresh chopped basil or ¼ teaspoon dried basil

Add the parsley, tarragon, and basil to the basic omelet recipe before cooking and follow the directions for the basic omelet.

Cheese and Rice

> 2 tablespoons Gruyère, Swiss, or Cheddar cheese, shredded
> ¼ cup cooked plain, fried or wild rice or wild rice mixture,
>   warmed in oven

Add the shredded cheese to the basic omelet recipe and cook according to directions until the eggs begin to set. Spread the eggs over the bottom of the pan. Spoon the rice over the omelet surface and tilt the pan. Turn the eggs over, inch by inch, covering the rice, and then turn the omelet out onto a warmed plate.

Spanish-Style Ground Beef

 1 tablespoon raisins
 1 tablespoon butter
 1 tablespoon finely chopped shallots
 ½ clove garlic, minced
 2 ounces ground beef
 ¼ teaspoon oregano
 1 tablespoon chili sauce
 Salt and freshly ground pepper to taste
 2 tablespoons toasted pine nuts

Soak the raisins in water for 15 minutes. Drain them and pat them dry. Heat the butter in a 9-inch skillet. Add the shallots and garlic and sauté, stirring for 4 minutes. Stir in the beef and cook it until its pink color disappears. Add the oregano, chili sauce, salt, and pepper. Stir and cook for 2 minutes. Add the raisins and pine nuts. Set the mixture aside. Follow the directions for the basic omelet to the point where the eggs are beginning to set. Spread the eggs over the bottom of the pan. Spoon the mixture across the center of the eggs. Tilt the pan and begin to fold the eggs over, completely covering the filling. Turn the omelet out onto a warmed plate.

Mushroom and Sausage

> 2 sausage links
> 1 tablespoon butter
> 4 fresh mushrooms, very thinly sliced

Sauté the sausage links until they are browned. Chop them and set them aside. Heat the butter in a 9-inch skillet and sauté the mushrooms over medium-high heat for 4 or 5 minutes. Combine the sausage and mushrooms. Follow the basic omelet directions until the eggs begin to set in the pan. Spread the eggs over the bottom of the pan. Spoon the sausage and mushroom mixture over the surface of the eggs, tilt the pan, and begin folding the eggs over, covering the filling. Turn the omelet out onto a warmed plate.

Mixed Julienne of Vegetables with Dill

> 10 thin julienne strips of fresh carrot, about 3 inches long
> 10 thin julienne strips of fresh celery, about 3 inches long
> 10 thin julienne strips of fresh zucchini, about 3 inches long
> 1 tablespoon butter
> 1 cup hot Chicken Stock (see index for recipe)
> 1 teaspoon finely chopped dill and several dill sprigs

Prepare the julienne vegetable strips. Heat the butter in a 9-inch skillet. Add the vegetables and sauté them over medium-low heat for 3 minutes. Add the dill sprigs and the chicken stock. Bring the liquid to a boil, then reduce heat and simmer for 5 minutes. Drain the vegetables and pat them dry. Prepare the basic omelet recipe to the point where the eggs are spread over the bottom of the pan. Line the vegetables in a row across the center of the omelet and sprinkle it with the chopped dill. Tilt the pan and fold the omelet over, completely covering the vegetables. Turn the omelet out onto a warmed plate.

Shrimp and Tomato

> Dash or two of Tabasco

¼ teaspoon basil
3 or 4 large cooked shrimp, chopped
1 small, ripe, firm tomato, peeled, seeded, and chopped

Add a dash or two of Tabasco and the basil to the basic omelet recipe and proceed with the recipe until the eggs begin to set in the pan. Spread them over the bottom of the pan and top them with the shrimp and tomato pieces. Tilt the pan and begin folding the eggs over until the filling ingredients are completely covered. Turn the omelet out onto a warmed plate.

Salami, Green Olives, and Onion

1 tablespoon butter
¼ cup diced salami
2 tablespoons green olive slivers
2 tablespoons chopped onion

Heat the butter in a 9-inch skillet. Sauté the diced salami over medium-high heat for 2 minutes. Remove the salami to a side dish and mix it with the olive slivers. Add the onions to the pan and cook them for about 3 minutes. Combine the onions with the salami and olive mixture. Follow the basic omelet recipe until the eggs are spread over the bottom of the pan. Top the eggs with the salami mixture, tilt the pan, and begin folding over the omelet until the filling ingredients are completely covered. Turn the omelet out onto a warmed plate.

Cranberry and Crème Fraîche

2 tablespoons Crème Fraîche (see index for recipe) or sour cream
3 tablespoons cranberry sauce
½ teaspoon grated orange rind

Follow the basic omelet recipe until the eggs are spread over the bottom of the pan. Spoon the *crème fraîche* and the cranberry sauce across the center of the eggs. Sprinkle the grated orange rind over the surface. Tilt the pan and begin folding the eggs over, completely covering the filling. Turn the omelet out onto a warmed plate.

Ham and Chutney

> ⅓ cup diced cooked ham
> 2 tablespoons chutney

Follow the basic omelet recipe until the eggs are spread over the bottom of the pan. Spoon the ham and chutney across the center of the eggs. Tilt the pan and begin folding the eggs over, completely covering the filling. Turn the omelet out onto a warmed plate.

Red Salmon Caviar, Sour Cream, and Chives

> 2 tablespoons sour cream
> 2 tablespoons red salmon caviar
> ½ teaspoon fresh snipped chives

Follow the basic omelet recipe until the eggs are spread over the bottom of the pan. Spoon the sour cream and red caviar across the center of the eggs. Sprinkle chives over the surface. Tilt the pan and begin folding the eggs over until the filling is completely covered. Turn the omelet out onto a warmed plate.

Sautéed Potatoes and Spinach

> 1 tablespoon butter
> 1 tablespoon vegetable oil
> ½ cup diced blanched potatoes, drained
> Salt and freshly ground pepper to taste
> ¼ cup cooked chopped spinach, well drained
> ½ teaspoon paprika

Heat the butter and oil in a 9-inch skillet. Sauté the potatoes until they are crisp and golden brown. Drain them and season them with salt and pepper. Follow the basic omelet recipe until the eggs are spread over the bottom of the pan. Spoon the potatoes and spinach across the center of the eggs. Tilt the pan and begin folding the eggs over until the filling is completely covered. Turn the omelet out onto a warmed plate.

EGG-WHITE OMELET

> 3 egg whites
> Salt and freshly ground pepper to taste
> 1 teaspoon fresh chopped parsley
> 1 tablespoon margarine
> 3 tablespoons fat-free cottage cheese, at room temperature
> 1 teaspoon fresh chopped chives

Beat the egg whites for 10 seconds. Add the salt, pepper, and parsley. Heat the margarine in an omelet pan. Add the egg whites and stir them in a circular motion until they begin to set. With the back of a spoon spread the whites so that they cover the pan evenly. Spoon the combined cottage cheese and chives onto the center of the egg whites. Tilt the pan and begin folding the omelet over the filling, a little at a time. Turn the omelet out onto a warmed plate.

ONE-EGG-YOLK OMELET

> 3 egg whites
> 1 egg yolk
> ½ teaspoon fresh chopped parsley
> ¼ teaspoon basil
> 1 tablespoon chopped pimiento
> Salt and freshly ground pepper to taste
> 1 tablespoon margarine

Beat together the egg whites, the yolk, the parsley, the basil, the pimiento, and the salt and pepper. Heat the margarine in the omelet pan. Pour the egg mixture into the pan. Stir in a circle until the eggs begin to set. Smooth the eggs over the pan bottom with the back of a spoon. Tilt the pan to one side and fold the eggs over a little at a time. Turn the omelet out onto a warmed plate.

Quiches

QUICHE LORRAINE

PASTRY:

> ½ cup all-purpose flour
> 2½ tablespoons cold butter
> ⅛ teaspoon salt
> 1 tablespoon ice-cold water
> ½ teaspoon all-purpose flour

FILLING:

> 1 tablespoon butter
> 2 tablespoons finely chopped onion
> 2 strips crisp cooked bacon
> ½ cup loosely packed shredded Swiss, Gruyère, or Cheddar
>   cheese
> 1 large egg
> ⅓ cup light cream
> ⅛ teaspoon salt
> Dash of nutmeg

Make the pastry half an hour before actually baking the quiche. In a bowl combine the ½ cup of flour, the butter (cut into little pieces), and the salt with a pastry blender or a table knife by chopping until the ingredients are incorporated into fine crumbs. Add the water and mix with a fork until the pastry rolls off the side of the bowl. Immediately form it into a ball. Roll it out on a lightly floured board to a circle 7 to 8 inches in diameter. Fit it into an individual 4- to 6-inch pie plate. Crimp the edges. Refrigerate the shell for 30 minutes.

Place an 8-inch sheet of aluminum foil in the pie shell and fill it with dried beans. Turn the edges of the foil over the beans. Bake the shell in a preheated 400°F oven for 10 minutes.

Remove the pie shell from the oven. Lift out the beans with the foil. (When cool, these beans may be stored in a jar and used for the same purpose again.) Sprinkle the remaining ½ teaspoon of flour onto the pie shell. This helps absorb the liquid filling and keeps the crust from becoming soggy.

Meanwhile, prepare the filling. Heat the butter in a small skillet and sauté the onion for 3 minutes, stirring occasionally. Remove the skillet from the heat. Sprinkle the onion, bacon, and cheese over the bottom of the pie shell. Combine the remaining ingredients and pour them over the pie filling. Reduce the heat to 350°F and bake for 25 to 30 minutes, until the filling is puffy. The quiche can be tested for doneness by inserting a knife in its center. When the knife comes out clean, the quiche is done.

QUICHE VARIATIONS

The onion, bacon, and cheese used in the basic Quiche Lorraine recipe can be replaced with any of the following ingredients. Put them in the partially baked pie shell before adding the egg and cream mixture.

Leek

Cut the white part of a small clean leek into thin slices. Sauté it in 1 tablespoon of butter for 5 minutes, stirring often. Sprinkle it over the bottom of the partially baked pie shell and sprinkle also 1 teaspoon of fresh chopped parsley.

Sausage

⅓ cup cooked crumbled bulk sausage

Mushroom

Thinly slice 3 fresh mushrooms and sauté them for 5 minutes in 1 tablespoon of butter. Chop them very fine and wrap them in one corner of a clean dish towel. Twist the cloth around the mushrooms, squeezing out as much liquid as possible. Spread them over the pie shell.

Spinach

⅓ cup well-drained chopped cooked spinach

Salmon and Dill

Line the partially baked pastry shell with 1½ ounces of chopped smoked salmon. Sprinkle over that 2 minced shallots and 1 teaspoon of chopped fresh dill or ¼ teaspoon of dried dill. Pour the egg mixture over these ingredients and bake according to the basic quiche Lorraine recipe.

4. Salads

Tossed and Mixed Green Salads

Every time I hear someone refer to his salad days, I think of a crisp, fresh, green salad with a good vinaigrette sauce, and the expression takes on a different meaning. Salad days should vary with the seasons of the year, not the seasons of life.

Depending on the season, the common available salad greens include arugula, Bibb, Boston, chicory, endive, Chinese cabbage, escarole, iceberg, leaf lettuce, romaine, dandelion, spinach, and watercress. When possible, shop for greens at local farm markets.

Never soak lettuce leaves in water. Instead, wash lettuce carefully under a gentle stream of cold running water. Either dry the leaves in a salad spinner or spread them out on a clean dishcloth or paper towels, roll them up, and refrigerate them until you are ready to use them. This second technique refreshes, or crisps, the lettuce.

After preparing a salad, use the highly perishable extra ingredients like lettuce and cucumbers as a base or addition to soups, cooked vegetables, or stir-fry dishes.

Even when cooking for one, you can expand your salad horizons far beyond greens and vegetables. Consider creative salads made of seafood, fish, meat, cheese, eggs, fruit, lentils, beans, or rice, and don't forget extras remaining from yesterday's meals that will perform well as salads today.

Avoid overburdening salads with sauces or dressings. Coat salad ingredients lightly so that there will not be a pool of dressing left in the bottom of the bowl.

ARUGULA AND ENDIVE SALAD

  1 small bunch fresh arugula, washed and dried
  1 small Belgian endive, cut into 1-inch lengths on a diagonal
  ¼ cup mandarin orange sections
  1 scallion, thinly sliced
  ¼ cup Mustard Vinaigrette Sauce (see index for recipe)

Combine the arugula, endive, mandarin orange sections, and scallion. Pour the sauce over the salad and toss.

MINI CAESAR SALAD

  3 to 4 medium-sized romaine lettuce leaves
  2 tablespoons olive oil
  1 clove garlic, quartered
  2 finely chopped anchovies
  Freshly ground pepper
  1 egg, boiled for 1 minute
  2 teaspoons fresh lemon juice
  1 teaspoon Worcestershire sauce
  ¼ cup fried or toasted croutons
  1½ tablespoons grated Parmesan cheese

Break the lettuce leaves into bite-sized pieces and put them in a salad bowl. In a blender or by hand in a small bowl, combine the oil, garlic, and anchovies. Season them with the freshly ground pepper. Pour this mixture over the lettuce and toss. Add the egg, lemon juice, and Worcestershire sauce and toss again. Sprinkle the salad with the croutons and Parmesan cheese and toss a final time. Serve immediately.

CREAMY COLESLAW

1 cup shredded cabbage
½ carrot, peeled and shredded
½ teaspoon celery seeds
¼ cup heavy cream
½ tablespoon sugar
1½ tablespoons white vinegar
Salt and freshly ground pepper

Combine the cabbage, carrot, and celery seeds in a bowl. Beat the cream with the sugar, vinegar, and salt and pepper to taste until it is thickened. Pour it over the cabbage, carrot, and celery seeds. Toss well.

PIQUANT CELERY SLAW

3 stalks celery, root ends trimmed and leaves removed
1 small onion, thinly sliced
½ small red pepper, trimmed, seeded, and cut into thin strips
2 tablespoons white vinegar
½ teaspoon sugar
¼ teaspoon salt
Freshly ground pepper to taste
⅓ cup sour cream
1 tablespoon vegetable oil
½ teaspoon Dijon-style mustard

Combine the celery, onion, and red pepper in a bowl. Mix the remaining ingredients well and pour them over the vegetables. Toss. Cover the slaw and refrigerate it for at least 2 hours. Mix it again and taste it for seasoning.

ENDIVE AND PIMIENTO SALAD

2 medium Belgian endives, cut into 1-inch lengths and separated
1 whole pimiento, diced
1 large scallion, thinly sliced
¼ cup Fresh Herb Vinaigrette Sauce (see index for recipe)

In a bowl combine the endives, pimiento, and scallion. Add the vinaigrette sauce and toss.

ROMAINE LETTUCE AND ORANGE SALAD

3 romaine lettuce leaves, broken into bite-sized pieces
1 navel orange, peeled and cut into sections
2 thin slices red onion, separated into rings
3 tablespoons Lemon Vinaigrette Sauce (see index for recipe)

Place the lettuce leaves, orange sections, and onion rings in a salad bowl. Pour the dressing over them and toss.

FRESH SPINACH SALAD

1½ cups cleaned spinach, broken into bite-sized pieces
4 mushrooms, thinly sliced
4 strips crisp cooked bacon, crumbled
2 tablespoons minced red onion
¼ cup Mustard Vinaigrette Sauce (see index for recipe)

Combine the salad ingredients and pour the sauce over them. Toss well.

NOTE: If I have any bean sprouts or water chestnuts, I add a small amount to this salad.

ROSS McCLENNAN'S TOMATO AND BASIL SALAD

When Ross McClennan was two years old, his family made a quick trip to New York. Julie, Ross's mother, and I had a chance to catch up on each other's lives while we lunched on salad and cold roast beef. Ross would have nothing to do with the roast beef, but he asked for a second salad of tomatoes and basil. He even helped himself to our salads while his second was being prepared. At that early age Ross was already blessed with good taste, because the tomatoes were perfectly ripe, fresh garden tomatoes and the leafy basil bits were fresh too. I'm waiting to see if he ends up with a career in food.

> 1 fresh ripe medium-sized tomato
> 2 basil leaves, cleaned and cut into small pieces
> ¼ cup Vinaigrette Sauce (see index for recipe)

Slice the tomato crosswise into about 8 slices and arrange the slices across a salad plate. Sprinkle the basil pieces over the tomato slices and pour the vinaigrette sauce over them.

SUZANNE EVANS LEVI'S SPINACH SALAD AND STRAWBERRY YOGURT LUNCHEON

My sister Suzanne belongs to the school of thought that believes in reading when you're eating alone. She told me, "Eating alone is a great indulgence. Only recently, when my youngest son, Jamie, started full school days was I able to eat a meal by myself at home. Part of the indulgence is eating the food I prefer, salads and yogurt mixed with fruit, but the main delight for me is having the time to read. There has never been or never will be enough time for reading all that I would like to. I always put my anticipated solitary lunch on a tray and eat it in front of the fireplace, on the patio, or in bed. It's very peaceful and cozy. I eat slowly and read in between bites for an hour or so."

Spinach Salad

> 2 cups fresh spinach pieces
> 1 hard-boiled egg, chopped
> 3 cooked asparagus spears, cut into 1-inch lengths
> 2 tablespoons sunflower seeds or unsalted natural chopped nuts
> Several thin rings of red onion

Safflower Vinaigrette:

> 2 tablespoons safflower oil
> 2 teaspoons fresh lemon juice
> 1 teaspoon Dijon-styled mustard
> Salt and freshly ground pepper to taste

Place the salad ingredients in a large individual salad bowl. Beat the vinaigrette ingredients in a small bowl with a wire whisk and pour the dressing over the salad. Toss.

Strawberry Yogurt

> 1 cup plain yogurt
> 5 fresh strawberries, chopped
> 1 tablespoon honey

Combine the ingredients in a blender.

Other fruits, such as a ripe peach or 2 apricots or ½ cup of blueberries or raspberries, can be substituted for the strawberries.

Vegetable Salads

BROCCOLI SALAD

1½ tablespoons olive oil
1 small clove garlic, finely minced (optional)
1 cup blanched broccoli, chopped into ½-inch pieces

DRESSING:

1½ tablespoons olive oil
1 tablespoon white wine vinegar
½ teaspoon Dijon-style mustard
⅛ teaspoon basil
⅛ teaspoon oregano
Salt and freshly ground pepper to taste

Heat the oil and sauté the garlic for 2 minutes over medium heat. Add the broccoli and cook it for 3 minutes, gently stirring every 30 seconds. Place the broccoli in a bowl.

Whisk together the dressing ingredients. Pour the dressing over the broccoli and gently toss. Cover the salad and refrigerate it for several hours or overnight.

CARROT AND POTATO SALAD

1 carrot, peeled, diced into ½-inch cubes
1 medium potato, peeled
1 tablespoon finely chopped onion
2 tablespoons Mayonnaise (see index for recipe)
1 tablespoon white vinegar
½ teaspoon Dijon-style mustard
1 teaspoon fresh chopped parsley
Salt and freshly ground pepper to taste

Cook the carrot and the potato in separate pans with 3 cups of boiling lightly salted water until they are tender. Drain them, and while the potato is still hot, cut it into 8 pieces. Place the carrot and the potato in a bowl with the remaining ingredients. Mix the salad gently but well. Cover it and refrigerate it for several hours before serving.

CARROT AND RAISIN SALAD

    1½ tablespoons Mayonnaise (see index for recipe)
    1½ tablespoons heavy cream
    ½ teaspoon sugar
    Pinch of salt
    Freshly ground pepper to taste
    2 medium carrots, peeled and grated
    ¼ cup raisins
    1 small scallion, thinly sliced

Beat together the mayonnaise, heavy cream, sugar, salt, and pepper. Add the carrots, raisins, and scallion. Toss, cover, and refrigerate for 1 hour. Toss again before serving.

LETTUCE COLESLAW

    1¼ cups shredded romaine lettuce
    1 small carrot, peeled and grated
    ½ small onion, cut into very thin slices
    1 tablespoon fresh chopped parsley
    2 tablespoons Mayonnaise (see index for recipe)
    2 tablespoons sour cream
    2 teaspoons vinegar
    1 teaspoon Dijon-style mustard
    ½ teaspoon sugar

Toss the lettuce, carrot, onion, and parsley in a salad bowl. Combine the remaining ingredients and pour them over the lettuce mixture. Combine well and serve immediately.

SWEET AND SOUR KRAUT SALAD

  1 8-ounce can sauerkraut
  ¼ cup golden raisins
  1 heaping tablespoon honey
  1 teaspoon grated orange rind
  ½ teaspoon caraway seeds

Place the sauerkraut in a colander and rinse it thoroughly under cold running water. Drain it well. Combine it with the remaining ingredients and refrigerate for 1 hour.
  Serve this salad with roast Cornish game hen or cold cuts.

CHERRY TOMATO, MUSHROOM, AND
CUCUMBER SALAD

  5 cherry tomatoes, halved
  4 fresh mushrooms, thinly sliced
  A 2-inch piece of fresh cucumber, peeled, seeded, and thinly
    sliced
  3 tablespoons Vinaigrette Sauce (see index for recipe)

Combine the vegetables, pour the dressing over them, and mix well. Serve immediately or chill for 1 hour and then serve.

TOMATO AND RED ONION SALAD

  1 medium-large ripe tomato, thinly sliced
  1 medium red onion, thinly sliced
  1 teaspoon fresh chopped parsley
  ¼ cup Mustard Vinaigrette Sauce (see index for recipe)

Make layers across a salad plate of alternating tomato and onion slices. Add the parsley to the vinaigrette sauce, mix, and pour it over the tomatoes and onions. Cover and refrigerate for 1 hour before serving.

TOMATO STUFFED WITH RICE AND MINT SALAD

> 1 large fresh ripe tomato
> ½ cup cold cooked rice
> 1 teaspoon finely chopped fresh mint or ½ teaspoon dried mint
> 1 teaspoon minced scallion
> 1 heaping tablespoon raisins
> 2 tablespoons vegetable oil
> 1 teaspoon white wine vinegar
> ½ teaspoon lemon juice
> Salt and freshly ground pepper to taste

Cut off the stem end of the tomato. Scoop out the inside of the tomato with a melon ball cutter or a teaspoon. Combine the remaining ingredients. Taste for seasoning. Cut 1/16 of an inch off the bottom end of the tomato so that it will stand up on a plate. Spoon the rice mixture into the tomato. Garnish with a sprig of mint.

MARINATED FRESH VEGETABLE SALAD

> 4 fresh mushrooms, sliced
> 4 snow pea pods, blanched and cut into 3 pieces each on the
>   diagonal
> ½ small red or green pepper, seeded, cored, and chopped
> ½ cup thinly sliced zucchini
> 4 water chestnuts, thinly sliced
> ½ cup fresh bean sprouts
> 5 cherry tomatoes, halved
> ½ cup Vinaigrette Sauce (see index for recipe)

Place all the vegetables in a bowl. Pour the vinaigrette sauce over them and toss well. Cover and refrigerate for several hours, tossing the mixture occasionally during that time.

Serve this salad on a fresh bed of lettuce.

E<small>XTRAS</small> S<small>UGGESTIONS</small>: Any previously cooked or blanched vegetable, such as lima beans, green beans, or broccoli pieces, may be added or substituted in this salad.

GREEK SALAD

 1 medium tomato, cut into wedges
 8 peeled cucumber slices, halved
 8 Greek olives or domestic black olives
 2 slices red onion, broken into rings
 1 teaspoon freshly chopped parsley
 ¼ cup crumbled feta cheese
 ¼ cup Lemon Vinaigrette Sauce (see index for recipe)
 2 romaine lettuce leaves

In a bowl combine the tomato, cucumber, olives, onion, parsley, and cheese. Pour the vinaigrette sauce over them and gently toss. Place the lettuce leaves on a salad plate and top them with the mixed salad.

Poultry, Rice, Seafood, and Beef Salads

CHINESE-STYLE CHICKEN SALAD

 ¾ cup cooked chicken, cut into thin julienne strips
 1 scallion, sliced
 2 tablespoons Mayonnaise (see index for recipe)
 1 teaspoon lemon juice
 ¼ teaspoon sesame oil (available in Chinese grocery stores and specialty food shops)
 ½ teaspoon Dijon-style mustard
 6 snow pea pods, blanched for 2 minutes in boiling water and cut into quarters on the diagonal

Salt and freshly ground pepper to taste
¾ cup shredded lettuce

Combine all the ingredients except the lettuce. Make a circle with the lettuce on a dinner plate and pile the chicken salad in the center.

CHICKEN, CAPER, AND ANCHOVY SALAD

1 cup cooked cubed chicken
1 tablespoon capers
3 or 4 anchovy fillets, chopped
¼ cup Vinaigrette Sauce (see index for recipe)
1 cup crisp lettuce pieces

Combine the chicken, capers, and anchovies. Pour the vinaigrette sauce over them and toss. Spoon the salad over the lettuce pieces on a large salad plate garnished with black olives and orange wedges.

CHICKEN AND ORANGE SALAD

1 cooked chicken breast, chopped into bite-sized pieces
½ cup fresh orange segments
3 water chestnuts, finely chopped
1½ tablespoons Mayonnaise (see index for recipe)
1 tablespoon orange juice
1 tablespoon chopped red onion

Combine the ingredients and chill the salad in the refrigerator, covered, for at least 1 hour.
Serve it on a bed of lettuce pieces.

DUCK AND ORANGE SALAD

    Meat from half a roast duck, cut into strips
    1 small orange, peeled and with pith removed, cut into sections
    1 scallion, thinly sliced
    3 tablespoons Lemon Vinaigrette Sauce (see index for recipe)

Combine the ingredients.
    Serve this salad on a bed of Chinese or other lettuce.

CURRIED DEVILED-EGG SALAD

    2 hard-boiled eggs, chopped
    2 tablespoons Mayonnaise (see index for recipe)
    1 teaspoon white vinegar
    ¼ teaspoon Dijon-style mustard
    ½ teaspoon curry powder
    ½ teaspoon minced onion
    2 sautéed fresh or 2 canned mushrooms, minced
    1 tablespoon minced green pepper
    Salt and freshly ground pepper to taste
    1 tablespoon chutney (optional)

Combine the ingredients and serve them on toast or in an avocado
half. Sprinkle the salad with paprika.

RICE SALAD

    1 cup cold cooked rice
    2 tablespoons diced green pepper
    1 scallion, sliced
    1 carrot, peeled and grated

1 small tomato, peeled, seeded, and chopped
1 tablespoon fresh chopped parsley
¼ cup Mustard Vinaigrette Sauce (see index for recipe)

Gently combine the rice and vegetables in a bowl with a fork, tossing them lightly. Pour the vinaigrette sauce over them and toss again.

LOBSTER SALAD

¼ pound cooked lobster meat, cut into bite-sized pieces
1 tablespoon Mayonnaise (see index for recipe)
1 tablespoon heavy cream
1 teaspoon lemon juice
1 teaspoon fresh chopped parsley
Salt and freshly ground pepper to taste
½ teaspoon fresh snipped chives

Combine the ingredients and chill well.

Serve on a bed of crisp lettuce leaves with a wedge of lemon and Pain Grillé. (See index for recipe.)

VARIATION: Add 1 teaspoon of fresh chopped tarragon or ¼ teaspoon of dried tarragon or ½ teaspoon of Pernod or to taste.

LOBSTER SALAD CARIBBEAN STYLE

1 1-pound cooked lobster, meat removed
1½ tablespoons Mayonnaise (see index for recipe)
1 tablespoon lime juice
½ teaspoon Dijon-style mustard
¼ teaspoon grated lime rind
½ teaspoon tarragon
Salt and freshly ground pepper to taste
2 romaine lettuce leaves, shredded
1 small tomato, peeled and cut into thin strips
2 teaspoons chopped onion
2 tablespoons Vinaigrette Sauce (see index for recipe)
1 whole romaine lettuce leaf

Cut the lobster meat into medallions or bite-sized pieces. Combine the mayonnaise, lime juice, mustard, lime rind, tarragon, salt, and pepper. Pour the mixture over the lobster and toss. Gently mix the shredded lettuce, tomato strips, and chopped onion with the vinaigrette sauce. Place the lobster salad in the center of the whole romaine lettuce leaf on a serving dish. Arrange the mixed shredded lettuce salad alongside the lobster-filled lettuce leaf. Serve at once.

SALADE NIÇOISE

3 romaine lettuce leaves, broken into bite-sized pieces
1 small tomato, cut into wedges
1 cold boiled potato, sliced
¼ pound cold cooked green beans
6 black olives
4 anchovy fillets, cut into ½-inch lengths
1 3½-ounce can white-meat tuna, drained
⅓ cup Mustard Vinaigrette Sauce or as needed (see index for recipe)

Cover the bottom of a large individual salad bowl with the lettuce pieces. Arrange the remaining ingredients except for the vinaigrette over the lettuce, with the tuna in the center. Pour the vinaigrette over the salad and toss just before serving.

EXTRAS SUGGESTIONS: Salade Niçoise is an excellent home for steamed extras such as asparagus, broccoli, snow pea pods, or zucchini.

NEW ORLEANS SHRIMP SALAD

    3 romaine lettuce leaves, broken into bite-sized pieces
    8 medium boiled shrimp, peeled, deveined, and cut into
        3 pieces each
    3 strips crisp cooked bacon, crumbled
    1 small tomato, cut into wedges
    2 tablespoons chopped green pepper
    1 small dill pickle, chopped
    1 scallion, thinly sliced
    1 stalk celery, sliced
    1 hard-boiled egg, sliced
    ¼ cup Mustard Vinaigrette Sauce plus a dash or two of Tabasco
        (see index for recipe)

Line a salad bowl with the lettuce leaves. Arrange the shrimp, bacon, vegetables, and egg on top. Pour the salad dressing over all and gently toss.

TUNA AND CHEESE SALAD

    1 3½-ounce can white-meat tuna, drained
    ¼ cup ¼-inch cubes of Cheddar cheese
    1 stalk celery, finely chopped

1 tablespoon grated onion
1 teaspoon lemon juice
1 teaspoon capers
3 tablespoons Mayonnaise (see index for recipe)
Salt and freshly ground pepper to taste

Flake the tuna thoroughly with a fork and combine it with the remaining ingredients.

Serve it on a bed of lettuce pieces with black olives

CURRIED TUNA SALAD

1 3½-ounce can white-meat tuna
2 tablespoons diced green pepper
2 tablespoons diced celery
1 teaspoon grated onion
1 teaspoon toasted sesame seeds
½ teaspoon curry powder
3 tablespoons Mayonnaise (see index for recipe)
½ teaspoon soy sauce
Salt and freshly ground pepper to taste
2 romaine lettuce leaves, shredded
1 small banana, peeled and sliced lengthwise
1 heaping tablespoon chutney (optional)

Combine well the ingredients through the soy sauce. Season the mixture with the salt and pepper. Arrange it on the lettuce leaves and garnish with the banana and chutney.

Curried tuna salad makes delicious sandwiches, too.

TUNA SALAD WITH SAUCE GRIBICHE

1 cup bite-sized Boston lettuce leaves
1 3½-ounce can white-meat tuna, drained

Sauce Gribiche:

¼ cup Mayonnaise (see index for recipe)
2 teaspoons minced onion
1 small gherkin, minced
1 teaspoon fresh chopped parsley
¼ teaspoon dill weed
¼ teaspoon tarragon
2 teaspoons lemon juice
1 hard-boiled egg
Salt and freshly ground pepper to taste

Combine all the sauce ingredients except for the egg and the salt and pepper. Separate the egg; mash the yolk and mince the white. Mix them both into the sauce. Season to taste with the salt and pepper. Refrigerate the sauce for several hours. Arrange the lettuce pieces on a salad plate. Invert the tuna from the can onto the lettuce, taking care to keep its shape. Spoon the sauce over the top.

COLD BEEF VINAIGRETTE

6 ounces cooked beef (roast beef, sirloin, London broil, or filet
mignon), thinly sliced and cut into julienne strips
1 tablespoon sliced cornichon or other pickle
1 tablespoon minced scallion
¼ cup Mustard Vinaigrette Sauce (see index for recipe)
Fresh watercress

Combine the beef, cornichon, and scallion. Pour the mustard vinaigrette sauce over the mixture and toss. Spoon the salad over a bed of watercress.

Serve it with French bread and butter and a dry red wine. Cheese is also a good accompaniment.

Dressings

I spent the summers of my youth on my grandparents' farm in northern Texas. All the food we ate was grown, raised, or prepared on the farm, and my grandmother was an excellent cook. The taste of everything was so good that I remember meals as the major events of my happy times there.

Curiously, the closest thing to salad we ever had was a platter of succulent, thickly sliced tomatoes or a bowl piled high with crisp sliced cucumbers in an icy marinade of vinegar water with salt and pepper. We never had a true salad dressing.

My family lived in Kansas, where I was introduced to the orange variety of bottled French dressing. Salad at home consisted of iceberg lettuce, grated carrots, tomato wedges, and rings of onions topped with the orange mystery blend. I never did like it.

The first authentic vinaigrette sauce I ever tasted was in a French restaurant in Chicago. From that day forward, using bottled dressings or mixing packaged concoctions would be only a last resort. Today I'd rather eliminate salad from a menu than ruin it with a premixed dressing.

Much to my dismay, I have found that the major reason people use premixed dressings is to save time. But freshly made dressing, which is far superior to, and less expensive than, commercial brands, takes only a minute or two to compose. If time is truly the disadvantage it has for you, make it by the pint.

The art of salad dressing is one of the least fearful aspects of cooking. Here are some suggestions aimed at converting users of commercial dressings.

1. Keep ingredients such as oils, vinegars, herbs, spices, and seasonings for salad dressing together in one specific area in the kitchen.

2. Make a pint of a particular favorite dressing at a time. Store it in a tightly sealed jar in the refrigerator.

3. Practice the art of salad dressings, creating your own original

blends. Demonstrate this talent for company at home or when you are visiting your family or friends.

I learned in a Cordon Bleu course in London to put all the ingredients in a small bowl or pitcher and mix them by rubbing the handle of a small wire whisk between both hands for 15 seconds. If the oil and vinegar proportions are right, the dressing will quickly emulsify.

BASIC VINAIGRETTE SAUCE

> 2 tablespoons olive or vegetable oil
> 1½ teaspoons red wine vinegar or to taste
> ½ teaspoon Dijon-style mustard
> Salt and freshly ground pepper to taste

Combine the ingredients in a small bowl or cup and beat with wire whisk.

Makes about ¼ cup.

VARIATIONS: The following ingredients may be added to or substituted for those in the basic vinaigrette sauce recipe to vary the flavor:

Anchovy: Add 1 mashed anchovy.

Blue Cheese: Add 1 tablespoon of crumbled blue cheese.

Caper and Red Onion: Add 1 tablespoon of capers and 2 teaspoons of finely chopped red onion.

Cornichon and Onion: Replace the vinegar in the basic vinaigrette recipe with 2 tablespoons of the liquid in a jar of cornichons. Add 1 tablespoon each of minced cornichon and cocktail onions.

Fresh Herb: Add 1 teaspoon of fresh chopped parsley, 1 teaspoon of fresh chopped tarragon, and 1 teaspoon of fresh chopped basil.

Garlic: Add 1 small clove of garlic, minced, to the basic vinaigrette. Beat and strain before using.

Italian: Add ½ clove of crushed garlic, ¼ teaspoon of oregano, ⅛ teaspoon basil, and a pinch of red pepper flakes.

Lemon: Replace the vinegar in basic vinaigrette recipe with 2 teaspoons of fresh lemon juice and ¼ teaspoon of grated lemon peel.

Mustard: Increase the mustard in the basic vinaigrette recipe to 1 teaspoon.

Oriental: Replace the vinegar in the basic vinaigrette recipe with 1 teaspoon of lemon juice, ¼ teaspoon of sesame oil, and 1 teaspoon of soy sauce.

Roquefort: Add 1 tablespoon of crumbled Roquefort cheese.

ONION VINAIGRETTE

    2 tablespoons olive or vegetable oil
    2 teaspoons red wine vinegar
    ¼ teaspoon Dijon-style mustard
    ½ tablespoon minced onion
    Salt and freshly ground pepper to taste
    1 teaspoon fresh chopped parsley

Mix the dressing well with a wire whisk.

Makes about ¼ cup.

Serve it with tomato and cucumber slices or Green Beans Cap Cruz. (See index for recipe.)

RUSSIAN DRESSING

    ¼ cup Mayonnaise (see index for recipe)
    1 tablespoon chili sauce
    2 teaspoons chopped gherkins
    ½ teaspoon gherkin pickle juice
    ½ teaspoon lemon juice
    1 teaspoon finely chopped scallion greens (optional)

Beat all the ingredients together in a bowl. Cover the bowl and refrigerate the dressing until it is well chilled.

Makes about ⅓ cup.

LOW-CALORIE TOMATO YOGURT DRESSING
WITH MINT

2 tablespoons plain yogurt
2 tablespoons peeled, seeded, and chopped tomato
1 teaspoon chopped fresh mint or ¼ teaspoon dried mint
1½ teaspoons fresh lemon juice
¼ teaspoon Seasoned Salt (see index for recipe)
Dash of Tabasco sauce
Freshly ground pepper to taste

Puree all the ingredients in a blender or force the tomatoes through a sieve and then blend them with the other ingredients. Taste for seasoning.

Makes a little over ⅓ cup.

DIET COTTAGE CHEESE DRESSING

¼ cup low-fat cottage cheese
1 tablespoon buttermilk or plain yogurt
½ scallion, minced
⅛ teaspoon celery seeds
½ clove garlic, crushed
1 tablespoon chopped green pepper
1 teaspoon fresh chopped parsley
1 teaspoon white wine vinegar
Salt and freshly ground pepper

Put all the ingredients in a blender and puree them. Taste the dressing for seasoning.

Makes a scant ½ cup.

MAYONNAISE

2 large egg yolks
½ teaspoon salt
1 teaspoon dry mustard
Dash of cayenne pepper
2 tablespoons white vinegar or to taste
2 cups vegetable, peanut, or olive oil or a combination of
    vegetable or peanut oil and olive oil (Mayonnaise made
    with olive oil will have stronger flavor.)

Beat the egg yolks in a large shallow bowl with a wire whisk until they are creamy and lemon-colored. Beat in the salt, dry mustard, cayenne pepper, and half of the vinegar. Blend thoroughly. Drop by drop, beat in the oil, continually whisking until the mixture thickens. Gradually increase the quantities of oil as you beat until it is completely used. Slowly beat in the remaining vinegar, tasting as you work. Place the mayonnaise in a jar, cover it tightly, and chill it. Store it in the refrigerator and use it as needed.

Makes a little over 1 pint.

NOTE: Since mayonnaise is something we keep on hand for many dishes, it is sensible to make a substantial amount. See also Curried Lemon Mayonnaise and Green Mayonnaise in the index.

HERB VINAIGRETTE SAUCE WITH DILL

2 tablespoons vegetable or olive oil
1 scant tablespoon red wine vinegar
¼ teaspoon tarragon
½ teaspoon dill weed
⅛ teaspoon basil
1 teaspoon freshly chopped parsley
¼ teaspoon salt
Freshly ground pepper to taste

Combine the ingredients in a small bowl or a glass. Beat them vigorously with a small wire whisk.

ONE PINT OF VINAIGRETTE WITH HERBS

> 1½ cups olive or vegetable oil
> ½ cup red wine vinegar
> 2½ tablespoons Dijon-style mustard or to taste
> 2 scant teaspoons salt
> Freshly ground pepper to taste
> 2 tablespoons fresh chopped parsley
> 1 teaspoon basil
> 1 or 2 fresh sprigs tarragon or 1 teaspoon dried tarragon
> 1 sprig fresh rosemary (if available; otherwise omit)

Put all the ingredients in a jar. Seal the lid tightly. Shake the jar vigorously. Store the dressing in the refrigerator, tightly covered. It will last for 2 weeks. Use it as needed.

CREAMY HORSERADISH DRESSING

> 2 tablespoons Mayonnaise (see opposite page for recipe)
> 1 tablespoon heavy cream, beaten until frothy
> 2 teaspoons fresh grated horseradish
> Salt and freshly ground white pepper to taste

Combine the ingredients well.

Makes about ⅓ cup.

CRANBERRY DRESSING

2 tablespoons Mayonnaise (see page 110 for recipe)
1 tablespoon cranberry sauce, drained and chopped
½ teaspoon grated orange rind
Pinch of fresh grated nutmeg
1 teaspoon grenadine

Blend the ingredients together and refrigerate the sauce for 1 hour. Mix it thoroughly before serving. Serve with sliced roast chicken, pork, or ham.

5. Fourteen Pasta Dishes

An embarrassingly insatiable desire for pasta has led me along many delicious avenues of northern and southern Italy and Sicily. I've also tasted marvelous pasta dishes in France, in England, and, of course, here at home.

I've learned that almost any food can go into properly cooked pasta to make an exciting dish. These dishes can range from simple spaghetti and butter seasoned with salt and pepper to hearty rigatoni and sardines with a basil and tomato sauce.

Pasta is great for the single cook because it can be cooked in any quantity and it stores well.

For me, the fourteen pasta recipes that make up this section are better reminders of past travels than any photograph or souvenir.

Store-bought pasta is available in numerous shapes and sizes, including ditali, fedelini, fettucine, fusilli, lasagne, linguini, orzo, penne, rigatoni, shells (conchiglie), spaghetti, spaghettini, tubettini, vermicelli, and ziti.

Most Italian imported pasta is really better in quality than domestic brands, so it is worth searching for.

Though all pasta is made with essentially the same dough, the shape determines how it tastes, how it should be served, and with what sauce. Thin, light pasta—orzo, ditali, or tubettini—takes a light sauce or can be served in soups. Heavy pasta—penne, lasagne, or rigatoni—needs a more substantial sauce to support it.

Pasta is extremely simple to cook for one if a few rules are observed.

1. Cook ¼ pound of pasta in 2½ quarts of rapidly boiling water.

2. Add 1 teaspoon of salt to the boiling water before adding the pasta.

3. Cooking times for pasta vary according to the size—anywhere from 4 to 10 minutes. Fresh pasta cooks very quickly—2 to 4 minutes. Keep testing pasta after 3 or 4 minutes until it is just tender, or *al dente*.

4. Immediately drain the cooked pasta and pour it into a preheated dish. Add the sauce right away and mix well, coating the pasta evenly. The sauce must be added immediately or the pasta will stick together.

MADAME CLAIRE'S SPAGHETTI WITH ROQUEFORT

I learned this recipe at a pasta-cooking contest in Cap d'Antibes in the south of France during the 1978 Cannes Film Festival. The sole judge was Mario Puzo. First place went to Sergio Leone, the director of spaghetti westerns, for his spaghetti marinara, spicy combination of virgin olive oil, garlic, pureed tomatoes, parsley, and hot peppers. Second prize went to Francis Ford Coppola for his spaghetti Matriciana, an aromatic blend of fresh tomatoes, onions, and bacon. Madame Claire, the chef at the villa where the contest was held, took third place for her spaghetti Roquefort.

¼ pound Roquefort cheese, at room temperature
½ cup Crème Fraîche, at room temperature (see index for
    recipe)
¼ teaspoon freshly ground white pepper or to taste. (Don't use
    tinned white pepper if you don't have white peppercorns.
    Use black freshly ground pepper instead.)
2 teaspoons salt
¼ pound spaghetti
1 tablespoon butter

With the back of a fork, mash the Roquefort until it is creamy. Mix it well with the crème fraîche and the white pepper. Bring 2½ quarts of water to a rolling boil and add the salt. Add the spaghetti and stir it with a wooden spoon. Boil the spaghetti moderately for 6 minutes or until it is just tender. Drain it well and place it in a serving bowl with the butter. Toss it to coat it with the butter. Immediately add the Roquefort mixture and toss until the sauce is blended thoroughly.

SPAGHETTI WITH BUTTER

Mario Puzo once told me that the purest and most satisfying pasta is plain, piping hot spaghetti bathed in butter and seasoned with salt and pepper. It's the only dish he cooks for himself—usually late at night after writing. Then he sleeps like a baby.

> ¼ pound spaghetti
> 2 tablespoons butter or to taste
> Salt and pepper

Cook the spaghetti in 2½ quarts of rapidly boiling lightly salted water for 6 minutes or until it is just tender. Drain the spaghetti, pour it into a bowl, and dot it with butter. Season it with salt and pepper. Toss it until the butter melts and coats each strand of spaghetti.

SPAGHETTI WITH A FRESH LEEK AND
PARMESAN CHEESE

> 1 large leek, trimmed and cleaned
> 1 tablespoon butter
> 2 tablespoons olive or vegetable oil
> 1 clove garlic, minced
> ⅓ cup Chicken Broth (see index for recipe)
> ¼ teaspoon basil
> ¼ pound spaghetti
> 1 tablespoon olive oil
> Salt and freshly ground pepper to taste
> 2 tablespoons grated Parmesan cheese or to taste

Cut the leek lengthwise into very fine julienne strips. Heat the butter and 1 tablespoon of olive oil in a 9-inch skillet. Add the garlic and the leek and cook them over medium heat, stirring, for 1 minute. Add the chicken broth and the basil. Reduce heat and simmer the sauce for 8 minutes. Meanwhile, cook the spaghetti in 2½ quarts of lightly salted boiling water for 6 minutes or until it is tender. Drain it. Toss it in a serving dish with 1 tablespoon of olive oil. Add the leek mixture and season the dish with the salt and pepper and the Parmesan cheese. Toss and serve immediately.

SPAGHETTI CARBONARA

¼ pound spaghetti
2 tablespoons olive oil
1 large clove garlic, crushed
1 small onion, minced
1 egg
Salt and freshly ground pepper to taste
¼ cup heavy cream, heated to a boil
2 tablespoons Romano or Parmesan cheese
4 strips crisp cooked bacon, crumbled
¼ cup cooked green peas, drained (optional)
1 teaspoon fresh chopped parsley

Drop the spaghetti into 2½ quarts of rapidly boiling, lightly salted water. Cook until it is just tender, about 6 minutes. Meanwhile, heat the olive oil in a small skillet and sauté the crushed garlic and onion for 2 or 3 minutes, stirring. Transfer the garlic and onion to a bowl and let them cool for 2 minutes. Add the egg, season it with salt and pepper, and beat. Heat the heavy cream. Drain the cooked spaghetti well. Transfer it to a heated bowl. Pour the egg mixture over the spaghetti, add the cheese, and toss. Add the bacon, heavy cream, peas, and parsley. Toss the spaghetti and taste it for seasoning. Serve immediately.

BURSA SPAGHETTI

Bursa, a city in Turkey about sixty miles from Istanbul, specializes in a dish which, naturally enough, bears its name, Bursa kebab. It is prepared with brown rice, tomatoes, mushrooms, onions, and yogurt and topped with sizzling slivers of spit-roasted pressed lamb. Craving the dish one day, but not having the rice or lamb, I experimented with the dish's remaining ingredients plus a few others and spaghetti. The delectable result follows.

> 1 cup Beef Stock or Broth (see index for recipes)
> 1 tablespoon olive oil
> 1 tablespoon butter
> 1 small onion, finely chopped
> 4 fresh mushrooms, chopped
> 1 medium firm ripe tomato, peeled, seeded, and chopped
> Salt and freshly ground pepper to taste
> 1 teaspoon fresh chopped parsley
> ½ cup plain yogurt
> ¼ pound spaghetti

Fill a large pot with 2½ quarts of water and bring it to a boil. Meanwhile, boil the stock in a small, heavy saucepan over high heat until it is reduced to ¼ cup. Set it aside. Heat the oil and butter in a 9-inch skillet. Sauté the onion for 5 minutes, stirring it occasionally. Add the mushrooms, tomato, salt, pepper, and parsley. Cook the mixture for 3 minutes. Pour in the reduced stock and simmer the sauce for 6 minutes. Season the boiling water in the large pot with salt and cook the spaghetti until it is just tender. Drain it. Remove the skillet with the sauce from the heat and stir in the yogurt. Pour the sauce over the well-drained spaghetti and toss it until the spaghetti is evenly covered.

SPAGHETTI PUTTANESCA

2 tablespoons olive oil
1 clove garlic, finely minced
1 medium-large tomato, peeled and diced, or ½ cup diced
    canned tomatoes
3 anchovy fillets, chopped
1 heaping tablespoon chopped dill pickles
2 tablespoons black olive slivers
1 dozen pickled pearl onions
1 tablespoon fresh chopped parsley
¼ teaspoon dried hot red pepper flakes (or less if you don't like
    hot, spicy sauce)
⅓ cup Chicken Stock (see index for recipe)
2 teaspoons salt
¼ pound spaghetti

Put 2½ quarts of water in a pot to boil. Heat the olive oil in a large
skillet. Sauté the garlic for 30 seconds. Add all the remaining ingredients except for the salt and spaghetti. Stir the mixture and heat it to
a boil; then reduce heat and simmer the sauce for 15 minutes, stirring
it occasionally. When the water boils, add the salt to it and cook the
spaghetti until it is tender. Drain the spaghetti well and transfer it to
a serving dish. Top it with the sauce and toss until the spaghetti is
evenly coated.

LINGUINI PRIMAVERA

½ cup chopped broccoli
2 tablespoons olive oil
1 clove garlic, minced
1 small onion, thinly sliced
1 tablespoon butter
1 tablespoon fresh chopped parsley
½ teaspoon basil
¼ teaspoon oregano
Salt and freshly ground pepper to taste
¼ pound linguini
½ cup cubed zucchini
4 fresh mushrooms, quartered
8 fresh snow pea pods, cut in half crosswise on a diagonal
½ cup heavy cream
1 tablespoon fresh grated Parmesan cheese or to taste

Bring 2½ quarts of water to a boil in a large pot. In a small saucepan bring 2 cups of lightly salted water to a boil. Blanch the broccoli for 3 minutes in the saucepan. Drain it and set it aside. Heat the oil in a 10- to 12-inch skillet and sauté the garlic and onion for 5 minutes. Add the butter and sprinkle in the parsley, basil, oregano, salt, and pepper. Remove the skillet from the heat. Add the linguini to the boiling water in the large pot and cook it until it is tender, about 6 minutes. Return the skillet to the heat and add the zucchini, mushrooms, and drained broccoli. Cook the mixture over medium-high heat, stirring, for 3 minutes. Add the snow pea pods and stir for 1 minute. Meanwhile, place the heavy cream in the cleaned small saucepan and bring it to a boil. Cook the cream for 3 minutes over medium-high heat, stirring it occasionally until it thickens. Remove the vegetables from the heat. Drain the linguini and pour it into a warmed dish. Pour the thickened heavy cream over the pasta and toss. Add the vegetables and Parmesan cheese and toss again. Taste for seasoning.

FETTUCINE WITH GROUND VEAL, PROSCIUTTO, AND CREAM SAUCE

1 tablespoon olive oil
2 ounces ground veal or beef
¼ pound fettucine
½ tablespoon butter
¾ cup heavy cream
2 slices prosciutto, minced
½ teaspoon fresh chopped parsley
2 tablespoons fresh grated Parmesan cheese
Salt and freshly ground pepper to taste

Heat the oil in a 9-inch skillet. Sauté the ground veal, stirring, until it is cooked but not browned. Crumble it with a fork. Set it aside. Cook the pasta in 2½ quarts of lightly salted, rapidly boiling water until it is just tender. Melt the butter in a small saucepan and add the cream. Cook the mixture over high heat, stirring it until it begins to thicken. Stir in the ground veal, the prosciutto, the parsley, and the Parmesan cheese. Season the mixture with the salt and pepper. Drain the pasta and pour the sauce over it. Toss and serve immediately.

BUTTERED FETTUCINE WITH HERBS

¼ pound fettucine or ribbon noodles
2 tablespoons melted butter
1 teaspoon fresh chooped parsley
¼ teaspoon chopped fresh dill weed or ¼ teaspoon dried dill
    weed
¼ teaspoon basil
Pinch of oregano
Pinch of thyme
Salt and freshly ground pepper to taste

Bring 2½ quarts of lightly salted water to a boil. Add the fettucine and stir it with a wooden spoon. Cook for about 6 minutes or until the noodles are just tender. Meanwhile, melt the butter in a saucepan. Drain the fettucine and add it to the heated butter in the saucepan. Toss. Sprinkle with the herbs, salt, and pepper.

VARIATIONS: Follow the recipe to the point of tossing the fettucine in the heated butter. Then do one of the following.

Parmesan: Add 2 tablespoons of heavy cream and 1 tablespoon of grated Parmesan cheese or to taste. Season with salt and pepper and toss.
Poppy Seed: Add 1 teaspoon of poppy seeds. Season with salt and pepper and toss.

VERMICELLI WITH ANCHOVY, TOMATO, AND ONION SAUCE

3 tablespoons olive oil
1 small onion, sliced
1 small clove garlic, minced

3 anchovy fillets, chopped
½ cup peeled and chopped tomato
¼ teaspoon basil
1 teaspoon fresh chopped parsley
Salt and freshly ground pepper to taste
¼ cup Chicken Broth (see index for recipe)
¼ pound vermicelli
1 tablespoon butter

Heat the olive oil in a 9-inch skillet. Sauté the onion and garlic for 5 minutes over medium heat, stirring. Stir in the anchovy pieces and cook for 1 minute. Add the tomato, basil, and parsley. Season with the salt and pepper. Pour in the chicken broth and simmer the sauce for 10 minutes over medium heat. Cook the vermicelli in 2½ quarts of lightly salted, rapidly boiling water for 4 or 5 minutes, until it is just tender. Drain it well. Toss the vermicelli with the butter and pour the sauce over it. Toss well and serve immediately.

CONSTANCE M. MADINA'S QUICK PASTA WITH
SICILIAN-STYLE TOMATO SAUCE

Constance M. Madina holds the highest position of any female in any district attorney's office in New York City. She is Queens County Executive Assistant District Attorney. Here is her pasta recipe for busy cooks.

"Since I was appointed to my present position, I usually stay in the office until 7:30 P.M. I then go home for a quick dinner and go out to a meeting. My duties as a nonpaid commissioner add to a full schedule.

"My husband, Sid Davidoff [former executive under Mayor Lindsay], is a busy attorney, interested in politics. We share the interest in politics, but, unfortunately, rarely the time for weekday dinners together.

"My Sicilian grandmother taught me the art of a great sauce, but it takes hours. So here is my quick recipe, after a long day, for a nice and easy home-cooked dish of pasta.

"Boiling water for pasta takes a lot of time. I pour 10 cups of water into our automatic coffee maker, which is very hot in 5 minutes.

"Pour this hot water into a pot and bring it to a boil. Add 2 teaspoons salt. While waiting for the water to boil, make the sauce.

"All the ingredients for the sauce are kept on a revolving cabinet near my stove. Once you get the hang of it, there is no need to measure."

> 1 small can imported tomato puree
> 1½ teaspoons sugar
> ¼ teaspoon freshly ground pepper
> Salt to taste
> 2 tablespoons minced onion
> ¼ teaspoon minced garlic
> ¼ teaspoon oregano
> 1 tablespoon fresh chopped parsley or 1 teaspoon dried parsley
>   flakes

Dash of dried basil
1 tablespoon olive oil
2 tablespoons water
4 to 6 ounces pasta (ditali)
Freshly grated Parmesan cheese

Combine the tomato puree, sugar, pepper, salt, onion, garlic, oregano, parsley, and basil in a small saucepan with the oil and water. Heat the sauce slowly, stirring it frequently. When the water for the pasta boils, add the ditali and cook it in rapidly boiling water until it is just tender. Drain it. Pour the sauce over the pasta and sprinkle it with Parmesan cheese.

FUSILLI WITH FRESH MARINARA SAUCE

¼ pound fusilli

Marinara Sauce:

3 tablespoons olive oil
1 medium onion, finely chopped
1 clove garlic, minced
2 whole tomatoes, peeled and chopped
½ teaspoon oregano
Salt and freshly ground pepper to taste
¼ cup Chicken Broth (see index for recipe)
Freshly grated Parmesan cheese (optional)

Heat the olive oil in a large saucepan. Add the onion and garlic, and stir and sauté them over medium heat for 5 minutes. Add the tomatoes, oregano, salt, pepper, and chicken broth. Bring the mixture to a boil, reduce heat, and simmer the sauce for 20 minutes, stirring it often. Cook the fusilli in 2½ quarts of lightly salted, rapidly boiling water for about 6 minutes or until it is just tender. Drain the pasta thoroughly and pour the sauce over it. Toss and serve plain or with freshly grated Parmesan cheese.

RIGATONI WITH SARDINES, TOMATOES, AND BASIL

> Marinara Sauce (see recipe above)
> 3 or 4 fresh chopped basil leaves or ¼ teaspoon dried basil
> 4 to 6 ounces rigatoni
> 3 ounces sardines, skinless, boneless, and drained

Prepare the marinara sauce, adding basil to the other ingredients in the recipe. Cook the rigatoni in 2½ quarts of rapidly boiling, lightly salted water. Drain it well. Place the pasta in a large bowl with the sauce and sardines. Gently toss.

BAKED ZITI WITH SAUSAGE

> 1 cup Marinara Sauce (see recipe before last)
> 6 ounces ziti
> 1 tablespoon olive oil
> 2 Italian sweet sausages, cut in half lengthwise
> 3 ounces mozzarella cheese, diced
> 2 tablespoons freshly grated Parmesan cheese

Heat the marinara sauce in a small saucepan. Cook the ziti in 2½ quarts of rapidly boiling, lightly salted water. Meanwhile, heat the olive oil in a skillet and sauté the sausages until they are lightly browned. Remove the sausage from the skillet and chop it. Drain the pasta well and toss it with all but ¼ cup of the marinara sauce. Add the sausage and toss again. Place half of the mixture in a lightly greased, shallow baking dish. Sprinkle half of each cheese over the pasta. Spoon the rest of the pasta into the dish and pour the reserved sauce on top. Sprinkle evenly with the remaining cheeses. Bake the ziti in a preheated 375°F oven for 15 minutes or until the cheese bubbles.

6. Glorious Black Bean Days

I have long fancied black beans, and because I cook for myself most of the time, I have worked out a formula for cooking one batch of black beans which provides four varied black bean dishes.

When I related this news to a single friend of mine, her response was "Isn't that a lot of trouble to go to for one person? The idea of four meals of black beans in a row isn't very appealing anyway."

First of all, cooking dried beans is easy, but they must be soaked in water for 10 hours. Start them in the morning before you leave for work or soak them overnight. Dried beans require about 3 hours cooking time. You can cook them whenever you know you're going to be home for that length of time. While cooking, the beans require little attention. You just have to stir them occasionally and, near the end of their cooking time, make sure there is enough water left in the pot.

The four following bean dishes needn't be eaten on consecutive days. You can freeze cooked beans in small containers and use them whenever you wish.

Aside from being extremely palatable, dried beans are inexpensive and nutritious, and in the dried state they keep indefinitely.

BASIC BLACK BEANS

2 cups dried black beans
1 medium-large onion, chopped

3 quarts water
1 teaspoon salt
Freshly ground pepper to taste
1 bay leaf

Cover the beans in a bowl with cold water and soak them for 10 hours or overnight. (There will be about 2½ cups of beans after soaking.) Drain the beans and remove any broken or discolored ones. Place the beans in a large pot with the onion, water, salt, pepper, and bay leaf. Bring the water to a boil, then reduce heat and simmer for 2½ to 3 hours, until the beans are tender. Stir the beans about once every hour, and after the 2 hours' cooking time check to make sure the beans still have enough water to cover the bottom of the pot. Discard the bay leaf.

Black beans can be eaten plain with rice and meat. Cool the remaining beans and liquid and divide them equally among 3 or 4 refrigerator containers. Freeze them. The size of an individual portion depends on your appetite. An average portion is ½ cup.

BLACK BEAN SOUP WITH CURRIED TOMATOES

½ cup cooked black beans
½ cup Chicken Stock or broth (see index for recipe)
1 tablespoon olive oil
1 small clove garlic, minced
1 scallion, thinly sliced
¼ teaspoon basil
1 teaspoon fresh chopped parsley
1 medium tomato, peeled, seeded, and chopped
½ teaspoon curry powder or to taste
Salt and freshly ground pepper to taste

Puree ¼ cup of the beans and put them in a small saucepan with the remaining ¼ cup of whole beans and the chicken stock. Stir the mixture and bring it to a boil; then reduce heat and simmer for 10 minutes. Meanwhile, heat the oil in a 9-inch skillet and sauté the garlic and scallion for 3 minutes, stirring. Add the basil, parsley, tomato, and curry powder and season with the salt and pepper. Cook the vegetables over medium-high heat for about 4 minutes, until most of the liquid has evaporated. Pour the hot soup into a serving bowl and spoon the curried tomato sauce into the center of it.

Serve this soup with grilled tortillas.

STIR-FRIED CHINESE BEEF WITH BLACK BEAN SAUCE

1 teaspoon cornstarch
1 tablespoon egg white
4 to 6 ounces sirloin or flank steak, cut into thin strips
1½ tablespoons peanut oil
1 scallion, thinly sliced
½ cup cooked black beans
2 teaspoons soy sauce

Mix the cornstarch and egg white in a bowl. Add the meat, toss, and refrigerate for 30 minutes. Heat the oil in a 9-inch skillet or a small wok. Add the meat and stir-fry it with a spoon and a fork until it browns. Remove the beef. Add the scallion and stir-fry it for 1 minute. Add the beans, soy sauce, and meat and cook them over medium-high heat for 3 minutes.

BLACK BEAN CHILI

    1 cup cooked black beans
    ½ cup black bean liquid or Beef Stock (see index for recipe)
    1½ tablespoons olive oil
    ½ small green pepper, seeded and chopped
    1 small clove garlic, minced
    1 small onion, chopped
    1 small tomato, peeled, seeded, and diced
    ½ teaspoon cumin
    2 teaspoons chili powder
    Salt and freshly ground pepper

Combine the beans and liquid or stock in a medium-sized saucepan. In a 9-inch skillet heat the oil and sauté the green pepper, garlic, and onion for 5 minutes, stirring. Add the tomato and sprinkle the vegetables with the cumin and chili powder. Stir and cook the vegetables for 2 minutes. Add the mixture to the beans and simmer for 15 minutes. Taste the chili for seasoning, adding salt and pepper to taste.
    Garnish the chili with diced raw green pepper and onion.

BLACK BEAN SALAD

¾ cup cooked black beans, cold and drained
2 tablespoons stuffed olive slices
1 tablespoon minced red onion
1 stalk celery, diced
1 tablespoon fresh chopped parsley
1 teaspoon lemon juice
2 tablespoons olive or vegetable oil
½ teaspoon Dijon-style mustard
Salt and freshly ground pepper to taste, if necessary
¾ cup shredded romaine lettuce
1 hard-boiled egg, quartered
2 hot peppers
¼ cup shredded Cheddar cheese

In a bowl combine the black beans, olive slices, red onion, celery, and parsley. Mix together the lemon juice, olive oil, and mustard. Pour the dressing over the salad and toss. Taste for seasoning. Line an individual salad plate with the shredded lettuce. Spoon the salad into the center. Place the egg quarters and hot peppers around the border, and sprinkle the beans with the cheese.

7. Birds

Fourteen Chicken Breast Entrées

FRANK PERDUE'S BREAST OF CHICKEN CHUNKS WITH MUSHROOMS AND LEMON

Frank Perdue, chairman of Perdue, Inc., told me, "I'm opposed to cooking and eating alone in principle, but when I have to, I do. If I'm going to go to the trouble to cook, it might as well be something that tastes great and is made with first-rate ingredients. I like breast of chicken and use the best available—mine. Lemon and chicken complement each other beautifully, and with the addition of fresh mushrooms and a little good wine, it makes a fine dish. Then I drink a glass of the chilled wine with my meal. Chicken is always good company when eating alone."

    1 chicken breast, skinned and boned
    Salt and freshly ground pepper
    2 tablespoons olive or vegetable oil
    1 clove garlic, crushed
    ½ lemon, cut into thin slices with rind
    6 fresh mushrooms, quartered
    ¼ cup dry white wine (I like Verdicchio)
    ¼ teaspoon oregano
    1 teaspoon fresh chopped parsley
    Salt and freshly ground pepper

Cut the chicken into bite-sized chunks and season it well with salt and pepper. Heat the oil in a skillet, add the chicken, and brown it all over. Add the garlic and sauté for about 5 minutes over medium heat. Turn the chicken pieces. Add the lemon slices, mushrooms, wine, oregano, and parsley. Season lightly with salt and pepper. Cook the chicken over low heat, partially covered, for 10 minutes.

 SUGGESTED MENU:

Onion and Anchovy Canapés
Frank Perdue's Breast of Chicken Chunks with Mushrooms and
    Lemon
Fresh Cooked Asparagus
Chilled Verdicchio
Fresh Strawberries with Crème Fraîche and Brown Sugar

SAUTÉED CHICKEN BREAST WITH WALNUTS AND SESAME OIL

1 chicken breast, halved, skinned, and boned
Salt and freshly ground pepper
Flour
2½ tablespoons butter
¼ cup chopped walnuts
½ teaspoon sesame oil
1 teaspoon soy sauce

Place half of the chicken breast between two pieces of waxed paper. Flatten it to a ¼-inch thickness with a meat pounder or the side of a cleaver. Repeat this process with the other half. Season the chicken on each side with the salt and pepper. Dust it with flour. Heat 2 tablespoons of the butter in a 9-inch skillet and sauté the chicken until it is browned on each side (about 5 minutes per side). Transfer the chicken to a warmed dish. Add the walnuts and sesame oil and the remaining ½ tablespoon of butter to the skillet. Cook and stir the nuts over medium-high heat until they are browned. Add the soy sauce. Stir and cook for 15 seconds. Spoon the walnut sauce over the chicken.

 SUGGESTED MENU:

Artichoke Soup
Sautéed Chicken Breast with Walnuts and Sesame Oil
Rice Salad
Cinnamon Ice Cream

CHICKEN POT PIE WITH INSTANT PUFF PASTRY

2 cups Chicken Stock (see index for recipe)
1 small chicken breast, halved, skinned, and boned

1 medium onion, halved
1 bay leaf
1½ tablespoons butter
1 tablespoon flour
1 carrot, peeled and diced
1 stalk celery, diced
⅛ teaspoon thyme
1 teaspoon finely chopped fresh parsley
Salt and freshly ground pepper
1 frozen patty shell
1 egg, beaten

Bring the chicken stock to a boil in a saucepan. Add the chicken, onion, and bay leaf. Reduce the heat and simmer for 15 minutes. Remove the chicken. Strain the stock and reserve it. Cut the chicken into bite-sized pieces. In a small saucepan heat the butter and then stir in the flour with a wire whisk. Cook over medium heat for 1 minute, stirring. Slowly pour in 1 cup of the chicken stock, constantly stirring, until the stock is smooth and thickened. Add the chicken to the stock. Add the carrot, celery, thyme, and parsley. Stir the mixture and season it with salt and pepper. Spoon it into an individual round ramekin or soufflé dish. Roll out a frozen patty shell into a 5-inch circle. Trim the edges to even the circle. Cut a ½-inch hole in the center of the pastry. Fit it over the dish, pressing the edge down against the dish about ½ inch. Trim off the excess dough. Brush the pastry with the beaten egg. Place the baking dish in a preheated 400°F oven for 20 minutes until the pastry is puffed and golden.

 SUGGESTED MENU:

Sautéed Tiny Sausages with Mustard
Chicken Pot Pie with Instant Puff Pastry
A mixed green salad
Chocolate ice cream

CHICKEN SATE WITH PEANUT SAUCE

 1 medium-sized whole chicken breast, skinned and boned
 1 clove garlic, crushed
 2 tablespoons soy sauce
 2 tablespoons dry sherry
 1 tablespoon water

Peanut Sauce:

 1 tablespoon grated onion
 1 tablespoon peach or apricot preserves
 ½ teaspoon chili powder
 1 tablespoon lemon juice
 3 tablespoons crunchy peanut butter
 2 teaspoons soy sauce

Cut the chicken into 1-inch cubes. Thread the cubes onto dampened wooden or metal skewers (dampening wooden skewers prevents them from burning), leaving 2 inches at each end of the skewers for holding them. Mix together the garlic, soy sauce, sherry, and water. Place the skewers in a shallow dish and pour the marinade over them, turning the skewers to coat them evenly. Marinate the chicken for 1 hour in the refrigerator. Combine the peanut sauce ingredients and leave it at room temperature until you are ready to use it. Broil the chicken on the skewers under the broiler, turning them once to cook them evenly.

 Serve the chicken sate with the peanut sauce.

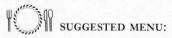 SUGGESTED MENU:

Fried Crepes with Honey Butter
Chicken Sate with Peanut Sauce
Curried Rice

Any green salad
Coconut Macaroons

COLD POACHED CHICKEN BREAST WITH SALMON SAUCE

  2 cups Chicken Broth (see index for recipe)
  1 medium onion, quartered
  1 chicken breast, skinned, boned, and halved

Salmon Sauce:

  ½ cup cooked salmon, boned and skinned (or canned salmon)
  ¼ cup olive or vegetable oil
  2 tablespoons Mayonnaise (see index for recipe)
  2 anchovy fillets, mashed with a fork
  1 teaspoon fresh lemon juice or to taste
  Freshly ground pepper
  Salt, if necessary
  1 heaping tablespoon capers

Bring the chicken broth and onion to a boil in a small saucepan. Add the chicken, reduce heat, and simmer for 15 minutes. To make the sauce, put the salmon in a blender. Turn the blender on and slowly add the oil through the hole in the cover. If you don't have a blender, force the salmon through a sieve or a food mill and slowly add the oil to it in a bowl while beating it vigorously. Add the mayonnaise, anchovy fillets, and lemon juice to the blender and puree, or beat these ingredients into the salmon mixture in the bowl. Taste the sauce and season it with pepper and, if necessary, salt.

Put the sauce in a bowl and refrigerate it. Cool the poached chicken in the broth to room temperature (about 30 minutes). Remove the chicken, trim it evenly, then cover and refrigerate it. Both the sauce and the chicken should be refrigerated for at least 2 hours or even overnight. When you are ready to dine, slice the chicken into ¼-inch-thick medallions. Arrange these attractively on a serving dish, spoon the sauce over them, and sprinkle the sauce with capers.

 SUGGESTED MENU:

English-Style Cucumber Tea Sandwich
Cold Poached Chicken Breast with Salmon Sauce
Rice Salad
Independence Day Fruit Sundae

JOY ROSSI'S CHICKEN PERI-PERI

Joy Rossi is an interior designer in Bridgetown, Barbados. Joy coaxed this recipe for chicken peri-peri out of her grandfather. She says, "I often eat alone and so I worked on reducing the recipe for one until it tasted like the giant batch I make for visiting guests and friends. It is difficult to find authentic native food in Barbados any longer. The Atlantis Hotel serves the best variety of native food on Sunday for lunch, but it's on the east end of the island in Bathsheba, and I can't always talk visitors into the hour trip. The Caribbean is known for spicy dishes, and this one is certainly hot. We use tiny little bulb peppers, locally grown. Substituting with Tabasco works quite well in the recipe. It is a hot, spicy dish, so reduce the amount of Tabasco according to your taste."

   1 large chicken breast, halved and skinned
   2 tablespoons butter
   1 medium green pepper, seeded and quartered
   1 small onion, thinly sliced
   1 medium firm ripe tomato, peeled and quartered
   1 tablespoon white wine vinegar
   2 tablespoons chili sauce

½ teaspoon Tabasco or less, according to taste
1 cup Chicken Stock or Broth (see index for recipe)
Salt and freshly ground pepper to taste

Bring 2 cups of lightly salted water to a boil in a small saucepan. Add the chicken and cook it over medium heat for 12 minutes. Drain it. Melt the butter in a 9-inch skillet and sauté the green pepper and onion for 5 minutes over medium heat. Pat the chicken dry. Add the chicken and tomato quarters to the onion and pepper in the skillet. Combine the white wine vinegar, chili sauce, Tabasco, and chicken stock in a saucepan and bring them to a boil. Season the sauce with salt and pepper and pour it over the chicken and vegetables. Cover the skillet and simmer slowly for about 1 hour, until the chicken falls from the bones.

SUGGESTED MENU:

Marinated Artichoke Hearts in Curry Sauce
Joy Rossi's Chicken Peri-Peri
Baked Yam
Pineapple Meringue Cake

BAKED CHICKEN BREAST IN SHERRIED
TOMATO SAUCE WITH CRISP CHEESE TOPPING

1 medium-large chicken breast, split, with breast bone removed
Salt and freshly ground pepper to taste
2 tablespoons olive or vegetable oil
1 medium onion, thinly sliced
1 small clove garlic, crushed
¼ cup dry sherry
¼ cup chopped tomato, peeled and seeded
1 teaspoon fresh chopped parsley
1 tablespoon bread crumbs
2 tablespoons shredded Cheddar cheese
1 teaspoon butter

Pat the chicken dry with absorbent paper and season it with the salt
and pepper. In a 9-inch skillet, heat the oil and brown the chicken on
the skin side. Remove the chicken to a side dish and sauté the onion
and garlic, stirring frequently, for 5 minutes. Add the sherry, tomato,
and parsley. Season with salt and pepper. Spread the mixture over
the bottom of an individual au gratin dish. Place the chicken, skin
side up, on the sauce. Sprinkle it with the combined bread crumbs
and cheese and dot it with the butter. Bake the chicken in a preheated
375°F oven for 30 minutes or until the top is golden brown and the
chicken is tender.

 SUGGESTED MENU:

Creamed Mushrooms on Fried Toast
Baked Chicken Breast in Sherried Tomato Sauce with Crisp Cheese
  Topping
Carrots Cooked in Chicken Broth
Dutch Apple Pancake

LOW-CALORIE POACHED CHICKEN BREAST WITH MUSTARD AND CAPERS

1 small onion, peeled and quartered
1½ cups Chicken Broth (see index for recipe)
2 tablespoons dry sherry
1 medium chicken breast, skinned and boned
1 tablespoon Dijon-style mustard
¼ teaspoon curry powder
1 teaspoon lemon juice
Freshly ground pepper to taste
1 small tomato, peeled, seeded, and diced
2 teaspoons capers
1 romaine lettuce leaf

Place the onion in a small saucepan with the broth and sherry and bring them to a boil. Add the chicken, bring the liquid back to the boil, reduce heat, and simmer for 15 minutes or until the chicken is cooked. Remove the chicken to a side dish. Combine the mustard, curry powder, lemon juice, and pepper in a bowl. Fold in the diced tomato and capers. Slice the chicken breast into medallions crosswise, about ¼ inch thick, and arrange them on the lettuce leaf. Spoon the mustard sauce over the chicken. This dish may be served at room temperature or chilled.

 SUGGESTED MENU:

Fresh melon with lemon
Low-Calorie Poached Chicken Breast with Mustard and Capers
Cherry Tomato, Mushroom, and Cucumber Salad
Fresh fruit with Brie

STUFFED CHICKEN BREAST

2 tablespoons butter
2 large shallots, finely chopped
1 small clove garlic, crushed
3 tablespoons fresh chopped parsley
¼ teaspoon tarragon
¼ cup dried bread crumbs
2 tablespoons dry white wine
1 medium chicken breast, halved and boned
¼ cup Chicken Broth, heated (see index for recipe)
1 tablespoon melted butter

Melt the butter in a small saucepan and sauté the shallots and garlic, stirring, for about 3 minutes. Add the parsley, tarragon, bread crumbs, and white wine. Mix thoroughly and remove from heat. Separate the skin from the chicken breast pieces and spread the mixture in the saucepan in equal amounts over the surface of meat. Cover the meat with the skin and tuck the ends in underneath. Place the chicken in a small, shallow baking dish just large enough to comfortably hold the chicken without the pieces touching each other. Pour in the heated broth and brush the skin of the chicken with the melted butter. Bake the chicken in a preheated 375°F oven for 15 minutes. Baste it with the remaining butter and cook it another 10 minutes, until the skin is nicely browned and the chicken is tender.

 SUGGESTED MENU:

Herring in Cream Sauce with Mustard and Capers
Stuffed Chicken Breast
Sautéed Potato Pancake with Cauliflower Puree
Poached Pear with Cranberry and Apricot Sauce

BONED CHICKEN BREAST FLORENTINE

¼ cup dry white wine or vermouth
1¼ cups chicken broth
1 small chicken breast, skinned, boned, and cut in half
1 small onion, quartered
½ pound fresh spinach, stems removed and washed well
¼ cup grated Cheddar cheese
1 tablespoon seasoned bread crumbs
1 tablespoon melted butter

Bring the white wine and broth to a boil in a small saucepan. Add the chicken breast halves and onion, cover the pan, and simmer for 15 minutes. Meanwhile, cook the spinach in 1 cup of lightly salted water in another covered saucepan for 5 minutes. Drain it well in a strainer by pressing it with the back of a tablespoon. Chop the spinach. Line the bottom of an individual au gratin dish with the spinach. Remove the chicken from the broth and place it on the spinach. Spoon 3 tablespoons of the broth from the pan over the chicken. Combine the cheese and bread crumbs and sprinkle them over the chicken. Drizzle the butter over the top. Place in a preheated 425°F oven for about 8 minutes, until the cheese topping is golden.

 SUGGESTED MENU:

Pimiento Cheese and Bacon Spread on Fried Butter Croutons
Boned Chicken Breast Florentine
Buttered Fettucine with Herbs
Fresh Figs with Dates and Crème Fraîche

BONED CHICKEN BREAST IN SHALLOT SAUCE

1 tablespoon butter
1 tablespoon vegetable oil
1 chicken breast, split in half, skinned, and boned
Salt and freshly ground pepper to taste
8 shallots, peeled and left whole
½ cup chicken stock
2 tablespoons dry white wine or vermouth
½ teaspoon cornstarch

Heat the butter and oil in a skillet. Season the chicken with the salt and pepper and brown it on each side. Turn the pieces of chicken and add the shallots, stock, and wine. Bring the liquid to the boil, cover the skillet, and simmer for 15 minutes. Remove the chicken and shallots. Stir the cornstarch dissolved in a little water into the sauce and boil for 1 minute, always stirring. Pour the thickened sauce over the chicken.

 SUGGESTED MENU:

Fresh Hot Tomato and Onion Soup
Boned Chicken Breast in Shallot Sauce
Endive and Pimiento Salad
Zucchini Cake

BREAST OF CHICKEN WITH BRIE FILLING KIEV STYLE

1 medium-sized chicken breast, skinned, boned, and halved
Salt and freshly ground pepper to taste
2 ounces cold Brie cheese
½ teaspoon tarragon
1 teaspoon fresh chopped parsley
Flour
1 egg, beaten
Bread crumbs
2 tablespoons Clarified Butter (see index for recipe)
½ cup vegetable oil

Place each breast half between two pieces of waxed paper and flatten it with a meat pounder or the side of a cleaver to a ¼-inch thickness. Remove the waxed paper. Season the inside of each breast with the salt and pepper. Place a 1-ounce slice of brie in the center of each half. Sprinkle it with equal amounts of tarragon and parsley. Enclose the filling by folding over 1 inch of chicken on each end. Fold the chicken over lengthwise so that the meat overlaps slightly, sealing the filling inside. Roll each breast in flour. Carefully dip them into the beaten egg, coating the entire surface. Then coat them with the bread crumbs. Place them on a plate seam side down and refrigerate them for 30 minutes. Heat the clarified butter and oil in a 9-inch skillet and fry the chicken pieces over medium heat until they are golden on all sides. Remove the chicken to a shallow baking dish and bake it in a preheated 375°F oven for 10 minutes. Serve immediately.

 SUGGESTED MENU:

Celery Root Rémoulade
Breast of Chicken with Brie Filling Kiev Style
Mushroom Brochettes
Fresh Strawberry Tart

LEMON-FLAVORED FRIED CHICKEN BREAST

3 tablespoons vegetable oil
2 tablespoons lemon juice
1 clove garlic, crushed
¼ teaspoon Seasoned Salt (see index for recipe)
1 medium-sized chicken breast, halved with breastbone
    removed
Salt and freshly ground pepper to taste
Flour
½ cup vegetable oil
1 juicy lemon wedge
½ teaspoon fresh chopped parsley

Whisk together the 3 tablespoons of oil, lemon juice, garlic, and seasoned salt. Turn the chicken breasts over in the marinade; then cover
the dish and refrigerate it for several hours. Remove the chicken from
the marinade and pat it dry. Season it with the salt and pepper. Coat
it with the flour. Heat the ½ cup of oil in an 8-inch skillet. Fry the
chicken over medium heat until it is golden brown on both sides.
Squeeze the lemon juice from the wedge over the chicken and sprinkle
it with the parsley.

 SUGGESTED MENU:

Ham and Bread Stick Rolls
Lemon-Flavored Fried Chicken Breast
Sautéed Cucumbers
Martin Rapp's Square Apple Tart with Instant Puff Pastry

CHICKEN LOAF

1 large chicken breast, boned and skinned
1 egg
8 soda crackers, crushed
2 tablespoons minced green pepper
1 small onion, minced
1 tablespoon fresh chopped parsley
½ teaspoon paprika
¼ teaspoon salt
Freshly ground pepper to taste
2 teaspoons butter

Cut the chicken breast into 1-inch cubes and grind them. Mix the ground chicken in a bowl with the remaining ingredients except for the butter. Lightly grease an individual loaf pan and fill it with the chicken mixture. Smooth the top with the back of a spoon and dot it with butter. Cover the loaf with foil. Place the loaf pan in a larger pan with enough hot water in it to come halfway up the side of the loaf pan. Bake in a preheated 350°F oven for 30 minutes. Remove the foil. Cook for another 15 minutes or until a knife comes out of the center of the loaf clean. Lift the loaf pan out of the water and let it sit for 10 minutes before slicing the loaf. You can also refrigerate this dish and serve it cold as a first course.

 SUGGESTED MENU:

Quick Black Bean Soup
Chicken Loaf
Fresh Green Beans with Parsley Butter
Cherry Vanilla Ice Cream

Chicken Legs, Thighs, and Wings

COKI BEACH FRIED CHICKEN LEG

Long before St. Thomas in the United States Virgin Islands saw its first condominiums, the snack bar at Coki Beach was an oasis for hungry snorkelers. Happiness on the beach was to hold a Coki fried chicken leg in one hand and a frosted Heineken's beer in the other.

> 1 chicken leg (leg and thigh attached)
> 1 clove garlic, crushed
> ¼ teaspoon Seasoned Salt (see index for recipe)
> 2 teaspoons vinegar
> 3 tablespoons vegetable oil
> 2 dashes of Tabasco sauce
> 1½ cups vegetable oil

Prick the chicken leg all over with the sharp point of a knife and place it in the center of double sheet of aluminum foil about 12 inches in length. Fold the edges of the foil up around the chicken leg so that liquid won't run out. Mix together the garlic, seasoned salt, vinegar, 3 tablespoons of oil, and Tabasco sauce. Pour the mixture over the chicken. Bring the edges of the foil together up over the chicken and press them together, sealing the chicken. Refrigerate it overnight. Heat the 1½ cups of oil in a medium-sized skillet. Pat the chicken leg dry. When the oil is hot, but not smoking, add the leg and cook it over medium-high heat until it is crisp on both sides, or about 20 minutes' total cooking time.

 SUGGESTED MENU:

Guacamole
Coki Beach Fried Chicken Leg

Creamy Coleslaw
Grilled Apricots with Pecan Filling

CRISP FRIED CHICKEN

> 3 or 4 pieces of chicken (example: 1 leg, 1 thigh, and 1 breast, split)
> Salt and freshly ground pepper to taste
> Flour
> 1 cup shortening or vegetable oil

Season chicken well with the salt and pepper and coat it lightly with the flour. Heat the fat in a 12-inch skillet. When it is hot, but not smoking, add the chicken and lower the heat to medium. Cook the chicken for 10 minutes, until it is browned on one side. Turn it and cook it for 10 minutes on the other side. Turn it and increase the heat for 2 or 3 minutes, until it is crisp and brown. Turn it again and cook for 2 more minutes. Total cooking time, about 25 minutes.

EXTRAS SUGGESTIONS: Cover and refrigerate any remaining chicken and eat it cold the following day, or slice it and make a sandwich or a salad.

 SUGGESTED MENU:

Tomato Stuffed with Rice and Mint
Crisp Fried Chicken
Corn on the Cob
Crisp Molasses Cookies

CHICKEN FRIED WITH BACON CUBES

½ cup ½-inch cubes of slab bacon (Do not cut up strips of
    bacon, because they will burn.)
2 or 3 pieces of chicken (example: ½ breast, 1 leg, and 1 thigh)
Flour

Place the bacon cubes in a skillet large enough to hold the chicken comfortably. Coat the chicken lightly with the flour and place it on top of the bacon cubes. Cook on very low heat for 30 minutes. Turn the chicken and make sure the bacon is out from under the chicken. Stir the bacon to cook it evenly. Cook for another 20 minutes and turn the chicken again. Cook for another 10 minutes. Remove the chicken and bacon cubes. You can either eat the bacon or discard it. It tends to be on the chewy side, but it is delicious.

A milk gravy can be made by pouring all the bacon fat out of the skillet, adding 1 tablespoon of butter, and stirring in 1 scant tablespoon of flour. Stir and cook for 1 minute over medium heat. Then pour in ½ cup of milk, constantly stirring with a wire whisk until the gravy is nicely thickened. Season it well with salt and freshly ground pepper.

Serve the milk gravy with the chicken or on hot biscuits or cornbread.

SUGGESTED MENU:

Chicken Fried with Bacon Cubes
Mashed Potatoes with Mushrooms and Onions
A tossed green salad with Herb Vinaigrette Sauce
Peach Cobbler

BUTTER-FRIED CHICKEN

3 pieces chicken
Salt and freshly ground pepper to taste
Flour
½ cup Clarified Butter (see index for recipe)
2 tablespoons vegetable oil

Season the chicken with the salt and pepper. Coat it with flour, shaking off any extra flour. Heat the butter and oil in a 9-inch skillet. Add the chicken and cook it over medium heat for 10 minutes. Turn it, lower the heat, and cook for another 10 minutes. Increase the heat slightly and turn the chicken. Cook for 5 minutes or until the chicken is crisp and tender.

 SUGGESTED MENU:

Pasta and Spinach Eggdrop Soup
Butter-Fried Chicken
Tomato and Red Onion Salad
Fresh fruit and cheese

POULET MUGUET

2 or 3 chicken parts (example: 1 leg, 1 thigh, and ½ breast)
Salt and freshly ground pepper to taste
2 tablespoons butter
2 teaspoons vegetable oil
2 tablespoons dry white wine
2 tablespoons Chicken Stock (see index for recipe)
½ cup heavy cream
½ cup fresh small button mushrooms, stemmed
½ teaspoon fresh chopped parsley

Season the chicken with the salt and pepper. Heat 1 tablespoon of the butter with the oil in a 9-inch skillet. Brown the chicken on each side. Add the wine and chicken stock. Partially cover the skillet and simmer for 15 minutes. Turn the chicken and cook it uncovered for 10 minutes. Meanwhile, bring the heavy cream to a boil in a small saucepan. Cook it for 5 minutes, stirring it occasionally with a wire whisk, over medium heat until it thickens. Add the mushrooms and cook for 2 minutes. Stir in the remaining tablespoon of butter. Taste the cream and mushrooms for seasoning. Remove the chicken pieces to a heated dish. Pour the cream and mushrooms over the chicken. Sprinkle with parsley.

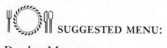 SUGGESTED MENU:

Poulet Muguet
Mini Caesar Salad
Lime Pie

SHEILAH RAE GROSS'S SWEET AND SOUR CHICKEN

Sheilah Rae Gross and I were in summer stock together years ago at the Goodspeed Opera House in East Haddam, Connecticut. During that summer the entire cast lived in a group of cottages, and we often had meals at a long table alfresco. We all had kitchens and we would each contribute a dish to the meals, which sometimes resulted in wonderful potluck dinners.

Sheilah loved tinned apricots then and still does. After several singles had asked me for an entrée made from an 8-ounce can of apricots, Sheilah had the recipe for me. Now a wife, mother, singer, and songwriter, she's married to Elliott Gross, a neurosurgeon, and has a daughter and son. She says, "Elliott's favorite dish is a cottage cheese omelet, which he always prepares for himself for lunch on weekends whether he's alone or the family is all together. When I get home late from a writing session and everyone else has eaten, I love sweet and sour chicken for a quick, easy dinner."

> 1 8-ounce can apricot halves, drained (reserve syrup)
> ¼ cup vinegar
> 2 tablespoons sugar
> 1 tablespoon ketchup
> Salt and freshly ground pepper to taste
> 2 teaspoons cornstarch
> 1 cup cooked cubed chicken
> ½ green pepper, cut into thin strips
> 1 small tomato, peeled and cut into 4 wedges

Set aside ¼ cup of the apricot syrup and pour the rest in a small saucepan with the vinegar, sugar, ketchup, salt, and pepper. Bring this sauce to a boil, then lower the heat and simmer for 5 minutes. Blend the cornstarch and reserved syrup. Stir it into the sauce. Cook and stir the mixture until it thickens. Add the apricots, chicken, green pepper, and tomato. Cook for about 3 minutes, until all the ingredients are heated thoroughly.

 SUGGESTED MENU:

Sheilah Rae Gross's Sweet and Sour Chicken
Hot cooked rice
Sugar and Almond Toasted Brioche

CHICKEN TARRAGON

2 pieces of chicken
Salt and freshly ground pepper to taste
2 teaspoons butter
2 teaspoons olive or vegetable oil
2 tablespoons finely chopped shallots
¼ cup dry white wine or vermouth
2 tablespoons Chicken Broth (see index for recipe)
½ teaspoon tarragon
¼ cup heavy cream

Pat the chicken dry and season it with the salt and pepper. Heat the butter and oil in a 9-inch skillet and brown the chicken on both sides over medium-high heat. Sprinkle the shallots around the chicken and stir. Add the wine, broth, and tarragon. Turn the chicken pieces over, cover the skillet, and slowly simmer for 15 minutes. Turn the chicken again and cook it without the cover for 10 minutes or until it is tender. Transfer the chicken to a heated dish. Pour the heavy cream into the skillet and, stirring, cook over high heat for 2 minutes, until the sauce thickens slightly. Spoon it over the chicken.

 SUGGESTED MENU:

Boiled Artichoke Heart (Plain or with Herbed Pepper Sour Cream
    Sauce)
Chicken Tarragon
Cherry Tomato, Mushroom, and Cucumber Salad
Baked Apple

DEVILED CHICKEN WINGS

2 tablespoons Dijon-style mustard
2 tablespoons brown sugar
2 tablespoons vegetable oil
1 clove garlic, crushed
2 dashes of Tabasco sauce
Freshly ground pepper to taste
4 chicken wings
Bread crumbs
¼ teaspoon salt

Combine the mustard, sugar, oil, garlic, Tabasco, and pepper. Fold each chicken pinion (wing tip) behind wing "drumstick" and dip the wings into the mixture. Then coat the wings with the combined bread crumbs and salt. Place them on a lightly oiled baking sheet and bake them in a preheated 350°F oven for 50 minutes or until they are crisp.

 SUGGESTED MENU:

Red Lentil, Red Pepper, and Tomato Soup
Deviled Chicken Wings
Piquant Celery Slaw
Sliced Bananas with Cream

SAUTÉED CHICKEN THIGHS WITH MUSHROOMS

3 medium-sized chicken thighs
Salt and freshly ground pepper to taste
1 tablespoon butter
2 teaspoons vegetable oil
1 small onion, finely chopped
¼ teaspoon thyme
¼ cup dry white wine
2 tablespoons Chicken Broth (see index for recipe)
6 fresh mushrooms, sliced
Freshly chopped parsley

Pat the chicken thighs dry and season them with the salt and pepper. Heat the butter and oil in a 9-inch skillet and brown the thighs on both sides over medium-high heat. Remove the thighs and sauté the onion, stirring it, for 3 minutes. Sprinkle the onion with thyme and pour in the wine and chicken broth. Add the chicken, cover the skillet, and simmer for 15 minutes. Turn the thighs, add the mushrooms, and recover the skillet. Cook for 10 more minutes over low heat. Sprinkle with parsley.

 SUGGESTED MENU:

Sautéed Chicken Thighs with Mushrooms
Risi Bisi
Zabaglione

The Whole Chicken (or Half)

CRISP BROILED CHICKEN

½ lemon
2 teaspoons vegetable oil
½ broiling chicken
½ teaspoon Seasoned Salt (see index for recipe)
⅛ teaspoon paprika
Freshly ground pepper to taste

Combine the juice of the lemon with the oil and rub it over the chicken. Sprinkle the chicken with the combined seasoned salt, paprika, and pepper. Place the chicken about 8 inches under a medium-hot broiler, skin side up. Cook it for 5 minutes, then turn it. Cook it for 8 more minutes, then turn it again and cook it until it is golden and tender.

 SUGGESTED MENU:

Fresh Green Pea Soup
Crisp Broiled Chicken
Ross McClennan's Tomato and Basil Salad
Cream Puff with Chocolate Ice Cream

ROAST CHICKEN HALF

½ roasting chicken (If purchased whole, cut it down the back,
 remove the backbone, and cut it through breast. Wrap and
 freeze the unused chicken half or wrap and use it in another
 recipe the following day.)
2 teaspoons vegetable oil
Seasoned Salt to taste (see index for recipe)
Freshly ground pepper to taste
2 tablespoons melted butter

Rub the chicken half on both sides with the oil. Sprinkle it with the
seasoned salt and pepper on both sides. Wrap it in aluminum foil and
place it in a baking pan, skin side up, in a preheated 400°F oven for
10 minutes. Unfold the foil, brush the chicken with some of the
butter, and cook it uncovered another 15 minutes. Baste it with more
butter and cook it until it is tender and golden.

 SUGGESTED MENU:

Clams Oreganato
Roast Chicken Half
Baby Lima Beans in Cheese and Cream Sauce
Lemon sherbet

ANGELA PAGLIAROLI'S ROAST CHICKEN

My aunt Angela Pagliaroli gave me this recipe for roasting chicken
several years ago. It requires practically no attention and is as juicy
and tender a roast chicken as I've ever eaten.

A 2½-pound roasting chicken
Salt

1 small lemon, quartered
1 clove garlic, crushed
1 teaspoon oregano

Season the chicken inside and out with salt. Rub the lemon quarters with the crushed garlic and sprinkle them with the oregano. Place the lemon quarters inside the chicken. Do not tie the legs together or truss the chicken, but fold the wings back. Roast the chicken in a preheated 325°F oven for 1½ hours. Turn off the oven and let the chicken remain inside for another 15 minutes. Do not baste the chicken or open the oven door during the cooking time.

EXTRAS SUGGESTIONS: Carve the desired amount of chicken for dinner. Then carve the remaining chicken and cover and refrigerate it. This chicken is excellent cold or in soups, salads, sandwiches, or any dish requiring cooked chicken.

 SUGGESTED MENU:

Spaghetti Carbonara
Angela Pagliaroli's Roast Chicken
Romaine Lettuce with Garlic Vinaigrette Sauce
Fresh Pear with Creamy Gorgonzola

One Dozen Cornish Game Hens

A whole roast Cornish game hen is a visual as well as a taste delicacy. It is great for the single cook, for it is portioned by nature for one person. It is economical too; per pound, it costs less than hamburger.

Like chicken, a Cornish game hen lends itself to various cooking methods: frying, braising, baking, roasting, poaching, sautéing, broiling, and grilling. And it can be enriched by the addition of various flavorings: herbs, spices, wine, sherry, lemon, lime, or orange.

If available, buy a fresh Cornish game hen for a more tender and better-flavored bird.

When using a frozen hen, thaw it completely before cooking it. Roasting time for a Cornish hen ranging in weight from 14 to 24 ounces is approximately 45 minutes in a 375°F oven. For further browning, pass it quickly under the broiler. Or, if you prefer, you can cook the bird at 350°F for 1 hour. Cooking time also varies from recipe to recipe, as you will see.

VERA KOCK'S ESCABECHE

Vera Kock, a consulting psychologist in New York, was born in Argentina, so her weekly meals are often comprised of specialties from her native country. An ambitious cook, Vera delights in entertaining a crowd of friends with unusual dinners, such as an impressive bouillabaisse party for sixteen, but she also dines well when eating alone. She says, "I look forward to meals I eat alone, especially after a hectic day of work that many times includes travel. Frequently these meals consist of a dish I have made when entertaining during the previous weekend or earlier, plus a tossed salad or fresh vegetables. Argentina's escabeche suits that purpose perfectly. It keeps indefinitely in the refrigerator if it is stored properly and covered tightly. Escabeche is normally made with partridges, but they aren't always available and are expensive when they are. I tried substituting Cornish game hens in the recipe and I was more than satisfied with the result. Pieces of firm fleshed fish can be used, too. This recipe is for six. I prepare it Friday night for a Saturday night dinner party for four, then refrigerate the two remaining Cornish hens with the sauce and eat them within the next few weeks. Yes, they keep that long, because they're pickled."

5 cloves garlic, peeled and left whole
6 bay leaves (or 3 if they are very strong)
8 carrots, peeled and cut into thin julienne strips

3 large onions, thinly sliced and broken into rings
1 whole lemon, thinly sliced, seeds removed but rind intact
2 teaspoons whole black peppercorns
1½ cups dry white wine
1½ cups red wine vinegar
2 cups vegetable oil
1 teaspoon salt
6 whole Cornish game hens, fresh if possible

Bring all the ingredients except the hens to a boil in a large heavy pot. (Don't use a metal pot, owing to the amount of acid in the dish. It will discolor the sauce. Use an enamel-lined pot.) Reduce the heat and simmer for 30 minutes. Add the hens and simmer for another 45 minutes. Remove the pot from the heat. Allow the hens to cool in their sauce in the pot. Cover and refrigerate them. Serve them the next day at room temperature.

Place each hen on a bed of crisp lettuce and serve it with the sauce. Refrigerate the remaining hens.

 SUGGESTED MENU:

Fresh Cooked Asparagus
Vera Kock's Escabeche
Fried Onion Rings
Yogurt with blueberries and walnuts

ROASTED-ALMOND-COATED CORNISH GAME HEN

 1 Cornish game hen, fresh if possible
 1 egg
 Salt and freshly ground pepper to taste
 ⅓ cup ground almond slivers
 2 tablespoons melted butter
 2 tablespoons vegetable oil

Cut the hen in half through the back and breastbone. Remove the back bone. Lightly beat the egg in a bowl with the salt and pepper. Coat each half of the hen on both sides with the egg. Coat each piece well with the ground almonds. Combine the butter and oil in a small roasting pan. Place the hen halves, skin side up, in the pan and cook them in a preheated 375°F oven for 45 minutes. Baste the pieces twice with the fat in the pan during the cooking time.

 SUGGESTED MENU:

Fruit cup
Roasted-Almond-Coated Cornish Game Hen
Lyonnaise Potatoes with Bacon Garnish
Butter pecan ice cream

BUTTER-ROASTED CORNISH GAME HEN

 1 Cornish game hen
 Salt and freshly ground pepper to taste
 3 tablespoons butter, at room temperature

Season the hen well inside and out with the salt and pepper. Place 1 tablespoon of the butter in the bird's cavity. Tie the legs together and fold the wings back. Smear the remaining 2 tablespoons of butter over the skin. Place the hen in a shallow au gratin dish just large enough to hold the bird comfortably. Roast the hen in a preheated 375°F oven for about 45 minutes, until it is well browned and tender. Baste it with the butter in the bottom of the dish several times during the roasting.

 SUGGESTED MENU:

Avocado with Vinaigrette Sauce
Butter-Roasted Cornish Game Hen
Broccoli with Hollandaise Sauce
Cantaloupe with Port

ROAST CORNISH GAME HEN WITH SHERRY

> 1 Cornish game hen, fresh or completely thawed
> Salt and freshly ground pepper to taste
> ¼ cup dry sherry
> ¼ cup chicken broth
> 2 tablespoons melted butter

Season the hen inside and out with the salt and pepper. Tie the hen's legs together and fold the wings back. Place it in a baking pan just large enough to hold it. Pour in the combined sherry and broth. Brush the bird with the butter. Roast it in a preheated 375°F oven for 45 minutes. Brush it with the butter once or twice during the cooking time.

 SUGGESTED MENU:

Caponata with Tuna
Roast Cornish Game Hen with Sherry
Sautéed Mushrooms
Raspberries with whipped cream

ROAST CORNISH GAME HEN WITH HONEY GLAZE

    1 Cornish game hen
    1 tablespoon vegetable oil
    1 tablespoon soy sauce
    2 tablespoons honey
    1 teaspoon Dijon-style mustard
    1 teaspoon butter, at room temperature
    1 slice white toast, crusts trimmed

Tie the hen's legs together and fold the wings back. Roast it in a
preheated 375°F oven for 15 minutes. Brush the hen generously with
the combined oil, soy sauce, honey, and mustard. Continue roasting
it for 30 more minutes, basting it often with the sauce during the
cooking time. Spread butter on the toast and top it with the roasted
bird. (Placing a piece of toast under the bird prevents it from skating
around on the plate.)

 SUGGESTED MENU:

Fresh Greens Soup
Roast Cornish Game Hen with Honey Glaze
Mashed Sweet Potato with Rum
Fresh Pear with Creamy Gorgonzola

DIET LEMON-FLAVORED ROAST CORNISH GAME HEN

1 Cornish game hen
Salt and freshly ground pepper to taste
½ lemon
¼ cup fresh lemon juice
¼ cup Chicken Stock (see index for recipe)

Season the hen inside and out with the salt and pepper. Place the ½ lemon inside the bird. Tie the legs together and fold the wings back. Put the hen in a shallow baking dish just large enough to hold it with the combined lemon juice and chicken stock. Roast it in a preheated 350°F oven for 1 hour. Do not baste.

 SUGGESTED MENU:

Boiled Artichoke Heart (Plain or with Herbed Pepper Sour Cream
  Sauce)
Diet Lemon-Flavored Roast Cornish Game Hen
Zucchini and Red Pepper Sauté
Dessert Crepe with Strawberries and Whipped Cream

A FRENCHWOMAN'S ROAST CORNISH GAME HEN
STUFFED WITH SPINACH

A charming and elegant French lady asked that she remain anonymous as she explained her philosophy of dining alone: "I am French. I am discreet. But I am happy to tell you how I plan my meals alone. They are many. Many by choice. People ask me if I take vitamins and I say, 'Never,' because I eat only well-balanced meals at home or in restaurants. I consider my mood and what is good in the markets each day as I plan my dinner. Fresh food is most important. The freezer is for ice. Often I begin my cooking—always comfortably dressed— with a glass of Dubonnet at my side in the kitchen. The menu for tonight, for example, is: radishes and carrot sticks (left from yesterday's dinner); pâté du Champagne (made last week); roast cornish hen stuffed with spinach; baked acorn squash; a Beaujolais to drink; and a baked apple.

"I never put just one dish in the oven when using it. You see, I cook the Cornish hen, the squash, and the apple in the oven. On the table I use only good china, crystal, and silver. The table will have two to six candles and flowers, or just one flower in a tiny bowl. Always a cloth napkin; my home is not a coffee shop. Just before I sit down to dinner, I turn on music I like, then I relax and concentrate on the food. I never read while eating alone."

> 1 Cornish game hen
> ½ cup cooked spinach, packed and chopped
> 2 teaspoons butter
> Salt and freshly ground pepper to taste
> A few grates of fresh nutmeg
> 1 tablespoon melted butter

Season the hen inside and out with the salt and pepper. Combine the hot spinach with the 2 teaspoons of butter and season it with salt, pepper, and nutmeg. Spoon the spinach mixture into the hen's cavity.

Fold the wings back and tie the legs together. Place the hen in a small roasting pan, breast side up. Brush it with the melted butter. Roast it in a preheated 400°F oven for 40 to 45 minutes, until it is golden brown. Baste it occasionally with butter.

POACHED CORNISH GAME HEN WITH VEGETABLES AND CREAMY HORSERADISH DRESSING

2½ cups Chicken Stock (see index for recipe)
1 Cornish game hem
1 medium onion, quartered
1 carrot, peeled and sliced
¼ pound green beans, trimmed
1 boiling potato, peeled
⅓ cup Creamy Horseradish Dressing (see index for recipe)

Bring the chicken stock to a boil in a medium-sized saucepan. Fold the hen's wings back. Put it and the onion in the stock. Cover the pan and simmer for 40 minutes. Meanwhile, cook the vegetables separately in boiling, lightly salted water until they are tender. Drain them immediately and set them aside. Remove the hen from the stock to a serving dish. Pour out any liquid in the body cavity. Place the vegetables in a strainer and dip it into the hot stock for 1 minute to reheat and flavor the vegetables. Drain them and arrange them around the hen.

Serve with the creamy horseradish dressing.

 SUGGESTED MENU:

Fried Butter Croutons with Peach-Flavored Cream Cheese
Poached Cornish Game Hen with Vegetables and Creamy
    Horseradish Dressing
A mixed green salad
Parfait of Fresh Papaya and Blueberries

FRIED CORNISH GAME HEN PIECES

Fried Cornish game hen pieces are incredibly tender and succulent. Since the pieces are quite small, they are really finger food. When you are entertaining, serve them as an appetizer.

    1 Cornish game hen
    ¼ cup seasoned bread crumbs
    ¼ cup flour
    ½ teaspoon Seasoned Salt (see index for recipe)
    ½ teaspoon oregano
    2 tablespoons fresh grated Parmesan cheese
    ½ cup milk
    Salt and freshly ground pepper to taste
    ¾ cup vegetable oil

Cut the hen into 8 pieces as you would cut up a whole chicken. In a bowl combine the bread crumbs, flour, seasoned salt, oregano, and Parmesan cheese. Dip the hen pieces in the milk and season them with the salt and pepper. Coat them with the bread-crumb mixture. Heat the oil in a 10- to 12-inch skillet and fry the pieces over medium-high heat until they are golden and crisp on both sides (about 15 minutes).

 SUGGESTED MENU:

Caponata
Fried Cornish Game Hen Pieces
Fresh Potato Salad with Sour Cream
Helen Abbott's Highland Toffee

BUTTERFLIED CORNISH GAME HEN WITH PARMESAN CHEESE AND BUTTER CRUMBS

1 Cornish game hen
1 tablespoon butter
Salt and freshly ground pepper to taste
1½ tablespoons seasoned bread crumbs
1½ tablespoons fresh grated Parmesan cheese
1 tablespoon melted butter

Turn the hen on its breast. Cut along both sides of the backbone with a kitchen shears and discard the bone. Turn the bird and bring the wings and breast areas towards you, breaking the shoulder bones. Fold the wings back. Make a ¾-inch incision in each side of the lower breast and fit the leg joints into the holes. Rub the bird with butter and season it with the salt and pepper. Roast it on a shallow roasting pan in a preheated 375°F oven for 30 minutes. Remove it from the oven. Sprinkle the combined bread crumbs and Parmesan cheese over the hen and drizzle melted butter over it. Return it to the oven and cook it for 20 more minutes or until it is golden and crisp.

 SUGGESTED MENU:

Fresh Crisp Vegetables with Green Mayonnaise
Butterflied Cornish Game Hen with Parmesan Cheese and Butter
    Crumbs
Sautéed Potatoes with Garlic
Sliced orange with pureed strawberries

CORNISH GAME HEN TANDOORI STYLE

½ cup plain yogurt
2 cloves garlic, crushed
1 teaspoon turmeric
1 teaspoon cumin
1 teaspoon coriander
½ teaspoon cinnamon
½ teaspoon nutmeg
Pinch of ground cloves
Pinch of cayenne pepper
2 tablespoons fresh lime juice
Salt and freshly ground pepper to taste
1 Cornish game hen
2 teaspoons melted butter

Combine the yogurt with the garlic, turmeric, cumin, coriander, cinnamon, nutmeg, cloves, cayenne pepper, lime juice, salt, and pepper. Place the hen in a bowl and pour the mixture over it. Cover the bowl and refrigerate it for 10 hours or overnight. Place the bird in a greased shallow baking dish just large enough to hold it comfortably. Sprinkle the butter over it and roast it in a preheated 375°F oven for 45 minutes or until it is tender.

Serve the hen with slices of fresh lime.

 SUGGESTED MENU:

English-Style Cucumber Tea Sandwich
Cornish Game Hen Tandoori Style
Deep-fried Onion Ring Garnish
Curried Rice
Fresh pineapple

CHINESE BARBECUED CORNISH GAME HEN

1 Cornish game hen

SAUCE:

1 tablespoon soy sauce
1 tablespoon dry sherry
1 tablespoon honey
1 tablespoon wine vinegar
1 clove garlic, crushed
½ teaspoon sugar
¼ teaspoon ginger
¼ cup Chicken Broth (see index for recipe)

Combine the sauce ingredients in a bowl. Add the hen and turn it until it is coated with the sauce. Cover the bowl and refrigerate it for several hours or overnight. Place the hen in a small roasting pan. Reserve the marinade. Roast the hen in a preheated 350°F oven for 1 hour, basting it with the marinade twice during the cooking time.

 SUGGESTED MENU:

Shrimp Wrapped in Snow Pea Pods
Chinese Barbecued Cornish Hen
Sautéed Broccoli with Garlic and Basil
Almond cookies and lime sherbert

Duck

A 4-pound duck will yield only two servings, so it is really quite reasonable for the single cook to prepare a duck. Half may be eaten for dinner, and the other half can be served in a variety of ways as a second meal. There are three useful techniques to remember when cooking a duck.

1. Remove all the fat from the body cavity.

2. Prick the duck all over except for the breast area, so that fat can escape freely while the duck cooks.

3. Place a large roasting pan filled to 1 inch with water on the floor of the oven. This pan will collect the fat that drips from the duck while it roasts on an oven rack directly overhead. This roasting method prevents the oven from smoking.

Fresh duck is always preferable to frozen, but it is not readily available. Most frozen ducks are excellent and need only to be thawed before cooking. This may be done by leaving the duck in the refrigerator overnight in the store wrapping, or by wrapping it in airtight plastic and thawing it in a large bowl of cold water, breast side down. This second procedure takes about 5 hours.

It is impossible to cook all the fat out of a duck. After the duck is cooked, cut away any excess fat from behind the skin before serving it. This is a Chinese technique used in preparing Peking duck, but it's a good rule to follow whenever you cook duck.

GLAZED ROAST DUCK

1 4-pound duck
2 tablespoons soy sauce
1 tablespoon honey

Remove all fat from the cavity opening of the duck. Prick the skin in all areas except the breast. Combine the soy sauce and honey and brush the duck with the mixture. Fill a roasting pan to 1 inch with water and place it on the floor of the oven. Place the duck on the middle oven rack directly over the pan in a preheated 375°F oven and roast it for 1½ hours. Remove the duck and cut it in half lengthwise. Cut the half you are serving in half again between the breast and the leg. This makes the duck easier to maneuver on your plate.

EXTRAS SUGGESTIONS: Cool the remaining duck while you are having dinner. Cover and refrigerate it for use the next day in a Sliced Duck, Bacon, and Mushroom Open-faced Sandwich or a Duck Salad. (See index for recipes.)

 SUGGESTED MENU:

Honeydew Melon with Curried Shrimp, Walnuts, and Apples
Glazed Roast Duck
Arugula and Endive Salad
Cinnamon Ice Cream

Turkey Breast

ROAST TURKEY BREAST WITH MUSHROOM AND HERB STUFFING

When I have an appetite for turkey with stuffing and I'm going to be eating alone, I roast a small whole turkey breast. It's really only the breast meat that I want anyway. A stuffed turkey breast cooked in foil at a high temperature produces moist, savory turkey meat for dinner and extras for several other meals. I don't mind having turkey a few days running in various other dishes, but if two consecutive turkey meals are your limit, cook the turkey when you are having company for dinner. You will then have one meal by yourself and another with as many as three guests, depending on the dish you make with the turkey. I don't recommend freezing cooked turkey, because the quality and texture of the meat suffer.

1 3½ pound turkey breast, fresh or frozen and thawed
1 tablespoon melted butter
Salt and freshly ground pepper to taste

Mushroom and Herb Stuffing:

3 tablespoons butter
1 stalk celery, chopped
1 small onion, chopped
6 fresh mushrooms, finely chopped
¼ teaspoon sage
¼ teaspoon marjoram
¼ teaspoon thyme
1 tablespoon dry white wine
½ cup water
2 cups herbed or seasoned stuffing mix
1 egg, beaten

First prepare the stuffing. Heat the 3 tablespoons of butter in a 10- to 12-inch skillet. Sauté the celery, onion, and mushrooms for 5 minutes over medium heat, stirring. Sprinkle them with the sage, marjoram, and thyme. Pour in the wine and stir. Add the water and stuffing mix. Remove the skillet from the heat, add the egg, and mix well. Make a pocket in the turkey breast by cutting against the bones of the rib section to the breast bone. Repeat this procedure on the other side, making another pocket. Line a roasting pan with a sheet of heavy-duty foil long enough to completely cover the turkey breast. Lightly butter the foil. Place the turkey on the foil, breast side up. Fit half of the stuffing between the meat and the rib section in one pocket, pressing down gently. Repeat this procedure on the other side of the breast with the remaining stuffing. Brush the entire breast with the melted butter and season it well with the salt and pepper. Cover it with the foil. Roast it in a preheated 425°F oven for 1 hour. Peel the foil covering the breast back and continue the cooking for about 30 minutes or until the turkey is browned and tender. Let it sit for 15 minutes before carving it. Serve it with Chicken Gravy (see recipe on page 178).

(After dinner, remove the remaining stuffing and store it, covered, separately in the refrigerator.)

EXTRAS SUGGESTIONS: Sliced cooked turkey topped with a generous slice of stuffing, cranberry sauce, and cheese makes an excellent sandwich. It also makes superb salads and creamed dishes. You can also substitute cooked turkey in any chicken salad recipe. Extra stuffing can be eaten cold or reheated and served with the extra turkey or any other meat.

 SUGGESTED MENU:
Tomato Mold with Vegetables and Fresh Basil
Roast Turkey Breast with Mushroom and Herb Stuffing
Chicken Gravy
Cranberry sauce
Elizabeth Ann McGinn's Georgia Peaches

CHICKEN GRAVY

2 pounds chicken backs, necks, wings, or giblets (never the
    liver)
1 onion, quartered
1 stalk celery, quartered
1 bay leaf
1 parsnip, quartered (optional)
4 peppercorns
1 teaspoon salt
2 cups Chicken Stock (see index for recipe)
¼ cup dry white wine
1 teaspoon flour or as needed
2 teaspoons butter or as needed

Place the chicken parts, onion, celery, bay leaf, parsnip, peppercorns, and salt into a large saucepan. Add the stock and enough cold water to just cover the ingredients. Bring the liquid to a boil, reduce the heat, and simmer for 1¼ hours, adding more water if necessary. Strain the stock. You should have 1¼ cups. Pour it into a small saucepan. Add the wine and reduce the mixture over high heat to ¾ cup. Combine the flour and butter with a fork and stir them into the stock with a wire whisk, until the gravy is smooth and thickened slightly. (For a thicker sauce, add a little more flour with butter.) Taste for seasoning.

8. Meats

A Roundup of Beef Dishes

JOHN BUNGE'S RESSAC ET GAZON

John Bunge, a research analyst in Chicago, relishes ten-hour work days. A few years back, after a successful business day, he created this savory dish.

"I wanted to relax at home and celebrate a new contract with a major client. Barbara, my friend, was working that evening, so I opened a bottle of chilled Pouilly Fuissé and headed for the kitchen. I'd shopped for steak and shrimp on my way home from work. Since I'm not an experienced cook, I always cook on top of the stove and concoct sauces that don't need to be cooked."

While sipping wine, John whipped up a quick meal for himself that is now multiplied and featured at the dinner parties he and his wife, Barbara, give. (*Ressac et gazon* is French for "surf and turf," a name John dislikes.)

> ½ bay leaf
> 4 peppercorns
> ¼ cup dry white wine
> 1 small onion, peeled and halved
> 4 extra-large shrimp, shelled and deveined
> 1 tablespoon vegetable oil
> 1 6-ounce filet mignon

In a small saucepan combine the bay leaf, peppercorns, white wine, onion, and 2½ cups of cold water. Bring the liquid to a rolling boil. Add the shrimp and bring it back to the boil. Reduce the heat slightly to a low boil and cook the shrimp for 5 more minutes or until they are just tender. Remove the shrimp with a slotted spoon to a plate. Let the broth the shrimp cooked in simmer over low heat. Heat the oil in a 9-inch heavy skillet. Brown the filet over high heat on one side for about 5 minutes. Turn it with tongs and cook it to the desired doneness; rare takes about 3 minutes. When the filet is done, remove it to a warmed plate. Drop the shrimp in the simmering broth to reheat them for 30 seconds. Remove them and drain them well.

Place the shrimp on the plate with the meat and serve the quick green herb sauce on the side.

Quick Green Herb Sauce

⅓ cup Mayonnaise (see index for recipe)
1 tablespoon fresh chopped parsley
2 teaspoons chopped chives
3 sprigs watercress, chopped
½ teaspoon tarragon
1 teaspoon vinegar
Salt and freshly ground pepper to taste

Combine all the ingredients in a food processor or blender.

 SUGGESTED MENU:

Fresh Crisp Vegetables with Green Mayonnaise
John Bunge's Ressac et Gazon
Fried Potatoes in Their Jackets
Strawberry Ice

BROILED FLANK STEAK WITH
MUSTARD PEPPER CRUST

1 1½-pound flank steak, cut in half crosswise on a diagonal,
    against the grain
Salt to taste
1½ tablespoons mustard
1 tablespoon honey
1 tablespoon fresh black peppercorns, coarsely crushed with the
    side of a cleaver or the back of a saucepan

Using only half the beef, season it with the salt and brush it evenly
with the combined mustard and honey. Press the crushed pepper into
the meat. Cook the steak under a hot broiler for 5 minutes. Turn it
and cook for 5 more minutes for rare; cook 2 or 3 minutes longer for
medium. (The meat will shrink considerably in size during the cooking.) Slice the steak on a diagonal, against the grain.

EXTRAS SUGGESTIONS: The remaining uncooked half of the flank steak
can be wrapped and frozen or used the next day in the recipe for
Stir-fried Chinese Beef with Black Bean Sauce. Any extra cooked
steak will make an elegant Cold Beef Vinaigrette or a Sliced Steak
Sandwich. (See index for recipes.)

 SUGGESTED MENU:

Fried Butter Croutons with Green Mayonnaise and Julienne of
    Cucumber
Broiled Flank Steak with Mustard Pepper Crust
Fresh Potato Chips
Sautéed Bananas with Brown Sugar

BROILED WINE-MARINATED SHELL STEAK

1 8-ounce shell steak
1 clove garlic, crushed
Salt and freshly ground pepper to taste
½ cup dry red wine
1 tablespoon vegetable oil
1 tablespoon melted butter

Rub the steak with the garlic, salt, and pepper. Combine the wine with the oil in a shallow dish just large enough to hold the steak. Place the steak in the wine mixture and turn it several times. Cover the dish and leave it at room temperature for 1 hour. Remove the steak and pat it dry. Brush each side with the butter and cook it 5 inches under a hot broiler for 5 minutes. Turn it and cook it 3 or 4 more minutes for rare; cook it 2 additional minutes for medium.

 SUGGESTED MENU:

Fresh Hot Tomato and Onion Soup
Broiled Wine-Marinated Shell Steak
Greek Salad
Crepes with Fruit Preserves

SAUTÉED TOURNEDOS OF BEEF WITH MADEIRA

1 6-ounce tournedos of beef
Salt and freshly ground pepper to taste
2 tablespoons Clarified Butter (see index for recipe)
¼ cup Madeira

Season the beef with the salt and pepper. Heat 1 tablespoon of the butter in a 9-inch skillet. Brown the meat on both sides over medium-high heat until it is cooked rare or to the desired doneness. Remove it to a heated plate. Pour the Madeira into the cleaned skillet and cook it for 1 minute over high heat. Whisk in the remaining tablespoon of butter. Pour the sauce over the filet. Serve at once.

 SUGGESTED MENU:

Creamed Mushrooms on Fried Toast
Sautéed Tournedos of Beef with Madeira
Stir-fried Fresh Vegetables
Fruit and cheese

CHICKEN FRIED STEAK

This dish was part of my weekly diet as a child in Kansas. It is to me what people today refer to as security food, but it still tastes wonderful, especially the crust.

¼ cup milk
1 small egg, beaten
1 6-ounce minute steak, tenderized
Flour
2 tablespoons butter
3 tablespoons vegetable oil
Salt and freshly ground pepper to taste

Beat together the milk and the egg. Dip the steak in this mixture, then dredge it in flour on both sides. Let it sit for several minutes. Heat the butter and oil in an 8-inch skillet and sauté the steak for about 5 minutes, until it is browned, over medium-high heat. Turn it, reduce the heat to medium, and brown it on the other side. Season it immediately with salt and pepper.

 SUGGESTED MENU:

Sautéed Tiny Smoked Sausages with Mustard
Chicken Fried Steak
Sautéed Cream of Fresh Corn
Whole Wheat Bread Pudding with Blueberries

Favorite Ground-Beef Recipes

MARION NEWBERG'S STUFFED CABBAGE

Esther Newberg, a literary agent, credits her mother for the dish she cooks most frequently. Esther has distinct views on cooking for one.

"Being single is a great advantage in cooking because it enables you to make a giant pot of stuffed cabbage and then eat it all. When my mother used to make it, as the cook, she was always faced with giving one of us the last stuffed cabbage. The martyrdom of motherhood. I usually make the cabbage on the weekend and then freeze half of it. I eat several the same day. Occasionally I cut the recipe in half and make smaller stuffed cabbages as hors d'oeuvres to eat prior to other meals. As a literary agent, I find that stuffed cabbage goes especially well with Travis McGee mysteries, S. J. Perelman *New Yorker* stories, and the sports page of the Boston *Globe*. I don't recommend eating stuffed cabbage and reading serious nonfiction."

> 1 large head cabbage
> 1 pound ground beef
> 1 cup cooked rice
> Salt and freshly ground pepper to taste
> 1 15-ounce can tomato sauce
> ½ cup brown sugar
> ¼ cup sugar
> The juice of half a lemon

Place the cored cabbage in a large pot of boiling water for 5 minutes. This will facilitate the removal of the leaves in whole pieces and blanch the cabbage. Drain it. Separate the leaves, using the 12 or 14 largest ones for stuffing. (Use the smaller, center leaves in coleslaw or salad.) Mix together the meat and rice, seasoning the mixture well with the salt and pepper. Place the meat and rice mixture in equal portions on the centers of the leaves. Fold the sides of one leaf over the mixture, then roll it up into a package about 2½ inches thick and 3 to 4 inches long. Repeat the procedure for the remaining stuffed cabbage leaves. As you make them, arrange them in a large skillet or pot. Combine the remaining ingredients plus 1 can of water and pour the mixture over the stuffed cabbage. Cover the skillet and cook the cabbage rolls over low heat on top of the stove for 1½ hours. Remove cover and transfer the skillet to a preheated 325°F oven and cook the cabbage for 30 more minutes, until the rolls are lightly browned.

SUGGESTED MENU:

Shrimp Wrapped in Snow Pea Pods
Marion Newberg's Stuffed Cabbage
Boiled Potatoes with Parsley
Raspberry Fool

MEAT LOAF

Meat loaf is really the Americanization of pâté. It is juicy and flavorful when it is served hot, but cold and sliced it makes a superb crude-style pâté for a first course or sandwich.

½ pound ground beef
¼ pound ground veal
¼ pound ground pork
1 medium onion, finely chopped
1 clove garlic, minced
1 tablespoon fresh chopped parsley
¼ teaspoon thyme
½ teaspoon oregano
¼ teaspoon rosemary
2 dashes of Tabasco sauce
½ cup seasoned bread crumbs

1 egg
Salt and freshly ground pepper to taste
6 strips bacon

Thoroughly combine all the ingredients except for the bacon. Line a 7½-by-3-by-¾-inch porcelain terrine or loaf pan with the bacon strips, arranged crosswise. Shape the beef mixture into a loaf and place it on the bacon. Press it evenly into the corners. Bring the ends of the bacon up over the top of the meat loaf. Cover the terrine with aluminum foil. Set it in a larger pan with water in it reaching halfway up the side of the terrine and bake it in a 350°F oven for 50 minutes. Pour out the fat. Let the loaf sit for 10 minutes before slicing it.

 SUGGESTED MENU:

Meat Loaf
Sautéed Broccoli with Garlic and Basil
Roasted Potatoes
Vanilla Ice Cream with Crème de Menthe and Chocolate Morsels

SPICY MEATBALLS

7 ounces ground beef
2 slices fresh bread, crusts trimmed
1 teaspoon fresh chopped parsley
¼ teaspoon oregano
1 tablespoon grated onion
Two dashes of Tabasco
Salt to taste
¼ teaspoon freshly ground pepper
2 tablespoons fresh grated Parmesan cheese
2 tablespoons olive oil

Soak the bread slices in water, squeeze them to remove all liquid, then shred them. Combine the bread with all the other ingredients except the olive oil. Divide the mixture into two parts. Shape each part into balls. Heat the oil in a 9-inch skillet and sauté the meatballs over medium heat until they are well browned, about 20 minutes.

 SUGGESTED MENU:

Fusilli with Fresh Marinara Sauce and Spicy Meatballs
A mixed green salad
Zucchini Cake

One Dozen Hamburgers

THE MASTER RECIPE FOR A GOOD HOMEMADE HAMBURGER

> 6 to 8 ounces good quality fresh ground chuck (Ground sirloin is good, too, but often it doesn't contain enough fat and turns out on the dry side.)
> Salt and freshly ground pepper to taste
> 1 tablespoon vegetable oil or Clarified Butter (see index for recipe)

Season the meat well with the salt and pepper. Shape it into an inch-thick patty. Heat the oil or clarified butter in a 9-inch cast-iron or other heavy skillet. Cook the patty over high heat for 4 minutes. Turn it and cook for another 4 minutes. The hamburger will now be medium rare. Cook it a minute longer if you prefer it medium. Remember, frying the hamburger over high heat in a heavy skillet is the only way to achieve a grill flavor and a browned crust if you are cooking on top of the stove.

Variations

Worcestershire-Flavored Hamburger

Add ½ teaspoon of Worcestershire sauce to 6 to 8 ounces of ground chuck seasoned with salt and pepper. Mix well and cook according to directions in the master recipe.

Soy Sauce and Onion Flavored Hamburger

Mix 1 teaspoon of grated onion and ½ teaspoon of soy sauce to 6 to 8 ounces of ground chuck and proceed as in the master recipe.

Mushroom Hamburger

Add 3 finely chopped fresh mushrooms to 6 to 8 ounces of ground chuck with ½ teaspoon of Worcestershire sauce, salt and pepper to taste, and 1 teaspoon of finely chopped parsley. Mix well and form the meat into a patty. Follow the cooking directions in the master recipe.

Cheeseburger

Place 1 slice of Cheddar, Swiss, mozzarella, or the cheese of your choice on the hamburger about 1 minute before it is done. Cover the pan with a lid. The cheese will heat and melt.

If you place a slice of cheese on the hamburger and put it under the broiler, it is likely that a crust will form if you let it turn golden. This crust is often chewy and bitter.

Hamburger Bread

Ordinary hamburger buns are usually tasteless unless they are made with high-quality ingredients and are very fresh. English muffins, bagels, French bread, or even good sliced whole-wheat or rye bread is superior to packaged hamburger buns. Whichever you select, butter it lightly and toast it until it is golden.

CONDIMENTS AND OTHER HAMBURGER ESCORTS

Ketchup is the generally accepted accompaniment to a hamburger. A mixture of ketchup and Dijon-style mustard or just mustard is preferred by some people. Across the country people's tastes vary; some like mayonnaise or a Thousand Island preparation with pickles, tomatoes, lettuce, and grilled or raw onions. To my mind, the perfect hamburger is the Worcestershire-Flavored Hamburger topped with Grilled Onion Slices (see index for recipe) and a generous amount of combined mustard and ketchup on hot buttered and toasted French bread.

PABLO BURGER

> 1 6- to 8-ounce hamburger patty
> 2 slices prosciutto
> 1 poached egg
> ¼ cup Béarnaise Sauce (see index for recipe)

Cook the hamburger according to the master recipe. Top it with the folded pieces of prosciutto, the poached egg, and Béarnaise sauce.

 SUGGESTED MENU:

Onion and Anchovy Canapés
Pablo Burger
Sautéed Green Beans
Banana Crown

AVOCADO AND BEAN SPROUTS BURGER

⅓ cup fresh bean sprouts
1 tablespoon minced scallion
1 tablespoon lemon juice
1 teaspoon mustard
1½ tablespoons olive oil
Salt and freshly ground pepper to taste
1 small ripe avocado
1 6- to 8-ounce hamburger patty

Combine the bean sprouts, scallion, lemon juice, mustard, and oil and season the mixture with the salt and pepper. Slice the avocado and arrange the slices on a plate. Top them with the burger cooked according to the master recipe and the bean sprouts mixture.

 SUGGESTED MENU:

Avocado and Bean Sprouts Burger
Fried Onion Rings
Caribbean Rum-Flavored Fruit

CRUSTY HAMBURGER

2 slices fresh bread, crusts removed
Freshly ground pepper to taste
¼ teaspoon Seasoned Salt (see index for recipe)
1 6- to 8-ounce hamburger patty
Flour
1 egg, beaten
2 tablespoons vegetable oil

Make bread crumbs from the two slices of fresh bread in a food processor or a blender, one at a time. Combine the crumbs with the pepper and seasoned salt. Coat the hamburger patty with the flour; dip it in the egg and cover it with bread crumbs. Heat the oil in a 9-inch skillet and sauté the hamburger until it is golden on each side and cooked to the desired doneness.

 SUGGESTED MENU:

Herring in Cream Sauce with Mustard and Capers
Crusty Hamburger
Carrots Vichy
Broiled Grapefruit with Maple Syrup

HERB HAMBURGER

To 6 to 8 ounces of ground chuck add ¼ teaspoon of oregano, ¼ teaspoon of basil, and 1 teaspoon of fresh chopped parsley. Season with salt and pepper and mix well. Form the hamburger into a patty and cook it according to the master recipe.

 SUGGESTED MENU:

Quick Black Bean Soup
Herb Hamburger
Cauliflower au Gratin
Peach Waffle Cake

GERMAN HAMBURGER

½ cup sauerkraut
2 teaspoons butter
¼ cup sour cream
¼ teaspoon caraway seeds
Freshly ground pepper to taste
1 6- to 8-ounce hamburger patty

Rinse the sauerkraut under cold running water in a colander and drain it well. Melt the butter in small saucepan, add the sauerkraut, and heat it, stirring constantly. Remove it from the heat. Stir in the sour cream and caraway seeds and season the mixture with the pepper. Spoon it over a hamburger cooked according to the master recipe.

 SUGGESTED MENU:

Sautéed Tiny Smoked Sausages with Mustard
German Hamburger
Fresh Potato Chips
Cinnamon Ice Cream with Toasted Almonds

PEPPER HAMBURGER

1 6- to 8-ounce hamburger patty
Salt
2 teaspoons fresh crushed black peppercorns

Season the hamburger patty with the salt and press the peppercorns evenly over the meat. Cook the hamburger according to the master recipe.

 SUGGESTED MENU:

Pepper Hamburger
Mini Caesar Salad
Fresh Strawberries with Crème Fraîche and Brown Sugar

HAMBURGER WITH SOUR CREAM AND RED CAVIAR

1 heaping tablespoon red caviar
⅓ cup sour cream
1 tablespoon chopped scallion
1 6- to 8-ounce hamburger patty

Combine the red caviar with the sour cream and scallion. Spoon the mixture on top of a hamburger cooked according to the master recipe.

 SUGGESTED MENU:

Hamburger with Sour Cream and Red Caviar
Fresh Cooked Asparagus
Sugar-and-Almond-Toasted Brioche

GROUND-BEEF PATTY EN CROÛTE

    6 to 8 ounces ground beef
    3 shallots, finely chopped
    ¼ teaspoon tarragon
    ½ teaspoon Worcestershire sauce
    Salt and freshly ground pepper to taste
    2 frozen patty shells, partially thawed for 5 minutes
    1 egg, beaten

Combine the ground beef, shallots, tarragon, Worcestershire sauce, salt, and pepper. Form a patty about 1 inch thick and 4½ inches in diameter. In a heavy 9-inch skillet, brown the patty quickly on each side over high heat. Cool it. Place one patty shell on top of the other and roll them out to about 9 inches. Place the ground-beef patty in the center of the pastry and bring up edges and seal them together by pressing. Place the sealed side down on a baking sheet. Brush the pastry with the beaten egg. Bake it in a preheated 400°F oven for 18 to 20 minutes, until the pastry is golden brown.

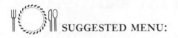 SUGGESTED MENU:

Melon Cubes Wrapped in Cheese and Prosciutto
Ground-Beef Patty en Croûte
Zucchini and Red Pepper Sauté
Zabaglione

Easy Veal for One

SAUTÉED HERB-STUFFED VEAL BIRDS

3 slices day-old white bread, crusts trimmed
2 tablespoons fresh chopped parsley
½ teaspoon dried tarragon
¼ teaspoon dried thyme
Salt and freshly ground pepper to taste
2 veal scallops, pounded till about ⅛-inch thick
Flour
1 egg, lightly beaten
2 tablespoons butter
2 tablespoons vegetable oil

Make bread crumbs with the bread in a food processor fitted with a steel blade or force the bread through a strainer. Add the herbs to the bread crumbs and season them well with the salt and pepper. Place 2 tablespoons of the bread-crumb mixture in the center of each veal scallop. Wrap the long sides of the meat over the stuffing. Fold the end pieces over the sealed edge of meat. Holding each veal bird together, dust it with the flour, roll it in the beaten egg, and coat it with the herbed bread-crumb mixture. Heat the butter and oil in a 9-inch skillet. Sauté the veal birds over medium heat until they are evenly browned and tender, about 10 minutes.

 SUGGESTED MENU:

Quiche Lorraine
Sautéed Herb-Stuffed Veal Birds
Lemon-Glazed Carrots
Dates Stuffed with Pecans and Cream Cheese

SAUTÉED VEAL STRIPS WITH LEMON AND TARRAGON

2 veal scallops, flattened to ¼-inch thickness with a meat
      pounder or the side of a cleaver
Salt and freshly ground pepper to taste
Flour
2 tablespoons butter
1 tablespoon olive or vegetable oil
1 teaspoon lemon juice
¼ cup Chicken Broth (see index for recipe)
¼ teaspoon tarragon

Season the veal scallops with the salt and freshly ground pepper. Cut them into ¼-inch-thick strips. Dust the strips with flour. Shake off any excess flour. Heat 1 tablespoon of the butter with the oil in a 9-inch skillet. When it is very hot, but not smoking, add the veal. Cook the veal until it is browned, turning the pieces with a fork. Remove the veal. Add the remaining tablespoon of butter to the skillet and stir to loosen any particles on the bottom of the pan. Pour the combined lemon juice and broth and tarragon into the pan and bring it to a boil, constantly whisking. Cook it for 2 minutes, until the sauce thickens. Add the veal. Toss the veal in the pan over high heat for 30 seconds.

 SUGGESTED MENU:

Fried Crepes with Honey Butter
Sautéed Veal Strips with Lemon and Tarragon
Baked Stuffed Potato
Four-Fruit Compote

VEAL MARSALA

> 2 veal scallops, flattened to ¼-inch thickness with a meat
>   pounder or the side of a cleaver
> Salt and freshly ground pepper to taste
> Flour
> 1 tablespoon butter
> 1 tablespoon olive or vegetable oil
> ¼ cup Marsala
> ½ teaspoon fresh chopped parsley

Season the veal scallops with the salt and pepper. Dust both sides with the flour. Heat the butter and oil in a 12-inch skillet. When the oil is very hot, but not smoking, add the veal and brown it quickly on both sides. Remove the veal to a warmed plate. Pour in the Marsala and stir it to release any meat particles on the bottom of the pan. Whisk over high heat for 1 minute until the sauce thickens. Pour the sauce over the veal and sprinkle it with parsley.

 SUGGESTED MENU:

Fettucine with Ground Veal, Prosciutto, and Cream Sauce
Veal Marsala
Arugula and Endive Salad
Fresh Pear with Creamy Gorgonzola

SAUTÉED VEAL CHOP WITH MUSHROOMS AND CREAM

1 veal chop
Salt and freshly ground pepper to taste
Flour
3 tablespoons butter
1 tablespoon vegetable oil
1 small onion, cut into thin slivers
4 fresh mushrooms, thinly sliced
1 tablespoon dry white wine
¼ cup Chicken Stock (see index for recipe)
¼ cup heavy cream

Season the chop with the salt and pepper. Dust it with the flour. Heat
1 tablespoon of the butter and the oil in a 9-inch skillet. Brown the
chop on both sides over medium-high heat. Remove it to a side dish.
Add the 2 remaining tablespoons of butter to the pan and sauté the
onion for 4 minutes. Stir in the mushrooms and cook for 3 more
minutes. Stir the vegetables occasionally. Pour in the dry white wine
and the chicken stock. Bring the liquid to a boil, reduce the heat, and
add the chop with the juices that have accumulated in the dish. Simmer the chop for 5 minutes. Transfer the chop with the onions and
mushrooms to a heated serving plate. Pour the heavy cream in the
skillet and bring to a boil, constantly whisking. Boil it for 3 minutes.
Taste it for seasoning. Pour the sauce over the chop and serve at once.

 SUGGESTED MENU:

Tomato Mold with Vegetables and Fresh Basil
Sautéed Veal Chop with Mushrooms and Cream
Potatoes à la Parisienne
Chocolate Soufflé

SAUTÉED CALF'S LIVER

2 slices thinly sliced calf's liver
Flour
Salt and freshly ground pepper to taste
1½ tablespoons butter
2 tablespoons vegetable oil
1 wedge fresh lemon

Coat the liver slices lightly with the flour and sprinkle them with the salt and pepper. Heat the butter and oil in a skillet. Sauté the liver over medium-high heat for 2 to 3 minutes on each side. The liver will be pink inside and tender. Transfer it from the pan to a heated dinner plate. Squeeze the juice from the lemon wedge into the pan. Stir and pour the sauce over the liver.

 SUGGESTED MENU:

Celery and Carrot Herb Soup
Sautéed Calf's Liver
Boiled Potatoes with Parsley
Grilled Apricots with Pecan Filling

WIENER SCHNITZEL À LA HOLSTEIN

2 medium-sized veal scallops (or 1 large), flattened to ¼-inch
      thickness
Salt and freshly ground pepper to taste
Flour
2 eggs
Bread crumbs
⅓ cup vegetable oil
½ tablespoon butter
Paprika

Season the veal with the salt and pepper. Dust it with flour on each
side. Beat 1 of the eggs in a bowl and dip the veal in the egg. Then
coat it with the bread crumbs. Heat the oil in a 10- to 12-inch skillet.
When it is hot, but not smoking, add the veal and cook it over
medium-high heat until it is browned on both sides. Transfer the veal
to a warmed plate. In a small, nonstick skillet heat the butter and fry
the second egg until the white is set. Top the veal with the fried egg.
Season it with paprika and pepper.
  Serve it with a seeded wedge of lemon.

 SUGGESTED MENU:

Herring in Cream Sauce with Mustard and Capers
Wiener Schnitzel à la Holstein
Sweet and Sour Kraut Salad
Martin Rapp's Square Apple Tart with Instant Puff Pastry

Great Lamb Solos

SUSAN ANGEL'S BROILED LAMB CHOPS

Susan Angel, a theatrical agent in London, did not hesitate when I asked her for her favorite dinner for one. "Broiled lamb chops with mint jelly, fresh green peas, and a baked potato with butter. It's a plain meal, but if all the dishes are cooked properly, it's glorious. To my taste, the lamb chops must be pink. This meal can also easily be doubled, tripled, or multiplied by the number of guests one has."

> 3 or 4 ¾-inch-thick rib lamb chops
> 1 clove garlic, halved
> Salt and freshly ground pepper

Rub the chops all over with the inside of the garlic halves and season them with the salt and pepper. Place them on a lightly oiled grill rack under a hot broiler for 3 to 4 minutes on each side, depending on the desired doneness.

Accompany them with mint jelly.

 SUGGESTED MENU:

Creamed Mushrooms on Fried Toast
Susan Angel's Broiled Lamb Chops with mint jelly
Hot cooked fresh peas
Baked potato with butter
Cantaloupe with Port

MARINATED LAMB KEBABS

> ¼ cup olive oil
> 2 tablespoons lemon juice
> 1 large clove garlic, crushed
> 2 tablespoons fresh chopped parsley
> 1 small onion, thinly sliced
> ¼ teaspoon thyme
> ¼ teaspoon basil
> ¼ teaspoon oregano
> ½ teaspoon salt
> ¼ teaspoon freshly ground pepper
> 6 to 8 ounces boneless shoulder or leg of lamb, cut into 1½-inch
>   cubes

Mix together all the ingredients except the lamb cubes in a bowl. Add
the lamb and toss. Cover and marinate the lamb in the refrigerator for
2 hours. Remove the meat and thread it onto a metal skewer. Broil it
until it is browned and tender to the desired doneness, turning it once
or twice.

 SUGGESTED MENU:

Marinated Artichoke Hearts in Curry Sauce
Marinated Lamb Kebabs
Sautéed Wild Rice
Strawberry Ice

BROILED LAMB SHANK

2 tablespoons vegetable oil
1 tablespoon lemon juice
1 clove garlic, crushed
1 tablespoon grated onion
¼ teaspoon rosemary
⅛ teaspoon thyme
Salt and freshly ground pepper to taste
1 lamb shank

Combine all the ingredients except the lamb and pour this mixture over the lamb. Turn the lamb several times, then cover and refrigerate it overnight. Remove the lamb and reserve the marinade. Place the lamb in a pan under a preheated broiler. Cook it for 4 minutes, turn it, and cook it for 4 more minutes or to the desired doneness. Heat the marinade in a small saucepan until it boils. Strain it and serve it with the lamb.

 SUGGESTED MENU:

Cold Cucumber and Yogurt Soup
Broiled Lamb Shank
Sautéed Eggplant with Garlic
Banana Crown

CURRIED LAMB STRIPS IN CREAM SAUCE

3 small lamb chops, cut into ¼-inch strips, fat removed
Salt and freshly ground pepper to taste
Flour
1 tablespoon butter
1 teaspoon vegetable oil
1 tablespoon fresh lime juice
1 scallion, sliced
½ teaspoon curry powder or to taste
½ cup heavy cream

Season the lamb strips with the salt and pepper and dust them with flour. Heat the butter and oil in a 9-inch skillet. Sauté the lamb over medium-high heat until it is browned on all sides. Pour in the lime juice. Cook for 30 seconds, stirring occasionally. Add the scallion and curry powder. Pour in the heavy cream and bring the liquid to a boil. Cook for about 3 minutes, stirring often, until the sauce thickens slightly. Taste for seasoning.

 SUGGESTED MENU:

Ham-Filled Biscuits
Curried Lamb Strips in Cream Sauce
Hot cooked rice
Green peas
Peach Cobbler

BROILED LAMB STEAK WITH MINT CHUTNEY

1 lamb steak
Seasoned Salt and freshly ground pepper to taste (see index for
    recipe)

Mint Chutney:

2 tablespoons chutney
1 teaspoon fresh chopped mint or ¼ teaspoon dried mint
1 teaspoon fresh lemon or lime juice

Cut through the fat along the border of the steak at several intervals
to prevent the steak from curling during cooking. Season it with the
seasoned salt and pepper on both sides. Broil it under a preheated
broiler about 4 minutes per side for medium rare; 1 minute longer per
side for medium. Place it on a warmed plate. Combine the chutney,
mint, and lemon juice. Serve the chutney with the steak.

 SUGGESTED MENU:

Celery Root Rémoulade
Broiled Lamb Steak with Mint Chutney
Boiled Potatoes with Parsley
Cointreau Dessert Omelet with Fresh Strawberries

GROUND-LAMB PATTY À LA LINDSTRØM

6 ounces ground lamb
2 tablespoons heavy cream
1 tablespoon finely chopped onion
1 tablespoon chopped capers
1 small potato, boiled and diced
Salt and freshly ground pepper to taste
2 teaspoons butter
1 tablespoon vegetable oil

Combine the lamb, cream, onion, capers, and potato. Season the mixture well with the salt and pepper. Shape it into 1-inch-thick patty. Heat the butter and oil in a 9-inch skillet and sauté the patty until it is brown on each side. It should be slightly pink inside.

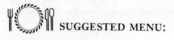 SUGGESTED MENU:

Carrot and Raisin Salad
Ground-Lamb Patty à la Lindstrøm
Fried Potatoes in Their Jackets
Broiled Grapefruit with Maple Syrup

LAMB HASH

2 tablespoons butter
2 tablespoons vegetable oil
1 small onion, chopped
⅔ cup diced parboiled potatoes
¾ cup cubed cooked lamb
Salt and freshly ground pepper to taste
Worcestershire sauce

Heat 1 tablespoon of the butter and 1 tablespoon of the oil in a 9-inch skillet. Sauté the onion for 5 minutes, stirring. Remove the onion with a slotted spoon. Add the remaining tablespoon of butter and of oil. Sauté the potatoes until they are lightly browned. Return the onion, add the lamb, and season with the salt and pepper. Sauté the hash for 5 or 6 minutes or until it is well heated. Sprinkle it with the Worcestershire sauce.

VARIATION: Instead of lamb, use cooked roast beef for roast beef hash.

 SUGGESTED MENU:

Cold Asparagus Vinaigrette
Lamb Hash
Pain Grillé with Butter
Poached Pear with Cranberry and Apricot Sauce

Singular Pork and Ham

SABINE SUGARMAN'S GINGERED PORK

Now residents of Atlanta, Sabine and Ron Sugarman lived in Tokyo for four years, so it's no wonder Sabine says, "Our taste buds have been seasoned by living in the Far East. I rarely eat alone, having two small children to look after, but when I do I usually cook dishes with oriental touches, like this stir-fried pork and ginger dish. It fits the three requirements that I wish all cooking would: quick, easy to prepare, and delicious to eat."

    1 tablespoon peanut or vegetable oil
    6 ounces boneless pork, thinly sliced or shredded
    1 tablespoon sugar
    1 tablespoon soy sauce
    1 teaspoon fresh grated ginger

Heat the oil in a 9-inch skillet and sauté the pork over high heat until it begins to brown, stirring. Sprinkle the sugar and soy sauce over the meat, stir, and cook for 1 minute. Add the ginger, stir, and cook for 2 minutes.

 SUGGESTED MENU:

Melon
Sabine Sugarman's Gingered Pork
Hot fluffy rice
Stir-fried Fresh Vegetables
Coconut Macaroons

BONELESS PORK ROAST

Even though I eat alone, boneless pork roast is a dish I refuse to do without.

A 3-pound boneless pork roast
Salt and freshly ground pepper to taste
1 tablespoon vegetable oil

Season the roast well with the salt and pepper. Heat the oil in a medium-sized skillet and brown the roast all over. Place it in a roasting pan and cook it in a preheated 350°F oven for 1½ hours. A meat thermometer should register 180°F.

EXTRAS SUGGESTIONS: Extra pork roast is delicious sliced cold with tomato, onion, and mustard or mayonnaise on black bread. Cold pork roast can also be substituted for the beef in Cold Beef Vinaigrette. (See index for recipe.)

 SUGGESTED MENU:

Boneless Pork Roast
Yams à la St. Thomas
Zucchini and Tomatoes
Raspberries sprinkled with framboise

ALSATIAN PORK CHOP

1 1-inch-thick pork chop
Salt and freshly ground pepper to taste
2 tablespoons vegetable oil
1 small onion, thinly sliced
1 8-ounce can sauerkraut, drained and rinsed in colander
½ teaspoon caraway seeds
½ cup Chicken Broth (see index for recipe)
2 tablespoons sour cream

Season the chop with the salt and pepper on each side. Heat the oil in an 8-inch skillet and brown the chop on both sides. Remove it to a plate. And the onion and sauté it, stirring, for 4 minutes. Add the sauerkraut, caraway seeds, and broth and stir. Return the chop to the pan, cover, and cook over low heat for 20 minutes. Turn the chop and stir the ingredients. Cook for 15 more minutes or until the chop is tender. Remove the pan from the heat. Place the chop on a heated serving dish. Stir the sour cream into the sauerkraut mixture. Spoon the mixture around the chop.

 SUGGESTED MENU:

Sardines with Red Onion Rings and Bacon
Alsatian Pork Chop
Bibb Lettuce Salad with Mustard Vinaigrette
Baked Apple

OVEN-BAKED PORK CHOP

⅓ cup herbed bread crumbs
½ teaspoon Seasoned Salt (see index for recipe)
½ teaspoon oregano
Freshly ground pepper to taste
1 1-inch-thick loin pork chop
Vegetable oil

Combine the bread crumbs, seasoned salt, oregano, and pepper. Coat the chop with the crumb mixture. Lightly grease a shallow ovenproof baking dish or ramekin just large enough to hold the chop. Bake the chop in a preheated 350°F oven for 30 minutes. Turn it and cook it about 20 minutes more or until it is crisp and tender.

SUGGESTED MENU:

Oven-Baked Pork Chop
Apple sauce
Baked Yam
A tossed green salad
Sliced Bananas with Cream

A THICK PORK CHOP BRAISED IN RED WINE

   1 1-inch-thick loin pork chop
   Flour
   1 tablespoon olive or vegetable oil
   1 small clove garlic, crushed
   1 whole medium-sized canned tomato, mashed
   ½ cup dry red wine
   ¼ cup Chicken Broth or water (see index for recipe)
   ¼ teaspoon oregano
   ¼ teaspoon crumbled sage
   Salt and freshly ground pepper to taste
   Fresh chopped parsley

Dust the chop with flour. Heat the olive oil in a heavy 8-inch skillet. Brown the chop quickly on both sides. Reduce the heat and add the garlic. Push the garlic around in the pan for 30 seconds. Add the tomato and pour in the wine and chicken broth or water. Sprinkle the oregano and sage over all and bring the liquid to a boil. Reduce the heat low as possible, cover, and simmer for 20 minutes. Turn the chop, recover the pan, and cook for 20 more minutes. Turn the chop again and cook for 20 more minutes. Remove the chop to a warmed dinner plate. Stir in the parsley and pour the sauce over the chop.

 SUGGESTED MENU:

Fried Butter Croutons with Pimiento Cheese and Bacon Spread
A Thick Pork Chop Braised in Red Wine
Baked Acorn Squash
Sugar-and-Almond-Toasted Brioche

SMOKED PORK CHOPS

Occasionally very easy foods are cloaked in mystery simply because they were never cooked in the household we grew up in. Smoked pork chops couldn't be simpler to prepare, and they are found in most special butcher shops.

    1 tablespoon butter or vegetable oil
    2 smoked pork chops
    1 teaspoon fresh chopped parsley

Heat the butter in a 9-inch skillet. Sauté the chops over medium heat for 4 or 5 minutes on each side. Sprinkle them with the parsley.

 SUGGESTED MENU:

Smoked Pork Chops
Baked Stuffed Potato
Sautéed Cream of Fresh Corn
Four-Fruit Compote

SAUTÉED PORK CHOP WITH RED CURRANT SWEET AND SOUR SAUCE

1 1-inch-thick pork chop
Salt and freshly ground pepper to taste
Flour
2½ tablespoons vegetable oil

SAUCE:

3 tablespoons sugar
2 tablespoons butter
1 tablespoon cornstarch
½ cup water
½ cup red currant jelly
2 teaspoons lemon juice
¼ teaspoon cinnamon
3 tablespoons brown sugar
⅓ cup sliced blanched almonds

Season the chop with the salt and pepper. Dust it with flour. Heat the oil in a heavy 9-inch skillet and sauté the chop for 15 minutes over low heat. Turn the chop and cook it until it is tender, about 15 minutes. Meanwhile, prepare the sauce. Combine the sugar and butter in a small saucepan and cook until they begin to turn light brown. Dissolve the cornstarch in a little water and stir it into the sugar-butter mixture. Cook for 1 minute. Add the remaining ingredients, stirring, and cook them over medium-low heat for 10 minutes. Taste the sauce for flavor. If more tartness is required, add a little more lemon juice. Pour the sauce over the chop.

 SUGGESTED MENU:

Sautéed Pork Chop with Red Currant Sweet and Sour Sauce
Tully Plesser's Baked Potato Latke

Fresh Spinach Salad
Chocolate ice cream with Kahlúa

BAKED PORK CHOP PIZZAOLA

   1 pork chop, cut 1-inch thick
   Salt and freshly ground pepper to taste
   1 tablespoon olive or vegetable oil
   1 tablespoon butter
   ¼ cup Chicken Broth (see index for recipe)
   1 medium onion, sliced into rings
   Pinch of oregano
   Pinch of thyme
   2 ¼-inch-thick slices mozzarella
   ¼ cup tomato sauce
   Freshly ground pepper to taste

Season the chop with the salt and pepper. Heat the oil in a 9-inch skillet and brown the chop on each side. Grease an au gratin dish just large enough to hold the ingredients comfortably. Sprinkle the onion rings on the bottom of the dish and place the chop on top. Season it lightly with the oregano and thyme. Cover it with the mozzarella and spoon the tomato sauce over the cheese. Grate fresh pepper over the top. Cook the chop in a preheated 375°F oven for 35 to 45 minutes, until it is tender.

EXTRAS SUGGESTIONS: Any remaining sauce can be covered and refrigerated for several days. Serve with grilled or sautéed ham steak.

 SUGGESTED MENU:

Clams Oreganato
Baked Pork Chop Pizzaola
Spaghetti with Butter
Caribbean Rum-Flavored Fruit

BARBECUED SPARERIBS

6 to 8 ribs (depending on their size and your appetite)

SAUCE:

1 small onion, thinly sliced
1 tablespoon olive oil
1 tablespoon butter
½ cup prepared barbecue sauce
1 teaspoon Worcestershire sauce
2 tablespoons honey
1 tablespoon vinegar
Dash of Tabasco
½ teaspoon Dijon-style mustard

Place the ribs in enough boiling water to cover them, reduce the heat, and simmer for 10 minutes. Meanwhile, combine the sauce ingredients in a small saucepan, bring the sauce to a boil, reduce the heat, and simmer for 8 minutes, stirring often. Remove the ribs, drain them, and place them in a shallow baking pan. Brush them with the sauce and bake them in a preheated 400°F oven for 10 minutes. Turn them and brush them again with the sauce. Place them under the broiler and cook them until they are golden brown and sizzling.

 SUGGESTED MENU:

Barbecued Spareribs
Fried Onion Rings
Zucchini and Red Pepper Sauté
Independence Day Fruit Sundae

BROILED HAM STEAK WITH MUSTARD
AND RED CURRANT JELLY

1 6- to 8-ounce ham steak, about ½ inch thick
1 tablespoon Dijon-style mustard
2 tablespoons red currant jelly
Pinch of ground cloves
Pinch of grated nutmeg
Freshly ground pepper to taste

Place the ham steak in a broiling pan. Combine the remaining ingredients in a bowl. Brush half of the mixture over the steak and cook it under a preheated broiler for 5 minutes. Turn the steak and brush it with the remaining mixture. Broil it for about 5 more minutes or until it is golden brown and sizzling.

 SUGGESTED MENU:

Fresh Greens Soup
Broiled Ham Steak with Mustard and Red Currant Jelly
Mashed Sweet Potato with Rum
Banana Crown

9. Seafood

Fish

I have always wanted to live at the seashore. Beaches, sunshine, salt air, a sense of spaciousness, and regular fresh seafood would add up to an ideal way of life.

With modern transportation, ice-packing and freezing methods, fish and seafood are available in all parts of the country. Fresh fish and seafood can be bought in small quantities, they cook rapidly, and they are extremely versatile. An endless array of easy delicious dishes that are low in calories and high in nutritional value makes fish and seafood even more desirable.

Fish fillets or steaks should be firm, with no discolored areas around the edges and no objectionable odor.

Fish and seafood cook quickly, so follow the timing in the following recipes carefully to avoid overdone, tasteless, and dry fish dishes.

Fresh is best, as always, but frozen fish and seafood can be very good indeed. If you are buying frozen fish fillets, don't accept swollen packages. They indicate that the fish has been thawed and refrozen.

Thaw frozen fish in the refrigerator, if possible. If it sits in liquid at room temperature for too long, it loses its flavor. Once the fish is thawed, cook it immediately.

If you haven't cooked with fish or seafood in the past, I encourage you to be fearless and try them. Not only are they great for one, but they offer a whole world of taste that no one should miss.

SAUTÉED COD TIDBITS

1 6-ounce fillet of cod, cut into 1-inch cubes
Salt and freshly ground pepper to taste
Paprika
Flour
2 tablespoons butter
2 tablespoons olive or vegetable oil
½ lemon

Season the cod cubes with the salt, pepper, and paprika. Dust them with flour. Heat the butter and oil in a 9-inch skillet and sauté the tidbits until they are browned evenly. Squeeze lemon juice over the fish.

 SUGGESTED MENU:

Sautéed Cod Tidbits with Curried Mayonnaise
Curried Rice
Zucchini and Tomatoes
Cinnamon Ice Cream

BETTY PAPPAS'S SNAPPER BAKED IN FOIL

1 6-ounce snapper fillet
¼ cup dry white wine
2 tablespoons minced onion
1 small tomato, peeled and diced
¼ teaspoon thyme
¼ teaspoon oregano
1 teaspoon fresh chopped parsley
Salt and freshly ground pepper to taste
2 teaspoons butter or margarine

Place the fillet on a 14-inch sheet of aluminum foil. Turn up the sides of the foil slightly. Pour the wine over the fish. Sprinkle it with the onion, tomato, herbs, salt, and pepper. Dot it with the butter. Seal the foil over the ingredients and place it on a baking sheet. Bake the fish in a preheated 375°F oven for 25 minutes. Peel back the foil and transfer the fish to a warmed plate. Pour the juices collected in the foil over the snapper.

 SUGGESTED MENU:

English-Style Cucumber Tea Sandwich
Betty Pappas's Snapper Baked in Foil
Creamed Broccoli
Dates Stuffed with Pecans and Cream Cheese

FRIED FLOUNDER FILLET WITH SAUTÉED ALMONDS

1 6-ounce flounder fillet
Salt and freshly ground pepper to taste
Flour
1 egg, beaten

¼ cup seasoned bread crumbs
½ teaspoon Seasoned Salt (see index for recipe)
½ cup vegetable oil
½ lime
1½ tablespoons butter
3 tablespoons sliced almonds

Season the fillet with the salt and pepper. Dust it with flour, dip it in the egg, and coat it with the combined bread crumbs and seasoned salt. Heat the vegetable oil in a 9-inch skillet until it is hot. Fry the fillet on both sides until it is crisp and tender. Squeeze the juice of the lime over the fillet and transfer it to a warmed dish. In a clean small skillet, heat the butter and sauté the almonds over medium-high heat for about 2 minutes, stirring, until they are golden brown. Sprinkle them over the fish.

 SUGGESTED MENU:

Guacamole
Fried Flounder Fillet with Sautéed Almonds
Tomato and Red Onion Salad
Whole Wheat Bread Pudding with Blueberries

LEMON-BAKED HALIBUT STEAK

    1 6-ounce halibut steak
    Salt and freshly ground pepper to taste
    1 tablespoon fresh lemon juice
    2 teaspoons butter
    Paprika
    3 thin slices of fresh lemon, peeled
    1 teaspoon fresh chopped parsley

Lightly butter an individual baking dish. Season the fish with the salt and pepper and place it in the dish. Pour the lemon juice over the halibut and dot it with the butter. Sprinkle it with the paprika. Bake the fish in a preheated 375°F oven for 20 minutes or until it flakes easily. Place the lemon slices across the fish and sprinkle it with the parsley.

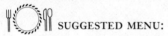 SUGGESTED MENU:

Artichoke Soup
Lemon-Baked Halibut Steak
Curried Rice
Fresh Strawberries with Crème Fraîche and Brown Sugar

FISH AND CHIPS

    1 medium potato, peeled and cut into ½-inch-thick sticks
        lengthwise
    2½ cups vegetable oil

Pat the potatoes dry and fry them in the hot oil in a medium skillet until they are lightly browned. Remove them with a spatula and set them aside. Transfer the pan with the oil to a burner not in use and prepare the fish.

6 to 8 ounces scrod, cut into 1-inch finger shapes

BATTER:

¼ cup flour
2 tablespoons cornstarch
¼ teaspoon baking powder
1 egg, beaten
¼ teaspoon salt
Freshly ground pepper to taste
½ cup milk

Mix together the batter ingredients in a bowl. Heat the oil in the skillet again, and when it is hot, dip the fish fingers into the batter and gently drop them into the oil. Fry them until they are crisp on all sides. Remove them and drain them on absorbent paper. Return the potatoes to the hot oil and fry them until they are golden brown.

Serve with a sprinkle of malt vinegar.

 SUGGESTED MENU:

Cantaloupe with Port
Fish and Chips
Creamy Coleslaw
Lime Pie

SOLE AMANDINE

1 6-ounce sole fillet
Flour
2½ tablespoons Clarified Butter (see index for recipe)
2 tablespoons almond slices
Salt and freshly ground pepper to taste
1 lemon wedge

Dust the sole with the flour. Heat 2 tablespoons of the butter in a 9-inch skillet. Sauté the sole over medium-high heat for 3 minutes. Turn it with a spatula and sauté it for about 3 minutes, until it is golden. Transfer it to a warmed dinner plate. Add the remaining ½ tablespoon of butter and the almonds to the pan and stir, cooking for about 2 minutes, until the nuts are toasted evenly. Season the fillet with the salt and pepper. Spoon the almonds over the fillet and squeeze the lemon juice over the top.

SUGGESTED MENU:

Dieter's Antipasto Plate
Sole Amandine
Carrots Cooked in Chicken Broth
Dutch Apple Pancake

SALMON STEAK WITH MUSTARD BUTTER

   1 6-ounce salmon steak
   1½ teaspoons vegetable oil

Mustard Butter:

   1 teaspoon Dijon-style mustard
   1 tablespoon butter, at room temperature
   ½ teaspoon lemon juice
   ½ teaspoon finely chopped dill
   Few grinds of freshly ground pepper

Mix together the mustard butter ingredients in a small bowl and put it in the freezer to harden. Brush the salmon with the oil on both sides. Broil it for about 4 minutes on each side or until it is just tender. Serve the mustard butter on top of the steak.

 SUGGESTED MENU:

Mixed Vegetable Terrine
Salmon Steak with Mustard Butter
Boiled Potatoes with Parsley
Yogurt with Golden Raisins, Fresh Fruit, and Honey

SALMON PATTIES

  1 3½-ounce can salmon, skin and bones removed
  ¼ cup Mayonnaise (see index for recipe)
  ½ teaspoon Dijon-style mustard
  3 soda crackers, crushed into fine crumbs
  1 scallion, minced
  1 teaspoon lemon juice
  1 teaspoon fresh chopped parsley
  Salt and freshly ground pepper to taste
  Bread crumbs
  3 tablespoons vegetable oil

Mix all the ingredients except the bread crumbs and oil. Shape the mixture into two equal-sized patties. Coat them evenly with bread crumbs. Heat the oil in a 9-inch skillet and sauté the patties until they are golden on both sides.

 SUGGESTED MENU:

Fresh Crisp Vegetables with Green Mayonnaise
Salmon Patties
Fresh Cooked Spinach
Cream Puff with Cinnamon Ice Cream

SAUTÉED TROUT FILLETS WITH LEMON CAPER SAUCE

  1 brook trout, filleted
  Flour
  3 tablespoons butter
  2 teaspoons lemon juice
  1 tablespoon capers
  1 teaspoon fresh chopped parsley

Dust the trout lightly with the flour. Heat 2 tablespoons of the butter in a medium skillet and brown the trout on both sides. Carefully remove the fillets to a warmed dish. Add the remaining tablespoon of butter, the capers, and the parsley to the skillet and cook the sauce over medium heat, stirring, for 2 minutes. Spoon the sauce over the fillets.

 SUGGESTED MENU:

Brioche Filled with Sour Cream and Black Lumpfish Caviar
Sautéed Trout Fillets with Lemon Caper Sauce
Carrot and Raisin Salad
Pineapple Meringue Cake

POACHED TROUT WITH CREAM SAUCE

    1 lake trout
    Milk
    ½ cup heavy cream
    1 egg yolk
    Salt and freshly ground pepper to taste

Bring enough milk to just cover the trout nearly to a boil in a medium skillet. Reduce the heat and add the trout. Cover the skillet and simmer the trout for about 12 minutes, or until it flakes easily. Remove the trout to a warmed serving dish. In a small saucepan bring the heavy cream to a boil and cook it, stirring, for about 3 minutes or until it thickens. Remove it from the heat and whisk in the egg yolk. Season the sauce with the salt and pepper. Fillet the trout and spoon the sauce over the fillets.

SUGGESTED MENU:

Fried Sesame Chicken Breast Bites

Poached Trout with Cream Sauce
Sautéed Broccoli with Garlic and Basil
Raspberry Fool

POTTED TUNA

> 1 3½-ounce can white-meat tuna, drained
> 3 ounces cream cheese, at room temperature
> 1 scallion, finely minced
> 1 tablespoon fresh chopped parsley
> ½ teaspoon tarragon
> 1 tablespoon lemon juice
> 1 teaspoon soy sauce

Flake the tuna very well with a fork. Add the remaining ingredients and pack the mixture into a small bowl or crock. Refrigerate the dish for several hours.

Serve with buttered toast.

 SUGGESTED MENU:

Potted Tuna
Stir-fried Mixed Vegetables
Grilled Apricots with Pecan Filling

BAKED SWORDFISH WITH LEMON BROTH AND BACON

1 6-ounce swordfish steak, ¾ to 1 inch thick
Salt and freshly ground pepper to taste
¼ cup Chicken Broth (see index for recipe)
1 tablespoon fresh lemon juice
Paprika
2 strips bacon

Sprinkle the swordfish lightly with the salt and pepper. Place it on a sheet of aluminum foil on a baking sheet. Turn the sides of the foil up into a 1-inch collar about 1 inch from the sides of the fish. Pour the combined chicken broth and lemon juice over fish. Sprinkle the fish with the paprika and place the bacon strips in a cross over it. Bake the fish in a preheated 375°F oven for 25 minutes or until the fish flakes easily but isn't dry. To further crisp the bacon, pass the fish under the broiler briefly.

 SUGGESTED MENU:

Cold Cucumber and Yogurt Soup
Baked Swordfish with Lemon Broth and Bacon
Sautéed Green Beans
Banana Crown

One Dozen Shrimp Recipes

SIX-MINUTE SHRIMP IN MARSALA AND BUTTER SAUCE

6 large shrimp, shelled and deveined
2 tablespoons butter
2 tablespoons Marsala
1 teaspoon lemon juice
Salt and freshly ground pepper to taste
1 slice toasted white bread, crusts trimmed

Cut the shrimp in half lengthwise. Simmer the butter, Marsala, and lemon juice in a 9-inch skillet over medium heat for 3 minutes. Add the shrimp; stir and cook for 1 minute. Stir again and cook for 1 more minute. Season the shrimp with the salt and pepper and cook for 1 more minute, stirring. Place the shrimp on the toast and pour the sauce over them.

 SUGGESTED MENU:

New England Creamy Clam Chowder
Six-Minute Shrimp in Marsala and Butter Sauce
Sautéed Cherry Tomatoes
Zucchini Cake

SHRIMP RISOTTO

1½ tablespoons butter
2 tablespoons minced shallot or onion
½ cup long-grain rice
¾ cup dry white wine

¾ cup Chicken Broth (see index for recipe)
Salt and freshly ground pepper to taste
6 medium shrimp, shelled, deveined, and cut into 4 pieces each
3 fresh mushrooms, finely chopped
1 teaspoon fresh chopped parsley
1 tablespoon fresh grated Parmesan cheese
1 teaspoon butter

Melt 1½ tablespoons of butter in a 9-inch skillet and sauté the shallot for 3 minutes. Add the rice and cook it, stirring, for 2 minutes. Pour in the white wine and broth and bring the liquid to a boil. Season with the salt and pepper. Reduce the heat, cover the skillet, and simmer the rice for 10 minutes. Add the shrimp, mushrooms, and parsley. Stir the mixture, recover the skillet, and cook until the rice is just tender, about 10 minutes. Stir in the Parmesan cheese and 1 teaspoon of butter. Serve immediately.

VARIATION: For Risotto Primavera (Rice with Vegetables), replace the shrimp in the recipe with ¼ cup of green peas; 2 stalks of fresh asparagus, sliced on a diagonal; 1 stalk of broccoli, chopped; and 1 small firm tomato, peeled and diced.

 SUGGESTED MENU:
Melon Cubes Wrapped in Cheese and Prosciutto
Shrimp Risotto
Pain Grillé with Herb Butter
Fresh Pear with Creamy Gorgonzola

SHRIMP WITH TOMATO AND LEMON SAUCE AND RICE

2 tablespoons olive oil
3 tablespoons finely chopped onion
1 small clove garlic, crushed
½ cup chopped, peeled fresh or canned tomato
¼ teaspoon basil
⅓ cup Chicken Broth (see index for recipe)
2 teaspoons lemon juice
½ teaspoon fresh chopped parsley
¼ pound medium-sized shrimp, shelled and deveined
¾ cup cooked rice
Salt and freshly ground pepper to taste
1 tablespoon grated Parmesan cheese

Heat the olive oil in a saucepan. Sauté the onion and garlic for 3 minutes over medium heat, stirring. Add the tomato and basil and bring the mixture to the boil. Add the broth, lemon juice, and parsley, stirring, and when the mixture boils, add the shrimp. Cook for 2 minutes. Add the rice, salt, and pepper. Stir and then simmer, covered, for 5 minutes. Sprinkle the dish with the Parmesan cheese, stir again, and serve at once with Italian bread.

 SUGGESTED MENU:

Ham and Bread Stick Rolls
Shrimp with Tomato and Lemon Sauce and Rice
Fresh Spinach Salad
Sugar-and-Almond-Toasted Brioche

SHRIMP TART

1 cooked individual pastry tart (see index for recipe)
½ cup Fish Velouté Sauce (see index for recipe)
8 medium shrimp, shelled, deveined, and boiled
2 tablespoons grated Swiss cheese

Spoon 3 tablespoons of the velouté sauce over the bottom of the tart. Top it with the shrimp. Spoon the remaining sauce over the shrimp and sprinkle it with the cheese. Quickly pass the tart under the broiler until the cheese melts and is golden.

 SUGGESTED MENU:

Caponata
Shrimp Tart
Sautéed and Braised Escarole
Peach Waffle Cake

SHRIMP SCAMPI

2 tablespoons melted Clarified Butter (see index for recipe)
1 tablespoon olive or vegetable oil
1 clove garlic, crushed
¼ teaspoon basil
¼ teaspoon oregano
1 teaspoon fresh chopped parsley
1 tablespoon dry white wine or dry vermouth
Salt and freshly ground pepper to taste
½ pound large shrimp, shelled and deveined, with tails intact

Combine all the ingredients except the shrimp in bowl. Place the shrimp in a single layer in a shallow ovenproof baking dish just large enough to hold them. Pour the mixture over the shrimp. Place the dish under a hot broiler for 3 minutes. Turn the shrimp. Cook them another 2 or 3 minutes or until they are tender.

SUGGESTED MENU:

Shrimp Scampi
Pain Grillé
Zucchini in Cream Sauce
Grilled Onion Slices
Zabaglione

SHRIMP MEUNIÈRE

> 6 jumbo shrimp, shelled and deveined, with tails intact
> Flour
> 3 tablespoons Clarified Butter (see index for recipe)
> 1 tablespoon olive or vegetable oil
> Salt and freshly ground pepper to taste
> 1 tablespoon lemon juice
> 1 teaspoon fresh chopped parsley

Coat the shrimp with flour. Heat the butter and oil in a 9-inch skillet. Sauté the shrimp over medium-high heat until they are lightly browned, about 3 minutes a side. Transfer them to a heated serving plate. Season them with the salt and pepper. Add the lemon juice and parsley to the pan. Cook the sauce for about 15 seconds, stirring, over high heat. Pour it over the shrimp.

Garnish this dish with a lemon wedge.

 SUGGESTED MENU:

Marinated Artichoke Hearts in Curry Sauce
Shrimp Meunière
Black Beans and Green Pepper with Rice
Vanilla Ice Cream with Crème de Menthe and Chocolate Morsels

SHRIMP MARIO

    1 tablespoon olive oil
    1 tablespoon butter
    2 tablespoons finely chopped onion
    1 small clove garlic, minced
    1 medium tomato, peeled, seeded, and chopped
    1 cup tomato sauce
    ¼ teaspoon oregano
    ¼ teaspoon basil
    1 teaspoon fresh chopped parsley
    2 tablespoons dry white wine
    8 medium shrimp, shelled and deveined
    3 slices mozzarella cheese
    1 tablespoon grated Parmesan cheese

Heat the oil and butter in an 8-inch skillet. Sauté the onion and garlic for 3 minutes over medium heat, stirring occasionally. Add the tomato and cook it, stirring, for 2 minutes. Add the tomato sauce, herbs, wine, and shrimp. Bring the liquid to a boil and cook for 2 minutes. Transfer the shrimp and sauce to a shallow baking dish. Top them with the mozzarella cheese and sprinkle the Parmesan over the top. Place the dish under a preheated broiler until the cheese is golden.

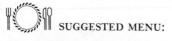 SUGGESTED MENU:

Lettuce Coleslaw
Shrimp Mario
Sautéed Potatoes with Garlic
Sautéed Banana with Brown Sugar

SHRIMP FRIED IN BEER BATTER

½ cup flour
⅔ cup beer
½ teaspoon baking soda
¼ teaspoon salt
Freshly ground pepper to taste
2 cups vegetable oil
8 medium-large shrimp, shelled and deveined, with the tails
   intact

In a small bowl beat together the flour, beer, and baking soda. Season the mixture with the salt and pepper. Heat the oil in a 9-inch skillet until it is hot but not smoking. Dip the shrimp by the tails into the batter and gently lower them into the oil. Cook them until they are golden, about 3 minutes on each side. Drain them.

Serve them with lemon wedges.

 SUGGESTED MENU:

Senegalese Soup
Shrimp Fried in Beer Batter
Mini Caesar Salad
Martin Rapp's Square Apple Tart with Instant Puff Pastry

COCONUT SHRIMP

½ cup beer
½ cup flour
½ teaspoon baking soda
Pinch of ginger
Salt and freshly ground pepper to taste
6 large shrimp, shelled and deveined, with the tails intact
½ cup shredded coconut
2 cups vegetable oil

Beat together the beer, flour, baking soda, and ginger with a wire whisk until they form a smooth batter. Season it with the salt and pepper. Dip each shrimp by the tail into the batter, coating it well, and roll it in the coconut. Heat the oil in a 9-inch skillet. When it is hot but not smoking, add the shrimp and cook them over medium-high heat until they are golden, about 3 minutes on each side.

Serve with Apricot Sauce. (See index for recipe.)

 SUGGESTED MENU:

Honeydew melon with lemon
Coconut Shrimp
Stir Fried Fresh Vegetables
Caribbean Rum-Flavored Fruit

SHRIMP CREOLE

1½ tablespoons bacon drippings or olive oil
1 small onion, finely chopped
1 small clove garlic, minced
2 stalks celery, chopped
1 small green pepper, chopped

1 whole ripe tomato, peeled and chopped
½ teaspoon Dijon-style mustard
2 teaspoons tomato paste
1 cup tomato sauce
Pinch of sugar
1 bay leaf
1 teaspoon fresh chopped parsley
Dash of Tabasco
Salt and freshly ground pepper to taste
6 large shrimp, shelled and deveined

Heat the bacon drippings in a medium-sized skillet and sauté the onion, garlic, celery, and green pepper for 5 minutes. Add all the remaining ingredients except the shrimp and bring to a boil. Reduce the heat and simmer for 20 minutes. Add the shrimp and continue simmering for 10 minutes.

 SUGGESTED MENU:

Ham-Filled Biscuits
Shrimp Creole
Hot fluffy rice
A mixed green salad
Sliced Bananas with Cream

SHRIMP WITH BLACK BEANS

¼ cup Chinese salted black beans (available in oriental food
    shops) or canned black beans
2 teaspoons soy sauce
1 clove garlic, crushed
1½ tablespoons peanut oil
8 medium shrimp, shelled and deveined
¼ cup Chicken Stock (see index for recipe)
1 teaspoon cornstarch
1 small scallion, minced
½ teaspoon fresh chopped parsley

Combine the beans, soy sauce, and garlic. Set them aside. Heat the
peanut oil in a small wok or skillet. Sauté the shrimp over medium-
high heat for 3 minutes, tossing. Add the black bean mixture, toss
again, and pour in the combined chicken stock and cornstarch. Toss
and cook for 2 minutes. Sprinkle scallion and parsley over the dish.

 SUGGESTED MENU:

Andrew Bergman's Hot and Sour Soup
Shrimp with Black Beans
Plain fried rice
Parfait of Fresh Papaya and Blueberries

SHRIMP WITH BOK CHOY, SNOW PEA PODS, AND
   WATER CHESTNUTS

1 egg white
2 teaspoons cornstarch
8 medium shrimp, shelled and deveined
1½ tablespoons peanut oil

1 cup bok choy, cut into 1-inch pieces (available in Chinese
    fresh vegetable markets)
¼ cup water chestnuts
¼ cup Chicken Stock (see index for recipe)
1 teaspoon soy sauce
1 dozen snow pea pods, trimmed
1 tablespoon sliced scallion

Combine the egg white and cornstarch. Add the shrimp and toss.
Cover the mixture and refrigerate it for 30 minutes. Heat the oil in a
small wok or skillet. Add the shrimp and toss, stir-frying. Remove
the shrimp with a slotted spoon. Add all the remaining ingredients
except the snow pea pods and the scallion. Toss, cover, and cook for
3 minutes. Add the shrimp and the snow pea pods. Stir-fry for 1
minute. Scatter the scallion slices over the mixture.

 SUGGESTED MENU:

Fried Butter Crouton with Orange-Flavored Cream Cheese
Shrimp with Bok Choy, Snow Pea Pods, and Water Chestnuts
Lemon sherbet

Crabmeat, Scallops, Mussels, Soft-Shell Crabs, and Lobster

CRABMEAT WITH COINTREAU

2 tablespoons butter
1 tablespoon chopped shallots
6 fresh mushrooms, thinly sliced
1 tablespoon flour
Salt and freshly ground pepper to taste
⅓ cup heavy cream
6 ounces crabmeat
1 tablespoon Cointreau
Fresh chopped parsley

Heat the butter in a 9-inch skillet. Sauté the shallots for 3 minutes. Add the mushrooms and cook over medium heat for 4 minutes. Sprinkle with the flour and season with the salt and pepper, stirring. Cook for 2 minutes. Stir in the heavy cream. When it comes to a boil, reduce the heat and add the crabmeat, Cointreau, and parsley. Cook the mixture for 2 minutes, stirring occasionally.

 SUGGESTED MENU:

Fried Crepes with Honey Butter
Crabmeat with Cointreau
Fresh Green Beans with Parsley Butter
Chocolate Soufflé

SAUTÉED CRABMEAT WITH SNOW PEA PODS AND WATER CHESTNUTS

1 tablespoon butter
6 ounces crabmeat
1 scallion, thinly sliced
4 water chestnuts, thinly sliced
1 tablespoon dry sherry
8 snow pea pods, cleaned and cut in half crosswise on a diagonal
Salt and freshly ground pepper to taste

Heat the butter in a 9-inch skillet. When the foaming of the butter subsides, add the crabmeat, scallion, and water chestnuts. Stir and pour in the sherry. Stir and cook the mixture over medium heat for 3 minutes. Add the snow pea pods, stir, and cover. Cook for 1 minute. Season with the salt and pepper and serve immediately.

 SUGGESTED MENU:

Clams Oreganato
Sautéed Crabmeat with Snow Pea Pods and Water Chestnuts
Romaine Lettuce and Orange Salad
Strawberry Ice

MARIAN FAUX'S BAY SCALLOPS AND SHRIMP WITH RICE

Marian Faux, a writer and editor, sees cooking for one as an opportunity for hedonism. She says, "In a pleasant, idle moment with friends, we began to speculate about what each of us would do if given a rare bottle of fine wine. Whom would we invite to share such a treasure? I confessed that I would drink such a bottle of wine alone. It would be an evening of reflection with an easy, elegant dish of my favorite seafood, scallops and shrimp; and that wine might be—well, an even better bottle than you would serve company. I honestly can't drink a full bottle of wine at one sitting, no matter how precious it is; recorked and refrigerated, it would be savored with dinner the following evening."

> 2 tablespoons butter
> 6 ounces bay scallops
> 2 tablespoons of dry white wine
> 4 large shrimp, shelled and deveined
> ½ cup diced fresh zucchini
> ½ teaspoon basil
> Salt and freshly ground pepper to taste
> ¾ cup cooked rice

Heat the butter in a 9-inch skillet and sauté the scallops until they are translucent, about 3 or 4 minutes. Add all the remaining ingredients except the rice and cook the mixture for about 5 minutes, stirring it occasionally. Stir in the rice and cook until the rice is hot. Taste for seasoning.

 SUGGESTED MENU:

Cold Asparagus Vinaigrette
Marian Faux's Bay Scallops and Shrimp with Rice
Dessert Crepes with Fruit Preserves

SCALLOPS SEBONAC

> ⅓ pound bay scallops

Flour
2 tablespoons butter
2 teaspoons olive oil
Salt and freshly ground pepper to taste
1 small onion, thinly sliced
1 small clove garlic, crushed
½ cup chopped canned tomatoes
Pinch of oregano
½ teaspoon fresh chopped parsley
2 tablespoons dry white wine
4 mushrooms, sliced
¼ cup spinach, cooked, drained, and chopped
2 ¾-inch-thick slices Italian bread

Dust the scallops with flour. Heat the butter and oil in 9-inch skillet. When the foaming subsides, add the scallops. Sauté them over medium-high heat for 30 seconds; then shake the pan and cook them for 30 more seconds. Shake the pan again and cook them for 1 more minute. Shake the pan and remove the scallops with a slotted spoon. Season them with the salt and pepper. Immediately add the onion and garlic to the pan. Stir them. Reduce the heat and sauté them for 3 minutes. Add the tomatoes, oregano, and parsley and cook, stirring, for 2 minutes. Pour in the white wine and bring it to the boil. Add the mushrooms and cover the pan. Cook the mixture over low heat for 3 minutes, stirring it once. Add the scallops and spinach. Season again with salt and pepper to taste. Cook uncovered for a minute or two until the ingredients are heated through. Spoon the mixture over toasted Italian bread slices.

 SUGGESTED MENU:

Scallops Sebonac
Arugula and Endive Salad
Sugar-and-Almond-Toasted Brioche

SAUTÉED SCALLOPS IN CREAM SAUCE

6 ounces bay scallops (if unavailable, use sea scallops and
    quarter them)
Flour
2 tablespoons butter
2 tablespoons dry white wine
¼ cup heavy cream
Salt and freshly ground white or black pepper to taste
½ teaspoon fresh chopped parsley

Dust the scallops lightly with flour. Heat the butter in a 9-inch skillet.
Brown the scallops over medium-high heat, shaking the pan often,
until they are cooked, about 5 minutes. Remove the scallops to a
warmed plate. Pour the wine into the skillet and cook it for 1 minute,
stirring up any browned particles on the bottom of the pan. Add the
heavy cream, stirring it until it boils. Season the sauce with the salt
and pepper and cook it, stirring, for 2 minutes. Pour it over the
scallops and sprinkle them with the parsley.

VARIATION: Add ½ teaspoon of tarragon or curry along with the wine
in the recipe.

 SUGGESTED MENU:

Tomato Mold with Vegetables and Fresh Basil
Sautéed Scallops in Cream Sauce
Potatoes à la Parisienne
Broiled Grapefruit with Maple Syrup

SAUTÉED BAY SCALLOPS WITH LEMON BUTTER

3 tablespoons Clarified Butter (see index for recipe)
1 teaspoon olive oil
6 ounces bay scallops
Flour
Salt and freshly ground pepper to taste
1 1-inch-thick slice toasted white bread, crusts trimmed
1 teaspoon lemon juice
1 teaspoon fresh chopped parsley

Heat 2 tablespoons of the butter and the oil in a 9-inch skillet. Coat the scallops with flour and sauté them over medium-high heat, shaking the pan every 30 seconds, until the scallops are evenly browned. Remove the scallops and season them with the salt and pepper. Place the toast in an individual ramekin and top it with the scallops. Add the remaining tablespoon of butter to the skillet with the lemon juice and parsley. Stir them for 30 seconds, then pour them over the scallops.

 SUGGESTED MENU:

Marinated Mussels
Sautéed Bay Scallops with Lemon Butter
Green Beans Cap Cruz
Peach Cobbler

SAUTÉED BREADED MUSSELS

1 dozen fresh mussels
Flour
1 egg, beaten
Seasoned bread crumbs
2 tablespoons butter
3 tablespoons vegetable oil

Steam the mussels in 1½ cups of boiling, lightly salted water for about 5 minutes or until the shells open. Remove the mussels from their shells when they have cooled. Dust them with flour, dip them in the egg, and roll them in the bread crumbs. Sauté them in the butter and oil in a medium-sized skillet until they are golden on both sides.

Garnish them with lemon wedges and serve them with Creamy Tartar Sauce. (See index for recipe.)

SUGGESTED MENU:

Celery Root Rémoulade
Sautéed Breaded Mussels
Cuban Fried Plantains
Zucchini Cake

STEAMED MUSSELS AND CURRIED TOMATO SAUCE

3 tablespoons olive or vegetable oil
¼ cup chopped shallots or onions
1 clove garlic, minced
1 teaspoon curry powder
1 ripe tomato, peeled and chopped
½ cup tomato sauce
2 teaspoons lemon juice
1 teaspoon fresh chopped parsley
¼ cup Beef Stock (see index for recipe)
1½ dozen mussels, cleaned
½ cup dry white wine

Heat the olive oil in a 9-inch skillet and sauté the shallots and garlic for 5 minutes, stirring. Sprinkle the curry powder over the mixture and add the tomato, tomato sauce, lemon juice, parsley, and stock. Bring the liquid to a boil, reduce the heat, and simmer for 10 minutes. Meanwhile, steam the mussels in the white wine and 1 cup of boiling water until they open. Remove them and place them in a large bowl. Pour the sauce over the mussels in their shells.

 SUGGESTED MENU:

Steamed Mussels and Curried Tomato Sauce
Pain Grillé
Sautéed Mushrooms
Cointreau Dessert Omelet with Fresh Strawberries

SAUTÉED SOFT-SHELL CRABS

> 3 or 4 small soft-shell crabs, cleaned (see below)
> Flour
> 4 tablespoons Clarified Butter (see index for recipe)
> 2 tablespoons lemon juice
> 1 tablespoon fresh chopped parsley

Lightly coat the crabs with flour. Heat 3 tablespoons of the butter in a skillet that will comfortably hold the crabs. Sauté them over medium-high heat until they are golden brown on each side, 3 or 4 minutes per side. Remove them to a heated serving platter. Add the remaining tablespoon of butter to the pan along with the lemon juice and parsley. Cook the mixture over medium-high heat until it is lightly browned. Immediately pour it over the crabs and serve.

 SUGGESTED MENU:

Mixed Vegetable Terrine
Sautéed Soft-shell Crabs
Boiled Potatoes with Parsley
Chocolate Soufflé

HOW TO CLEAN SOFT-SHELL CRABS

Cut off each crab's head, located just behind the eyes. Press out the green bubble there. Raise the pointed side of the soft shell and remove the spongy white gills. Turn the crab on its back and peel back and cut off the apron with the sharp point of a small knife. Rinse the crab under cold running water and pat it dry.

BOILED LOBSTER

Simple boiled lobster, unencumbered by an elaborate sauce, is wonderful. When buying a fresh live lobster, see to it that it actively moves when it is gently touched.

1 1¼- to 1½-pound lobster

Bring 1½ quarts of lightly salted water to a rapid boil in a large saucepan or pot. Lower the lobster into the pot, cover, and cook over medium-high heat for 15 to 18 minutes, until the lobster is bright red. Remove the lobster with tongs or a hot pad and rest it in a colander to drain for a few minutes. Crack the claws to release the water held there. The lobster can be eaten immediately or chilled. It can also be cut in half for easy handling on a plate. To accomplish this, turn the lobster on its back and cut through it lengthwise.

Serve boiled lobster with Clarified Butter and lemon wedges. (See index for recipe.)

 SUGGESTED MENU:

Swordfish Chowder
Boiled Lobster
Baked Stuffed Potato
Banana Crown

LOBSTER BROCHETTE BASTED WITH
PERNOD AND BUTTER

 3 strips bacon, halved crosswise
 2 frozen rock lobster tails, thawed
 1 tablespoon Pernod
 2 tablespoons melted butter

Partially cook the bacon for 3 minutes on each side in a 9-inch skillet. Remove it and drain it on paper towels. Cut each lobster tail into 3 equal parts. Fold one strip of bacon in half and thread it onto a skewer; then fold one piece of lobster in half and thread it onto the skewer. Repeat the process until the bacon and lobster pieces are all skewered. Combine the Pernod and butter. Brush the mixture over the lobster. Broil the lobster until it is evenly cooked, turning and basting it with the Pernod mixture once, about 4 minutes per side.

 SUGGESTED MENU:

Italian Chicken Salad Cocktail
Lobster Brochette Basted with Pernod and Butter
Fresh Cooked Asparagus
Dessert Crepe with Strawberries and Whipped Cream

10. Meal-in-One Dishes

Hearty Soups

ANDREW BERGMAN'S HOT AND SOUR SOUP

Andrew Bergman, a writer, offers this soup as a meal in itself. He says, "Although I like almost any Chinese food, all I ever really want to eat in a Chinese restaurant is hot and sour soup. Four or six portions, a little tea, a friendly fortune, and I'd leave the restaurant a happy man. Usually, self-consciousness inhibits me from such unbridled monomania—in public. But with this recipe I can indulge myself happily at home. With its delicate mix of vegetables, its searching tartness, and its smooth consistency, hot and sour soup is like a rich, satisfying stew and makes a fine evening meal. Here is a recipe based on many hours of contented experimentation. Caution: I like my soup very spicy; if the room temperature doesn't seem to rise, something has gone haywire. If your taste runs to milder dishes, just cut back a little on the red pepper."

6 large dried Chinese mushrooms
6 dried wood ears (black fungus)
2 dozen dried lily flowers
2 tablespoons vegetable or peanut oil
2 finely shredded pork chops, lean meat only
2 tablespoons light soy sauce

½ cup finely sliced bamboo shoots
6 cups Beef Stock or broth (see index for recipe)
Salt to taste
Red pepper flakes, to taste
3 tablespoons red wine vinegar, to taste
2 tablespoons dark soy sauce
1½ tablespoons cornstarch with 3 tablespoons water
2 squares of bean curd, sliced into thin strips
1 tablespoon sesame oil or to taste
Freshly ground black pepper to taste
3 eggs
2 tablespoons minced green scallions

Soak the mushrooms, wood ears, and lily flowers in hot water for 30 minutes; then drain them. Remove the mushroom stems and discard them. Cut the mushrooms and wood ears into thin slices. Shred the lily flowers. Heat the oil in a large skillet, wok, or pot and cook the pork thoroughly, stirring. Add the light soy sauce, mushrooms, wood ears, lily flowers, and bamboo shoots. Stir the mixture over medium-high heat for several minutes. Add the stock. Sprinkle in the salt and red pepper; stir in the vinegar and dark soy sauce and simmer the soup for 10 minutes. Dissolve the cornstarch in the water and stir it into the soup. After the soup thickens slightly, add the bean curd and bring it to a boil. Add the sesame oil and pepper. Beat the eggs in a small bowl and drizzle them into the soup, constantly stirring. Sprinkle the soup with the chopped scallions.

This will make two filling dinner servings. There is enough for a second, trouble-free meal, or, by another measure, enough so that if another hot-and-sour-soup fan should drop by, you'll both be able to eat without having to keep an eye on the size of each other's portion.

Cold beer or white wine nicely complements this soup.

PENNSYLVANIA DUTCH CHICKEN AND CORN SOUP

    1 chicken breast, skinned, boned, and cut into bite-sized pieces
    1 stalk celery, chopped
    1 carrot, peeled and chopped
    1 medium onion, chopped
    Salt to taste
    ⅛ teaspoon fresh grated pepper
    1 cup Chicken Broth (see index for recipe)
    1 ear of corn, cooked, with the kernels cut off the cob
    ¼ cup diced cooked ham
    1 teaspoon fresh chopped parsley

Put the chicken, celery, carrot, onion, salt, pepper, and broth in a medium-sized saucepan. Add enough water to cover the ingredients. Bring the soup to the boil, reduce the heat, and simmer for 20 minutes. Add the corn, ham, and parsley. Bring the soup to a rolling boil and serve it immediately.

THICK CHICKEN NOODLE SOUP AU GRATIN

    1½ cups chicken broth
    ½ chicken breast, boned, skinned, and cut into bite-sized pieces
    ½ cup small thin egg noodles
    1 carrot, peeled and diced
    4 mushrooms, sliced
    1 tablespoon minced onion
    2 tablespoons green peas
    ⅛ teaspoon oregano
    Salt and freshly ground pepper to taste
    1 tablespoon grated Swiss cheese
    1 teaspoon grated Parmesan cheese

1 teaspoon bread crumbs
1 1-inch-thick slice French bread, toasted

Bring the chicken broth to a boil in a saucepan. Add the chicken, noodles, carrot, mushrooms, onion, peas, oregano, salt, and pepper. Return the liquid to the boil, reduce the heat, and cook the soup at a slow boil for 10 minutes. Pour it into a heatproof individual crock or bowl. Combine the cheeses and bread crumbs and sprinkle them over the toasted French bread. Float the bread on the soup. Set the bowl under the broiler until the cheese turns golden.

PASTA AND SPINACH EGGDROP SOUP

2 cups Chicken Stock (see index for recipe)
¼ cup tubettini
⅛ teaspoon oregano
Pinch of rosemary
½ teaspoon fresh chopped parsley
½ cup finely chopped fresh spinach
Salt and freshly ground pepper to taste
1 egg, beaten
2 teaspoons fresh grated Parmesan cheese

Bring the chicken stock to a boil in a small saucepan. Add the tubettini, oregano, rosemary, and parsley. Boil the soup until the tubettini is tender, about 5 minutes. Add the spinach, salt, and pepper and cook for 3 more minutes. Slowly drizzle in the beaten egg, stirring. Sprinkle the soup with the Parmesan cheese to taste.

CELERY AND CARROT HERB SOUP

1 tablespoon butter
1 small onion, chopped
1 large stalk celery with leaves, chopped
1 large carrot, peeled and sliced
⅛ teaspoon thyme
⅛ teaspoon dill weed
⅛ teaspoon tarragon
1 teaspoon fresh chopped parsley
1 cup Chicken Broth (see index for recipe)
½ cup milk
Salt and freshly ground pepper to taste

Melt the butter in a saucepan. Add the onion and celery and sauté them for 5 minutes, stirring often. Add the carrot and herbs, stirring. Pour in the broth and milk. Season the soup lightly with salt and pepper. Bring it to a boil, then reduce the heat and simmer it for 25 minutes. Puree the soup in a blender or force it through a sieve a few cupfuls at a time.

This recipe yields about 1½ cups, enough for a hearty meal or two ¾-cup servings as a first course.

MINESTRONE

2 tablespoons olive oil
1 clove garlic, crushed
1 medium onion, chopped
1 stalk celery, chopped
2½ cups Beef Stock (see index for recipe)
¼ cup canned chick-peas
¼ cup cooked kidney beans
½ cup raw shredded cabbage

    1 medium tomato, peeled and chopped
    ¼ teaspoon basil
    ¼ teaspoon oregano
    1 teaspoon fresh chopped parsley
    Salt and freshly ground pepper to taste
    ¼ cup ditali (pasta)
    Fresh grated Parmesan cheese

Heat the oil in a medium-sized saucepan. Sauté the garlic, onion, and celery for 5 minutes, stirring. Add the stock and all the remaining ingredients except the ditali and Parmesan cheese. Bring the liquid to a boil, stirring occasionally. Add the ditali and cook the soup over medium heat for 20 minutes. Sprinkle it with the cheese.

    Serve it with crusty Italian bread and a mixed green salad.

LENTIL SOUP

    1 cup lentils
    1¼ cups cold water
    3 cups cold Beef Stock or Broth (see index for recipe)
    1 medium onion, chopped
    1 carrot, peeled and diced
    1 bay leaf, crumbled
    ½ teaspoon thyme
    Freshly ground pepper to taste
    ½ teaspoon salt

Bring all the ingredients to a boil in a large saucepan. Reduce the heat and simmer for 1¼ hours, until the lentils are tender. Stir the soup several times while it is cooking.

VARIATIONS: Add 4 ounces of chopped cooked ham to the recipe. Or add 1 teaspoon of curry powder and 1 chopped peeled tomato to the recipe.

NEW ENGLAND CREAMY CLAM CHOWDER

1 ounce salt pork, cubed
1 small onion, chopped
1 boiling potato, peeled and cut into ¼-inch cubes
1 8-ounce bottle clam juice
6 fresh clams, quartered
½ cup heavy cream
Salt and freshly ground pepper to taste
Butter

Fry the salt pork until its fat is released. Discard the bits of pork. Add the onion to the fat and sauté it for 5 minutes. Add the potato, clam juice, and clams. Bring the liquid to a boil, reduce the heat, and simmer the soup for 12 minutes. Add the heavy cream, season with salt and pepper, and cook, stirring, for 5 minutes over medium heat until the soup is hot and the potatoes are tender. Pour the chowder into a bowl and top it with a pat of butter.

FRESH HADDOCK AND RICE SOUP WITH
PARMESAN CHEESE

1½ tablespoons olive or vegetable oil
1 small clove garlic, minced
1 small onion, finely chopped
1 4-ounce haddock fillet, cut into 12 small pieces
1 teaspoon fresh chopped parsley
Pinch of thyme
1 teaspoon lemon juice
Salt and freshly ground pepper to taste
1½ cups bottled clam juice
½ cup cooked rice
1 tablespoon fresh grated Parmesan cheese

Heat the oil in a small, heavy saucepan and sauté the garlic and onion for 4 minutes over medium heat, stirring. Add the haddock, parsley, thyme, and lemon juice. Season the mixture with the salt and pepper. Pour in the clam juice and bring the liquid to a boil. Reduce the heat and simmer the soup for 10 minutes. Stir in the rice and cook until it is thoroughly heated, about 3 minutes. Taste the soup for seasoning. Sprinkle it with the Parmesan cheese.

QUICK STRIPED BASS SOUP

    1½ cups bottled clam juice
    3 tablespoons butter
    1 small onion, finely chopped
    1 scant tablespoon flour
    ⅓ pound striped bass fillet, cut into bite-sized pieces
    ½ cup heavy cream
    Salt and freshly ground pepper to taste

Heat the clam juice in a small saucepan. In a 9-inch skillet heat 2 tablespoons of the butter and sauté the onion for 5 minutes over medium-low heat. Sprinkle the flour over the onions and stir. Cook the mixture for 2 minutes, stirring often. Slowly stir in the hot clam juice. Add the bass and bring the soup to a boil. Reduce the heat and simmer the soup for 10 minutes. Add the cream and season with the salt and pepper. Cook the soup for 2 minutes over very high heat. Ladle it into a soup bowl and float the remaining tablespoon of butter in the center of it.

SWORDFISH CHOWDER

1 tablespoon butter
2 tablespoons minced onion
1 small clove garlic, minced
1 tablespoon vegetable or olive oil
¾ cup tomato, peeled and chopped
2 tablespoons dry white wine
¼ teaspoon thyme
2 teaspoons fresh chopped parsley
1½ cups Chicken Broth (see index for recipe)
Salt and freshly ground pepper to taste
⅓ pound swordfish, cut into bite-sized pieces
1 1½-inch-thick slice toasted French bread
Fresh grated Parmesan cheese

Heat the butter and oil in a saucepan. Sauté the onion and garlic for 5 minutes, stirring occasionally. Add the tomato, wine, thyme, parsley, and broth. Bring the liquid to a boil. Reduce the heat and simmer the soup for 15 minutes. Season it with the salt and pepper. Add the swordfish and cook the soup over medium heat for 5 minutes, until the fish is tender. Place the toasted bread in a deep soup bowl and ladle the chowder over it. Sprinkle it with the Parmesan cheese.

Stews, a Ragout, Chilies, and a Casserole

BEEF STEW

    2 slices bacon, chopped
    1 tablespoon vegetable oil
    ½ pound stewing beef, cut into bite-sized pieces
    Salt and freshly ground pepper to taste
    Flour
    3 cups Beef Broth (see index for recipe)
    1 clove garlic, quartered
    1 bay leaf
    ¼ teaspoon thyme
    1 teaspoon Worcestershire sauce
    ½ cup water
    2 tablespoons red wine
    1 carrot, peeled and sliced
    1 boiling potato, peeled and halved
    2 small onions, peeled and left whole

In a heavy 2-quart saucepan fry the bacon in the oil until it is crisp. Discard the bacon. Season the beef with the salt and pepper. Dust it with flour and fry it in the fat until it is browned on all sides. Drain off the fat. Pour in the broth and add the garlic, bay leaf, thyme, and Worcestershire sauce. Bring the liquid to a boil, reduce the heat, and simmer the mixture for 1 hour. Add the water and wine and simmer for 25 more minutes. Add the vegetables and simmer for about 25 more minutes or until the vegetables are tender. Taste the stew for seasoning.

IRISH STEW

½ pound lamb shoulder, cut into bite-sized pieces
Salt and freshly ground pepper to taste
Flour
2 tablespoons vegetable oil
2 cups water
1 bay leaf
⅛ teaspoon rosemary
⅛ teaspoon thyme
1 cup water
2 small onions, peeled and left whole
1 carrot, peeled and sliced
1 stalk celery, sliced
1 boiling potato, quartered
¼ teaspoon dill weed

Season the lamb pieces with the salt and pepper. Dust them with flour. Heat the oil in a heavy 2-quart saucepan and brown the lamb on all sides. Pour off the fat. Add the 2 cups of water and the bay leaf, rosemary, and thyme. Bring the liquid to a boil, reduce the heat, and simmer the mixture for 30 minutes. Add the 1 cup of water and simmer for 30 more minutes. Now add the vegetables and dill weed and simmer for 25 more minutes or until the vegetables are tender. Add a little more water if necessary, but stew sauce should be slightly thick.

This stew is excellent if it is refrigerated overnight and eaten the next day.

BEEF AND CARROT RAGOUT

½ pound stewing beef, cut into 1-inch cubes
Salt and freshly ground pepper to taste
2 tablespoons butter
1 tablespoon vegetable oil
1 small onion, chopped
1 tablespoon flour
1 cup Beef Broth (see index for recipe)
1 cup dry red wine
1 teaspoon tomato paste
¼ teaspoon thyme
1 bay leaf
2 carrots, peeled and cut into 1-inch lengths

Season the beef cubes with the salt and pepper. Heat the butter and oil in a medium-sized skillet and brown the beef over medium-high heat. Add the onion and continue cooking for 5 minutes. Sprinkle in the flour and stir. Pour in the broth and wine slowly, stirring. Add the tomato paste, thyme, and bay leaf. Season the mixture with additional salt and pepper. Bring the liquid to a boil, reduce the heat, and cover the skillet. Simmer the ragout for 1 hour. Stir it twice during the cooking time. Add the carrots and cook for another 20 minutes. Taste the ragout for seasoning.

GRINGO CHILI

>   1 tablespoon vegetable oil
>   1 medium onion, finely chopped
>   1 clove garlic, minced
>   ½ small green pepper, chopped
>   6 ounces ground beef
>   2 teaspoons chili powder
>   ½ teaspoon cumin
>   1 teaspoon Worcestershire sauce
>   1 8-ounce can whole tomatoes, chopped (Save the liquid.)
>   ½ cup kidney beans, cooked or drained
>   Salt and freshly ground pepper to taste

Heat the oil in a 9-inch skillet. Sauté the onion, garlic, and green pepper for 3 minutes, stirring often. Remove the vegetables and sauté the beef, crumbling it with a fork, for 5 minutes, stirring. Sprinkle the chili powder, cumin, and Worcestershire sauce over the meat, stirring. Add the sautéed vegetables with the tomatoes and their liquid. Combine the ingredients and bring the chili to the boil; then reduce the heat and simmer for 20 minutes. Add the beans, stir, and cook for 5 more minutes. Season to taste with the salt and pepper.

Garnish the chili with grated Cheddar cheese and chopped onion and green pepper.

GEORGE WILLIG'S CHILIES RELLENOS

George Willig is a mountaineer, actor, stunt man, and author, but to most New Yorkers he is the hero and living superman who climbed the World Trade Center one morning in 1977. George Willig is the most fearless man I know, and cooking for himself poses no problem. He enjoys collecting recipes and retesting them until he's satisfied with the dish. George says, "I worked on chilies rellenos for two years, perfecting the recipe. Now it's one of my favorites. It's best to eat the chilies immediately after they are cooked. Freezing them will cause the peppers to soften slightly, but they're still very good. Be sure to serve them with plenty of fresh Italian bread and iced beer."

3 Italian frying peppers (chilies)
1 cup shredded mild Cheddar cheese
Peanut oil for deep frying
Flour
2 eggs, separated

SAUCE:

¼ cup chopped onions
1 small clove garlic, minced
1 8-ounce can tomato sauce
1 6-ounce can tomato paste
1 tablespoon peanut oil
¾ cup Chicken Broth (see index for recipe)

Mix the sauce ingredients and puree them in a blender or force them through a food mill until they are smooth. Pour the sauce into a skillet and simmer it while you are cooking the chilies. Slit the chilies down one side lengthwise, leaving them whole. Carefully cut away the white pith and remove the seeds, but leave the stems intact. Stuff the peppers with equal amounts of the cheese and close them. Rub the peppers lightly with peanut oil and dust them with flour. Beat the egg whites until they are stiff but not dry. Fold in the beaten egg yolks. Dip the stuffed peppers in the egg mixture and fry them in 1 inch of hot oil in a skillet until they are golden brown on all sides. Drain them on absorbent paper. Put them in the simmering sauce and cook them for a few minutes until they are heated through. Serve them immediately.

PAELLA-STYLE OPEN RICE CASSEROLE

    1 sweet Italian sausage
    4 tablespoons olive oil
    1 chicken leg and thigh, separated
    Salt and freshly ground pepper to taste
    1 medium onion, finely chopped
    1 clove garlic, minced
    1 ripe tomato, peeled and diced
    1 small green pepper, seeded and diced
    ¾ cup long-grain rice
    ¼ cup green peas
    ⅛ teaspoon saffron
    1¾ cups boiling Chicken Broth (see index for recipe)

Place the sausage in a small skillet with ½ inch of boiling water. Prick
the sausage in several places with a fork and simmer it for 10 minutes.
Turn it and cook it for another 10 minutes. Remove the sausage and
drain it on absorbent paper. In the cleaned skillet, heat 2 tablespoons
of the oil. Season the chicken with the salt and pepper and brown it
on both sides in the oil. Remove the chicken from the skillet and add
the 2 remaining tablespoons of olive oil. Sauté the onion, garlic, tomato, and pepper for 8 minutes over medium heat. Remove the skillet
from the heat. In a heavy ovenproof 9-inch skillet combine the rice,
the sautéed vegetables, the green peas, and the saffron. Season the
mixture with salt and pepper. Pour in the boiling chicken broth. Stir
and bring the liquid to a boil. Place the chicken pieces and the sliced
sausage in the pan and bake it in a preheated 375°F oven for about 25
minutes or until the rice is cooked and the chicken is tender.

Sandwiches

For busy single cooks who don't want to go out for a quick meal, a delicious sandwich provides an easy answer. In fact, it was invented for and named after such a man, John Montagu, the Earl of Sandwich, who refused to leave the gambling table long enough to dine. Food was brought to him in the casino and was served, for convenience, between slices of bread.

There are hot and cold sandwiches, open-faced, finger, and meal-in-one sandwiches, even diet sandwiches.

Extras from previously cooked dishes of vegetables, fish, seafood, and meat, plus cheese, eggs, nuts, and a myriad fresh vegetables, all provide interesting sandwich possibilities.

The bread used in making sandwiches needn't be limited to white, whole wheat, or rye. There are infinite varieties to select from: French bread, Italian hero rolls, English muffins, pita bread, kaiser rolls, bagels, croissants, brioches, corn muffins, biscuits, even crepes.

Vary spreads to complement sandwich ingredients by changing from the regulars—butter, Mayonnaise, and mustard—to Russian dressing, Lemon Curried Mayonnaise, fresh tartar sauce, oil and vinegar with herbs or hearty bread, whipped cream cheese, Crème Fraîche, pureed cottage cheese, pureed vegetables, herb and seafood butter, jams, preserves, chutney, or plain virgin olive oil. Creamy Horseradish Dressing and Cranberry Dressing are two of my favorites. (See index for recipes.)

CRISTIN TORBERT'S FRESH TOMATO AND
BASIL PANNINIS

Cristin Torbert, a home decorator and designer in Washington, D.C., eats in any room of her Chevy Chase home, and because of her work schedule a meal may be at any hour of the day. Cristin always sets a proper place to eat wherever she dines, even when she's having her quick favorite summertime sandwich, a pannini. Cristin says, "I never really eat alone, because my Persians, Kazak and Tschebouc, are ever constant companions. And there are always kittens."

    2 individual French rolls
    Olive oil
    Red wine vinegar
    1 fresh ripe tomato
    2 thin slices red onion
    Fresh basil leaves
    Salt and freshly ground pepper to taste

Cut the French rolls in half. Sprinkle the inside of rolls with oil and vinegar. Arrange a layer of sliced tomato, onion, and basil leaves on the bottom half of the rolls. Season the vegetables with salt and plenty of pepper. Sprinkle a little more oil and vinegar over the basil leaves. Close the sandwiches with the tops of the rolls.
    Serve panninis with dry white wine.

CAESAR SALAD SANDWICH

    1 hero roll
    2 teaspoons butter
    2 teaspoons fresh grated Parmesan cheese
    A mini Caesar salad (see index for recipe)
    2 ounces mozzarella cheese, shredded

Cut the hero roll in half lengthwise. Spread the butter over the inside of the roll and sprinkle it with the Parmesan cheese. Toast the roll under the broiler until the cheese is golden. Pile the mini Caesar salad on the bread and sprinkle it with the mozzarella cheese.

AVOCADO GRILLED CHEESE SANDWICH

1 4-inch piece French bread
1 tablespoon Curried Lemon Mayonnaise (see index for recipe)
4 ¼-inch-thick slices avocado
3 strips cooked bacon, crumbled
2 slices Muenster cheese

Cut the bread in half lengthwise. Spread the mayonnaise over the slices. Place 2 slices of avocado on each half and sprinkle them with equal amounts of the bacon. Top each half with a slice of cheese. Place the sandwich under the broiler and cook it until the cheese just melts. (Don't allow the cheese to form a crust.)

SLICED DUCK, BACON, AND MUSHROOM OPEN-FACED SANDWICH

1½ tablespoons butter
4 mushrooms, sliced
Meat from half a roast duck
½ teaspoon Dijon-style mustard
1 teaspoon orange marmalade
¼ teaspoon soy sauce
1 slice pumpernickel
3 strips crisp cooked bacon

Heat the butter in a 9-inch skillet and sauté the mushrooms for 5 minutes, shaking the pan occasionally to turn them. Set them aside. Cut the meat into slices. Combine the mustard, marmalade, and soy sauce. Spread this mixture over the bread and top it with the duck meat, the mushroom slices, and the bacon strips.

MUSHROOM AND CREAM CHEESE SANDWICH
WITH BACON

2 tablespoons butter
2 tablespoons grated onion
6 medium-sized fresh mushrooms, finely chopped
3 tablespoons cream cheese, at room temperature
1 teaspoon fresh chopped parsley
Salt and freshly ground pepper to taste
1 sandwich roll or French roll, halved and toasted
3 strips crisp cooked bacon
2 slices fresh ripe tomato

Heat the butter in a 9-inch skillet and sauté the onion, stirring, for about 4 minutes. Add the mushrooms and cook them over medium heat for 5 minutes, stirring them often. With a slotted spoon, transfer the mushrooms and onions to a plate to cool. Beat the cream cheese until it is fluffy. Add the cooled mushrooms and onions, parsley, salt, and pepper to it and mix well. Spread it on the bottom half of the toasted sandwich roll and top it with the bacon and tomato slices. Close the sandwich with the top of the roll.

GRILLED MOZZARELLA, PROSCIUTTO, AND
BASIL SANDWICH

2 slices firm white bread
1 teaspoon butter
4 thin slices mozzarella
2 thin slices prosciutto
2 fresh basil leaves or ¼ teaspoon dried basil
2 thin slices fresh ripe tomato

Freshly ground pepper to taste
1 tablespoon Clarified Butter (see index for recipe)
1 tablespoon olive oil

Butter the bread. On one slice stack 2 slices of the mozzarella, the prosciutto, the basil leaves, and the tomato slices. Season this with pepper. Top the stack with the 2 remaining slices of cheese. Add the other slice of bread, buttered side down. Heat the butter and oil in a 9-inch skillet and cook the sandwich over medium heat until it is browned. Turn it with a spatula and brown it on the other side. Press the top down with the spatula.

Slice the sandwich into 3 rectangles and serve it with a salad.

EXTRAS SUGGESTIONS: Mozzarella and prosciutto enhance any pasta dish. Melon Cubes Wrapped in Cheese and Prosciutto makes an easy, delicious first course. (See index for recipe.)

ROAST BEEF AND WATERCRESS CROISSANT SANDWICH

1 large fresh croissant
Sweet butter
Dijon-style mustard
¼ pound rare roast beef
4 sprigs watercress

With a serrated knife, gently cut the croissant in half. Butter one side and spread the other side with mustard. Place the roast beef and watercress on one half and close the sandwich.

Serve with Carrot and Potato Salad. (See index for recipe.)

SLICED STEAK SANDWICH

    2 slices fresh rye or pumpernickel bread
    1½ tablespoons Creamy Horseradish Dressing (see index for
        recipe)
    4 ⅛-inch-thick slices cooked flank steak, London broil, or sirloin
    Fresh watercress sprigs
    3 or 4 red onion rings (optional)
    Salt and freshly ground pepper to taste

Spread both slices of the bread with creamy horseradish dressing.
Arrange the steak slices across one slice of bread, top it with the
watercress and onion rings, and season it with the salt and pepper.
Place the other bread slice on top.
    Serve this with black olives or cherry tomatoes.

MARIA URTUBEY'S TUNA CREPE SANDWICH TORT

Maria Urtubey, an Argentine, is a busy New York City housewife.
"When I consider food in general," Maria says, "the question I must
first ask myself is, Will I have to reduce or enlarge the recipe? The
easier the recipe is, the happier I am. But, of course, I complicate
matters by wanting the dish to be delicious. My crepe sandwich can
be made with either 6-inch individual crepes or giant 12-inch ones.
The latter is cut into wedges and serves 4 to 6 people. A combination
of tuna, lettuce, tomato, and ham is my specialty, which I'd like to
share with you, but by all means encourage everyone to investigate
all the wonderful options."

    5 Basic Crepes (see index for recipe)
    2 tablespoons Mayonnaise (see index for recipe)
    3 thin slices boiled ham
    2 ounces white-meat tuna
    ½ cup shredded lettuce

1 ripe tomato, thinly sliced
Salt and freshly ground pepper to taste

Spread each crepe lightly with mayonnaise. On the first crepe place the ham; top it with another crepe and sprinkle that with flaked tuna; top that with another crepe and sprinkle it with lettuce; top that with another crepe, arrange the tomato slices on it, and season them well with the salt and pepper. Place the last crepe on the tomatoes, mayonnaise side down. Press the top down slightly and cut the sandwich into wedges.

Serve it with pickles, large green olives, or carrot sticks.

VARIATION: On Maria's advice I tried her crepe sandwich with layers of shredded lettuce, thinly sliced cucumbers, Danish butter cheese, roasted red peppers, and thin slices of onion. It's superb.

POOR BOY SANDWICH

½ dozen shucked raw oysters
Flour
Vegetable oil for frying
1 6-inch piece of French bread, halved
Mayonnaise (see index for recipe) or ketchup
½ cup shredded lettuce
Salt and freshly ground pepper to taste
Hot pepper sauce (optional)

Coat the oysters with flour. Heat ¾ of an inch of oil in a frying pan and fry the oysters for about 3 minutes. Turn them and cook them for another 3 minutes, until they are golden and crisp. Drain them. Spread the mayonnaise or ketchup on the top half of the bread and arrange the lettuce on the bottom half. Top it with the oysters. Sprinkle them with the salt and pepper, and the hot sauce, if you wish. Close the sandwich with the other half of the bread.

NERO'S HERO SANDWICH

1 small onion
1 Italian hero roll
6 thin slices salami
6 thin slices prosciutto or boiled ham
4 slices provolone
4 thin tomato slices
½ cup shredded romaine lettuce

DRESSING:

2 tablespoons olive oil
1 teaspoon red wine vinegar
½ teaspoon Dijon-style mustard
⅛ teaspoon basil
⅛ teaspoon oregano
⅛ teaspoon rosemary
Salt and freshly ground pepper to taste

Cut the onion into very thin slices. Break these apart into rings and soak them in cold water for 30 minutes. Drain them and pat them dry. Cut open the hero roll. On the bottom half place rows of salami, prosciutto, provolone, and tomato slices, and scatter the lettuce and onions over the top. Combine the dressing ingredients in a bowl, mixing them well with a wire whisk. Sprinkle the dressing over the other sandwich ingredients and top them with the other half of the roll.

GOUJONNETTES OF SOLE SANDWICH

> 6 to 8 ounces sole fillet, cut into strips ⅓-inch thick on a
>   diagonal
> Flour
> 1 egg, beaten
> Bread crumbs
> 2 cups vegetable oil
> Salt and freshly ground pepper to taste
> ¼ fresh lemon
> 1 kaiser or Italian roll
> ¼ cup Creamy Horseradish Dressing (see index for recipe)

Dust the sole strips with flour. Coat them with the beaten egg and roll them in the bread crumbs. Heat the oil in a medium-sized saucepan and fry the fish until it is crisp and golden brown. Drain it. Immediately season it with the salt and pepper and sprinkle it with the juice of the lemon. Split open the roll. Spread creamy horseradish dressing liberally over each half of the roll and top it with the fried sole strips.

VARIATION: Creamy Tartar Sauce (see index for recipe) can be substituted for the creamy horseradish dressing.

Rice Dishes, Crepes, and Pizzas

FRIED RICE WITH SHRIMP

This dish accompanied by a fresh green salad makes an excellent
lunch or light dinner. The meal can be prepared in about 15 unhur-
ried minutes.

  1½ tablespoons vegetable or peanut oil
  1 cup cooked cold rice
  2 tablespoons thinly sliced scallions
  ½ cup cooked cubed shrimp
  1 tablespoon soy sauce
  1 egg, lightly beaten
  1 teaspoon fresh chopped parsley
  2 tablespoons diced cooked ham or bacon (optional)

Heat the oil in a 9-inch skillet and add the rice. Cook the rice, stirring
often, for 5 minutes. Add the scallions, shrimp, and soy sauce. Stir
and cook the mixture for 4 minutes. Stir in the egg, parsley, and ham
and cook, still stirring, until the egg is set, about 1 minute. Check the
seasoning.

ARANCINI
(Fried Rice and Cheese Balls)

¾ cup cooked rice, at room temperature
1 tablespoon melted butter
½ cup grated mozzarella
2 tablespoons fresh grated Parmesan cheese
1 teaspoon fresh chopped parsley
Salt and freshly ground pepper to taste
2 eggs, beaten
2 1-inch cubes mozzarella
Flour
Bread crumbs
2 cups vegetable oil

Combine the rice, butter, grated mozzarella, Parmesan cheese, parsley, salt, pepper, and half the beaten eggs. Divide the mixture in half. Form a ball out of each half, putting a cube of mozzarella in the center of each ball. Refrigerate the balls for 1 hour. Then dust the balls with flour and dip them in the remaining beaten egg. Coat them with bread crumbs and fry them in the oil in a 9-inch skillet until they are crisp and golden brown.

Serve arancini with Veal Marsala or as a light meal with the salad of your choice. (See index for recipe.)

EXTRAS SUGGESTION: Vegetable oil can be saved and used again. Just strain it through a fine sieve. Then pour it into a wide-mouthed jar and add a 1½-inch piece of peeled raw potato. (The potato will absorb any cooking odor.) Use the oil as soon as possible for frying or sautéeing, not in salads. Discard the potato.

BASIC CREPES

½ cup water
¼ cup milk
⅓ cup flour
1 whole egg
1 egg yolk
½ tablespoon oil
⅛ teaspoon salt
2½ tablespoons butter or as needed

Beat together all the ingredients except the butter until they are well blended. Cover the batter and refrigerate it for 30 minutes. Heat 1 tablespoon of butter and coat the bottom of a 7-inch crepe pan. When the butter is hot, pour about ¼ cup of the crepe batter into the pan. Immediately tilt the pan in a circle until the batter coats the bottom of the pan evenly. When the edges of the crepe begin to turn light brown, turn the crepe over with a spatula. Cook it for about 30 more seconds and transfer it to a plate. Add 1 teaspoon of butter to the pan and proceed making crepes in this fashion with the rest of the batter.

This recipe makes about 6 crepes.

Use the crepes immediately or cover and refrigerate them. Crepes can also be wrapped in airtight foil and frozen.

VARIATION: To make herb crepes, add 2 teaspoons of finely chopped fresh parsley and ½ teaspoon of your favorite herb, such as dill or tarragon, to the basic crepe recipe.

CREPES WITH SAUSAGE AND CHEESE

6 basic crepes (see above)
½ cup Mornay Sauce (see index for recipe)
½ cup cooked bulk sausage, crumbled

2 tablespoons freshly grated Swiss cheese
Freshly chopped parsley

Spread 1 tablespoon of mornay sauce over each crepe and top it with 1 tablespoon of sausage. Roll the crepes up. Place them in a lightly buttered baking dish. Sprinkle them with the cheese and pass them under the broiler until the cheese sizzles. Garnish them with parsley.

CREPES WITH SHRIMP AND MUSHROOMS

6 basic crepes (see above)
6 medium shrimp, shelled, deveined, and boiled
3 tablespoons butter
2 tablespoons chopped onions
6 fresh mushrooms, thinly sliced
½ teaspoon tarragon
Salt and freshly ground pepper
½ cup Fish Velouté Sauce (see index for recipe)

Chop the shrimp and set them aside. Heat the butter and sauté the onions and mushrooms for 5 minutes. Add the shrimp and cook for 4 more minutes. Sprinkle the mixture with the tarragon, salt, and pepper. Stir it and mix it with the hot fish velouté. Spoon the filling in equal amounts into the crepes and roll them up. Place them in a shallow baking dish and heat them in a preheated 350°F oven for 5 minutes. Serve them immediately.

COMBINATION FILLINGS

Combine the suggested ingredients and fill basic crepes with them.

Tuna and Green Peas

Combine ½ cup of hot Velouté Sauce (see index for recipe), ¼ cup hot cooked green peas, and 2 ounces of flaked tuna.

Sour Cream and Red Caviar

Combine ½ cup of sour cream, 1 tablespoon of minced scallion, and 2 ounces of red salmon caviar.

Creamed Broccoli and Ham

Combine ¾ cup of hot Creamed Broccoli (see index for recipe) and ¼ cup diced cooked ham.

HOMEMADE PIZZA

The Chicago area has the best pizza in this country. It is most famous for deep-dish pizza, a rich, thick concoction served originally in the Café Uno in the Loop. I worked briefly for a newspaper, *The Suburban Life*, in La Grange Park. Right next door, Johnny's Pizza made a miraculously crisp, thin-crusted pizza that they cut into 2-inch squares. It was so delicious that it wasn't possible to leave one morsel on the plate. I made many pizzas at home before I was satisfied with the crust as compared with Johnny's. I don't know why people say pizza is difficult to make. Try it once and you'll realize that you've been depriving yourself.

DOUGH:

>   1 envelope dry yeast
>   ½ cup warm water
>   1¼ cups flour
>   ¼ teaspoon salt
>   1 tablespoon olive oil

Dissolve the yeast in the water. Pour it in a bowl along with the flour, salt, and oil. Stir with a wooden spoon until the ingredients are well mixed, scraping the sides of the bowl as you stir. Cover the dough and let it rise in a warm area of the kitchen for about 40 minutes or until the dough doubles in size.

PREPARATION FOR BASIC CHEESE PIZZA

    2 teaspoons olive oil
    Flour
    ¾ cup canned tomato sauce
    ½ teaspoon oregano
    ¼ teaspoon basil
    ¾ cup shredded mozzarella cheese
    2 teaspoons fresh grated Parmesan cheese
    1 tablespoon olive oil

Grease a 13-inch pizza pan with the 2 teaspoons of oil. Flour your fingers and shape the pizza dough into a ball. Then flour your fingers again and shape the dough into a circle. Place it on the pizza pan. Work the dough with your fingers and pat it until it fills the pan to the outer edges as evenly as possible. Spoon the tomato sauce over the surface and sprinkle it evenly with the remaining ingredients in the order in which they are listed. Bake the pizza in a preheated 375°F oven for 15 minutes or until the top sizzles and the crust is golden and crisp. Cut it into 2-inch squares or large wedges and serve.

Mushroom Pizza

Prepare the pizza exactly as directed in the cheese pizza recipe and scatter ¾ cup of thinly sliced mushrooms over the pizza after adding the mozzarella cheese. Proceed with the rest of the recipe as directed.

Onion and Green Pepper Pizza

Prepare the pizza exactly as directed in the cheese pizza recipe and scatter 1 medium onion cut into thin slices and 1 small green pepper cut into thin strips over the pizza after adding the mozzarella cheese. Proceed with the rest of the recipe as directed.

Sausage Pizza

Prepare the pizza exactly as directed in the cheese pizza recipe and scatter ¾ cup of cooked crumbled Italian sweet sausage or bulk sausage evenly over the pizza after adding the mozzarella cheese. Proceed with the rest of the recipe as directed.

Ham, Caper, and Anchovy Pizza

Prepare the pizza exactly as directed in the cheese pizza recipe and scatter 2 chopped slices of boiled ham, 2 tablespoons of capers, and 3 chopped anchovy fillets over the pizza after adding the mozzarella cheese. Proceed with the rest of the recipe as directed.

Specialties

EGGPLANT AND HAM TART

> ½ cup flour
> ½ teaspoon baking soda
> ⅛ teaspoon salt
> Freshly ground pepper to taste
> 2 teaspoons fresh chopped parsley
> ¼ teaspoon oregano
> ¼ cup minced onion
> 1 small clove garlic, crushed
> 2 eggs
> ¼ cup vegetable oil
> ¼ cup fresh grated Parmesan cheese
> 1¼ cups thinly sliced eggplant (use the smallest eggplant
>   available)
> ¼ cup diced cooked ham

Combine all ingredients except the eggplant and ham in a bowl and mix them well. Fold in the eggplant and ham and coat them evenly with the mixture. Lightly grease an 8-by-8-inch baking pan. Turn the mixture into the pan and smooth it evenly on top. Bake it in a pre-heated 350°F oven for 25 minutes. Cut it into wedges and serve.

EXTRAS SUGGESTION: Extra tart can be served the next day cold or reheated. This recipe also makes a superb appetizer for 4.

HARRY BARON'S ANCHOVY FETE DISHES

Harry Baron, a writer, reports: "As one who works at home, normally prepares his own brunch, and is no threat to the great chefs of Europe, I have a simple kitchen philosophy: An enjoyable meal for one should not take longer to fix than to eat. Which works out very well for me since I am a fast fixer and a slow eater—and happen to like anchovies.

"In my view, there are two ways to eat anchovies: straight and diminished. Eating them straight (even in incompatible combination with pizza), you are eating hors d'oeuvres. Eating them diminished, you may discover the truly subtle and unique flavor of anchovies for the first time.

"As an example of what I mean by a diminished anchovy dish, take one of my favorite brunches: two flat fillets of anchovies cut up into quarter-inch sections; a side dish of several halved little red-skinned new potatoes, boiled 8 to 10 minutes; and a scoop of sour cream for potato dipping. The concept is as simple as the meal itself. The high sapidity of the anchovy is reduced by a comparatively bland side dish. This brings out the delicate flavor, titillating the taste buds instead of assaulting them, and creates a most palatable mix.

"In a different mode, diminished anchovies also make a great mid-afternoon or midnight snack—for example, anchovy bits of 2 or 3 fillets with cream cheese and thin slices of tomato on toast.

"For those who think they don't like anchovies, perhaps my an-chovy omelet will convert them—as it recently did my teenage daughter. In a bowl combine 2 or 3 eggs, 2 tablespoons of milk, 2 tablespoons of corn-flake crumbs (optional), the anchovy bits of 3 flat fillets, and dashes of pepper to taste. Stir well and pour into a hot, well-buttered (1 tablespoon) omelet or similar type of pan. Stir with a fork until the mixture begins to solidify. Smooth the egg mixture over the surface of the pan with the back of a spoon. Tilt the pan and start folding the omelet over, finally turning it out onto a heated plate. Do not overcook the omelet. Total cooking should not take more than 20 to 30 seconds. Serve the omelet on the toasted halves of an English muffin or with toasted French bread."

Harry's recipes should convert the uninitiated, but for those who would like anchovies with a less harsh flavor, try soaking the fillets in milk for 10 minutes before using them. Then pat the fillets dry with absorbent paper and proceed. This soaking also reduces some of the saltiness.

Extras Suggestions: Anchovies are pick-me-ups in salads, pasta, and sandwiches.

DUTCH APPLE PANCAKE

¼ cup flour
¼ cup milk
1 egg, beaten
½ teaspoon lemon juice
Pinch of salt
2 tablespoons butter
½ Delicious apple, peeled and cut into very thin slices
1 teaspoon sugar
⅛ teaspoon cinnamon

Lightly beat together the flour, milk, egg, lemon juice, and salt. The mixture should have a few small lumps in it. Melt the butter in a 9-inch ovenproof skillet. When the butter is hot, pour in the flour mixture and quickly arrange the apple slices over the top. Bake the pancake in a preheated 425°F oven for 15 to 18 minutes or until the batter is golden and puffy. Sprinkle it with the combined sugar and cinnamon.

TABOULEH
(Middle Eastern Salad)

½ cup raw bulgur wheat
1⅔ cups boiling, lightly salted water
¼ cup fresh chopped parsley
¼ cup chopped scallion or onion
1 small tomato, diced
1 tablespoon fresh chopped mint leaves or 1 teaspoon dried mint
1½ tablespoons fresh lemon juice
1 tablespoon olive or vegetable oil
Salt and freshly ground pepper to taste

Put the bulgur wheat in a bowl and pour the boiling water over it. Let it sit for 1½ to 2 hours, until it is fluffy. Drain it. Combine it with the remaining ingredients and chill the mixture thoroughly before serving it.

Serve this salad with toasted pita bread for a light luncheon. For a heartier meal, add ½ cup of chopped cooked shrimp or chicken to it.

SANDRA STEWART'S TORTILLA DINNER

My spirited cousin Sandra Stewart, a bank manager in San Leandro, California, loves Mexican food. She says her recipe is probably the world's easiest, because it requires little talent, measuring, or "real" cooking, plus it has an advantage that few recipes can boast: the ingredients can be changed. "You can eat as few or as many as your hunger demands. When I or either of my two daughters is dining alone at home, the menu 90 percent of the time will be some variation of tortillas. I should buy stock in the company."

> 2 tablespoons finely chopped green pepper
> Chopped hot pepper to taste
> 3 tablespoons crisp cooked crumbled bacon
> 2 tablespoons chopped stuffed green olives
> 1 scallion, minced
> Butter
> 3 flour tortillas
> ⅔ cup shredded Monterey Jack cheese

Combine the green pepper, hot pepper, bacon, olives, and scallion. Melt a little butter on a griddle or in a large frying pan. Add the tortillas. Sprinkle them with equal amounts of the cheese and top them with the pepper mixture. As the cheese begins to melt, fold the tortillas and turn them. Cook them until they are crisp and the cheese is melted through.

Serve tortillas with refried beans with hot pepper sauce and a green salad.

VARIATIONS: Add chopped ham, cooked crumbled ground beef, or sausage to the pepper mixture.

CHEESE FONDUE

   1 small clove garlic, halved
   ¾ cup dry white wine
   7 ounces shredded Gruyère or Swiss cheese
   1 tablespoon flour
   Pinch of freshly ground nutmeg
   Pepper to taste (white if possible)
   1 small loaf French bread, cut into 1-inch cubes

Rub a small fondue pot with the garlic halves and then discard them. Pour in the wine and heat it slowly. Do *not* boil it. Meanwhile, sprinkle the shredded cheese into a bowl with the flour and toss them. Add the floured cheese a little at a time to the hot wine, stirring with a wooden spoon. Season the mixture with the nutmeg and pepper. It should be creamy. Now bring it to a boil and immediately place it over the lighted flame in a fondue burner holder.

Using a fondue fork or a fork with a wooden handle, spear the bread cubes and dip them into the fondue.

Serve fondue with pickles, boiled potatoes, pickled onions, and dry white wine.

DIETER'S ANTIPASTO PLATE

    4 crisp lettuce leaves
    4 small cooked whole beets
    2 hot peppers
    1 hard-boiled egg, quartered
    1 stalk celery, cut in half
    1 raw carrot, peeled and quartered lengthwise
    4 marinated mushrooms
    1 3½-ounce can white-meat tuna packed in water, drained
    ½ lemon, cut into wedges
    1 cooked carrot, cut into julienne strips

Line a dinner plate with the lettuce leaves and arrange the other ingredients over the lettuce, the julienned carrot last.

MELISSA AVILDSEN'S GREEN LIQUID SALAD

Melissa Avildsen teaches exercise classes and trains professional athletes in a stretching program that she developed. Melissa is also a dedicated jogger and is working her way up to running the marathon. The mother of two young and energetic boys, she finds that she frequently eats alone during the week, usually between her exercise classes. By necessity the meals must be light but nourishing. If she doesn't have a salad of cucumber, sprouts, and romaine lettuce with a small wedge of cheese, she prepares her green liquid salad and takes it with her to class in a thermos.

    ½ green pepper, chopped
    3 stalks celery, chopped
    ½ cucumber, chopped
    1 ripe tomato, peeled and chopped
    Fresh lemon juice to taste
    Freshly ground black pepper to taste

Puree the ingredients in a blender and serve the salad with unsalted natural nuts.

IMPROVED CANNED BAKED BEANS

When you don't have time to cook dried beans from scratch, you can substitute a good-quality can of beans. Beans are one of the best canned products on the market if the skins aren't broken and the beans are whole. One word of caution when buying beans for this recipe: Never buy pork and beans, because they aren't truly baked beans. Look for a can whose label reads "Oven-Baked Beans." These are the best canned baked beans available, but their flavor can be improved by the addition of a few ingredients.

  2 teaspoons vegetable oil
  2 tablespoons finely chopped onion
  1 8-ounce can oven-baked beans
  1 tablespoon molasses
  1 teaspoon Dijon-style mustard
  3 tablespoons chili sauce

In a medium-sized saucepan, heat the oil and sauté the onion for 4 minutes, stirring. Add the remaining ingredients and bring the mixture to a boil. Reduce the heat to medium and cook the beans for 10 minutes, stirring occasionally, until the liquid has reduced and thickened.

Serve the beans with a baked pork chop, boiled knockwurst, or sautéed sausages.

EXTRAS SUGGESTIONS: Puree extra beans in a blender or force them through a sieve after refrigeration for an appetizer dip or spread. Baked beans can also be reheated and used as a topping for hamburger. Chili sauce and molasses are good staples to have on hand. Chili sauce added to mayonnaise with lemon juice can be used as a barbecue sauce for chicken, ribs, or fish. Molasses is needed in many cookie and pie recipes. It may also be used to enhance sweet and sour dishes.

BLACK BEANS AND GREEN PEPPER WITH RICE

> 2 tablespoons olive oil
> ¼ cup finely chopped onion
> ½ green pepper, cored, seeded, and chopped
> 1 small clove garlic, crushed
> Dash of Tabasco sauce
> ¼ teaspoon cumin
> ¾ cup canned black beans, drained
> ¾ cup hot, fluffy cooked rice

Heat the olive oil and sauté the onion, pepper, and garlic for 5 minutes, stirring. Add the Tabasco, cumin, and black beans. Stir and cook the mixture over medium-low heat for 8 minutes. Serve it over the hot rice.

A fried pork chop or sautéed Italian sweet sausages are a good accompaniment. For a vegetarian meal, serve the beans with Fried Plantains. (See index for recipe.)

EXTRAS SUGGESTIONS: Any remaining cooked rice or green peppers can be used in Fried Rice, a salad, or a soup. (See index for recipe.)

FRENCH BREAD

1¼ cups lukewarm water
1½ teaspoons dry yeast
1½ teaspoons sugar
1¼ teaspoons salt
3½ cups all-purpose flour
1 egg white

Combine the water and yeast in a bowl, stir them, and let them sit a few minutes until the yeast dissolves. Add the sugar and salt, stirring. Add the flour and stir the mixture with a wooden spoon until the dough rolls off the side of the bowl. Knead the dough on a lightly floured board for 10 minutes, adding a little flour to the board as it is worked into the dough. Shape the dough into a ball, put it in a bowl, and cover it. When it is doubled in size, press down on it and shape it into a long loaf by rolling it back and forth on a lightly floured board. Cut ⅓-inch-deep slashes on a diagonal in it at 2-inch intervals. Place it on a baking sheet, cover it with a towel, and let it rise again, about 35 minutes. Beat together the egg white and 1 tablespoon of water and brush the liquid over the dough. Bake the bread in a preheated 350°F oven for about 25 minutes, until it is golden. Remove it from the oven and let it sit for 30 minutes before serving it.

FRESH ENGLISH MUFFINS

Making English muffins at home is a Saturday and Sunday ritual for me. The thought that I'm probably the only one on the block savoring fresh English muffins is selfishly pleasing, but the pleasure derived from eating them is far greater.

¼ cup milk
¼ cup very hot water
1 teaspoon dry yeast
¾ cup plus 1 tablespoon all-purpose flour
¼ teaspoon sugar
¼ teaspoon salt
¼ teaspoon baking soda.

Heat the combined milk and water. Add the yeast and stir until it is dissolved. Combine the remaining ingredients and beat them into the liquid for 1 minute with a wooden spoon. Cover the batter and let it rise until it is doubled in size. Beat it for 10 seconds. Place 2 nonstick muffin rings (or 2 7-ounce cleaned tuna cans, top and bottom removed) in a lightly greased heavy 9-inch skillet or on a lightly greased griddle. Spoon equal portions of the batter into the rings. Cook the muffins over medium heat until bubbles form on their surface. Remove the rings and turn the muffins. Brown them on the other side. Cool them for 5 minutes. Split them, spread them with butter, and toast them.

English muffins can be topped with any number of ingredients: sautéed sausage patties, scrambled eggs and bacon, cream cheese and smoked salmon, or any fruit preserve. They are also the foundation on which Eggs Benedict rest—topped with grilled smoked ham, poached eggs, and Hollandaise Sauce. (See index for recipes.)

11. Fresh Seasonal Vegetables, A-Z

BAKED ACORN SQUASH

> 1 tablespoon melted butter
> 1 tablespoon brown sugar
> 1 tablespoon dry sherry, bourbon, or scotch
> 1 acorn squash, cut in half lengthwise, with the seeds and
>   membrane removed
> Salt to taste

Combine the melted butter, brown sugar, and sherry. Spoon half of the mixture into the center of each squash half and brush the entire cut surface with it. Season the squash lightly with salt. Cover each half with foil and cook them on a baking sheet in a preheated 350°F oven for 30 minutes. Remove the foil and cook them about 15 minutes longer or until they are tender.

EXTRAS SUGGESTIONS: The remaining half of a baked acorn squash is excellent served cold. Or peel it, cut it into cubes, and sauté it with apple slices.

FRESH COOKED ASPARAGUS

> 5 or 6 fresh asparagus spears
> Salt and freshly ground pepper to taste

Cut off the tough ends of the asparagus stalks and discard them. Peel the lower parts of the stalks with a small, sharp knife or a sharp vegetable peeler. Bring to a boil 1½ inches of lightly salted water in a 10-inch skillet. Lower the asparagus into the boiling water and cook it at a medium boil for 6 minutes or until it is just tender. Drain it and season it with the salt and pepper.

Serve it with butter and/or lemon juice.

COLD ASPARAGUS VINAIGRETTE

> 5 or 6 cooked asparagus spears
> ¼ cup Vinaigrette Sauce (see index for recipe)

Arrange the asparagus on a vegetable plate and spoon the vinaigrette sauce over it. Cover and refrigerate it for at least 1 hour.

CREAMED BROCCOLI

> 1 tablespoon butter
> 1 shallot, minced
> ¾ cup chopped cooked fresh broccoli
> Salt and freshly ground pepper to taste
> ¼ cup sour cream

Heat the butter in a 9-inch skillet and sauté the shallot for 2 minutes, stirring often. Add the broccoli and season it with the salt and pepper. Cook it over medium-high heat for 3 or 4 minutes, until it is thoroughly heated. Remove it from the heat and stir in the sour cream.

SAUTÉED BROCCOLI WITH GARLIC AND BASIL

2 stalks fresh broccoli (Frozen broccoli can be used. Cook it half
      the time suggested in the package directions and drain it.)
1 tablespoon butter
1 small clove garlic, minced
¼ teaspoon basil
Salt and freshly ground pepper to taste

Cook the broccoli for 5 minutes in enough lightly salted boiling water
to cover it. Drain and cool it. Cut it into 1-inch lengths. Heat the
butter in a 9-inch skillet and sauté the garlic for 1 minute over medium
heat. Add the broccoli and basil. Season the mixture with the salt and
pepper. Stir it gently and cook it for about 2 minutes or until it is
heated through.

CARROTS COOKED IN CHICKEN BROTH

¾ cup Chicken Stock (see index for recipe)
2 medium carrots, peeled and sliced on the diagonal
1 tablespoon butter
Salt and freshly ground pepper to taste
½ teaspoon fresh chopped parsley

Bring the stock to a boil in a small saucepan. Add the carrots, reduce
the heat, and cover the pan. Simmer the carrots for 6 minutes. Drain
them. Heat the butter in a small skillet, add the carrots, season them
with the salt and pepper, and toss them with a fork for 1 minute.
Sprinkle them with the parsley.

LEMON-GLAZED CARROTS

2 medium carrots, peeled and cut into ¼-inch slices
Salt
1½ tablespoons butter
1 tablespoon brown sugar
1 teaspoon lemon juice

Cook the carrots in 3 cups of lightly salted boiling water for 8 minutes. Drain them. In a 9-inch skillet heat the butter; then stir in the sugar and lemon juice. Add the carrots and cook them, stirring gently, for 2 minutes or until a light glaze forms on them.

Excellent with fried pork chops or roast chicken.

CARROTS VICHY

2 carrots, peeled and thinly sliced
Salt
1½ tablespoons butter
¼ teaspoon sugar
Pinch of marjoram
½ teaspoon fresh chopped parsley

Cook the carrots in 3 cups of lightly salted, boiling water for 5 minutes. Drain them. In a 9-inch skillet heat the butter. Add the carrots, sugar, marjoram, and parsley. Toss them with a fork over medium heat for 2 minutes.

CAULIFLOWER AU GRATIN

½ small head cauliflower, broken into small pieces
Salt
½ cup Mornay Sauce (see index for recipe)
1 tablespoon Sautéed Bread Crumbs (see index for recipe)

Cook the cauliflower in 3 cups of lightly salted boiling water in a medium-sized saucepan for 6 minutes. Drain it. Spoon ¼ cup of the mornay sauce into an individual au gratin dish, top it with the cauliflower, and spoon the remaining ¼ cup of the mornay sauce over the cauliflower. Sprinkle the bread crumbs over the top and pass the dish under heated broiler for a few minutes until the sauce bubbles.

EXTRAS SUGGESTION: Use the remaining cauliflower in Sautéed Potato Pancakes with Cauliflower Puree. (See index for recipe.)

CORN ON THE COB

Corn on the cob is extremely simple to prepare, but also easy to ruin if two important directions aren't followed: (1) Do not put the corn in the water until the water is rapidly boiling. (2) Do not leave it in the hot water longer than 5 minutes after it has cooked.

1 quart water
1 tablespoon sugar
1 ear of corn, husked

Bring the water to a boil in a saucepan. Stir in the sugar. Put the corn in the water and cook it for 5 minutes. Turn off the heat, cover the pan, and leave the corn in the water for 5 minutes. Drain it well.
    Serve it with plenty of butter, salt, and pepper.

SAUTÉED CREAM OF FRESH CORN

1 ear of corn, husked
1 tablespoon butter
⅓ cup heavy cream
Salt and freshly ground pepper

Remove the kernels from the cob by standing it on end and slicing them off with downward strokes of a sharp knife. Heat the butter in a 9-inch skillet and sauté the corn for 5 minutes over medium heat. Remove the skillet from the heat. Bring the cream to a boil in a small saucepan. Cook it, stirring often, for 3 minutes or until it thickens over medium-high heat. Add the corn. Season it to taste with the salt and pepper. Serve immediately.

SAUTÉED CUCUMBERS

½ cucumber
Salt
1 tablespoon butter
½ tablespoon vegetable oil
Freshly ground white or black pepper to taste

Peel the cucumber and cut it in half lengthwise. Remove the seeds with a teaspoon. Slice it into ½-inch pieces. Season it with salt and let it drain in a colander for 30 minutes. Pat it dry. Heat the butter and oil in a 9-inch skillet until they are hot but not smoking. Sauté the cucumber slices over medium-high heat for 5 minutes, shaking the pan to turn them. Season them with the pepper.

Serve them with a fish dish.

EXTRAS SUGGESTIONS: Use any remaining cucumber in a mixed salad, an English-Style Cucumber Tea Sandwich, or Cold Cucumber and Yogurt Soup. (See index for recipes.)

VARIATION: Add ¼ teaspoon of tarragon or mint to the cucumber while you are sautéeing it.

SAUTÉED EGGPLANT WITH GARLIC

3 tablespoons peanut or vegetable oil
1 clove garlic, minced
1 small eggplant, stemmed and cut into ½-by-1½-inch sticks
1 teaspoon light soy sauce
⅛ teaspoon sesame oil

Heat the peanut oil in a small wok or a 9-inch skillet. When it is hot but not smoking, add the garlic and cook it, stirring, for 30 seconds. Add the eggplant. Stir and then cook it for 3 minutes, covered. Sprinkle the soy sauce combined with the sesame oil over the eggplant. Reduce the heat to medium, stir the eggplant, and cook it for 3 more minutes.

SAUTÉED AND BRAISED ESCAROLE

½ small head of escarole
Salt
1 tablespoon olive oil
1 small clove garlic, crushed
¼ cup Chicken Broth (see index for recipe)
Salt and freshly ground pepper to taste

Cut off the stem end of the escarole and wash the leaves. Pile up the leaves with the largest on the bottom. Bring 2 quarts of lightly salted water to a boil. Immerse the escarole in the boiling water for 3 minutes. Drain it well, pressing it in a towel to remove any excess water. Gently arrange the blanched leaves in a pile, again with the largest leaves on the bottom. Fold the pile of leaves in half, tucking the ends underneath and making a packet. Heat the olive oil in an 8-inch skillet and add the garlic. Push it around in the pan for 30 seconds. Add the escarole, pour in the broth, and sprinkle them with the salt and pepper. Cover the skillet and cook the escarole over medium-low heat for 12 minutes.

GREEN BEANS CAP CRUZ

¼ pound green beans, ends trimmed, cut into 1-inch lengths
4 mushrooms, thinly sliced
5 pitted black olives, quartered
¼ cup Onion Vinaigrette (see index for recipe)

Bring 3 cups of lightly salted water to a boil. Add the green beans and cook them at a medium boil for 6 minutes. Add the mushrooms and cook for another 2 minutes. Drain the vegetables and cool them in a bowl. Add the black olive slices and onion vinaigrette. Toss, cover, and refrigerate the mixture for several hours before serving it.

FRESH GREEN BEANS WITH PARSLEY BUTTER

¼ pound fresh green beans, ends trimmed
1 tablespoon butter
1 teaspoon fresh chopped parsley
Freshly ground pepper to taste

Bring 3 cups of lightly salted water to a boil. Add the green beans and cook them at a medium boil for 8 minutes. Drain them. Melt the butter in an 8-inch skillet and add the beans, parsley, and pepper. Toss the beans gently and cook them for 1 minute.

SAUTÉED GREEN BEANS

¼ pound fresh green beans, ends trimmed
2 teaspoons butter
2 teaspoons vegetable oil
1 small clove garlic, peeled and quartered
Salt and freshly ground pepper to taste

Bring 3 cups of lightly salted water to a boil in a saucepan. Add the green beans and cook them at a slow boil for 6 minutes. Drain them. Heat the butter and oil in an 8-inch skillet and sauté the garlic for 1 minute, pushing the pieces around in the pan with a fork. Add the green beans and toss them over medium-high heat for 2 minutes. Discard the garlic. Season the beans with the salt and pepper.

BABY LIMA BEANS IN CHEESE AND CREAM SAUCE

¾ cup shelled fresh or frozen lima beans
1 teaspoon lemon juice
¼ cup heavy cream
2 scant tablespoons grated Swiss or Gruyère cheese
Salt and freshly ground pepper to taste

Cook the lima beans in boiling water until they are tender, about 20 minutes if they are fresh, or 6 to 8 minutes if they are frozen. Drain them. In a small saucepan, cook the lemon juice over medium heat for 30 seconds. Whisk in the cream and cook it for 4 or 5 minutes over high heat, stirring with a wire whisk until it thickens slightly. Add the cheese, stirring, and then the cooked lima beans. Season the beans with the salt and pepper.

EXTRAS SUGGESTIONS: Use extra lima beans in Minestrone Soup (see index for recipe), in a vegetable side dish mixed with another vegetable such as carrots or green beans, or in a mixed salad.

MUSHROOM BROCHETTES

    5 medium-sized fresh mushrooms, stemmed
    2 tablespoons butter
    2 teaspoons lemon juice
    1 teaspoon Dijon-style mustard
    ½ teaspoon soy sauce
    3 tablespoons seasoned bread crumbs
    1 tablespoon grated Parmesan cheese

Thread the mushrooms on an 8-inch metal or dampened wooden skewer. (Dampening the skewer prevents it from burning.) Combine the butter, lemon juice, mustard, and soy sauce. Brush the mixture over all sides of the mushrooms several times. Roll the mushrooms in a mixture of the bread crumbs and Parmesan cheese. Place the skewer under a heated broiler. Cook it for about 5 minutes, turning it several times, until the mushrooms are golden brown.

SAUTÉED MUSHROOMS

    2 tablespoons Clarified Butter (see index for recipe)
    ¼ pound medium-small fresh mushrooms
    Salt and freshly ground pepper to taste

Heat the butter in a 9-inch skillet. Add the mushrooms and cook them over medium-high heat for 5 minutes, shaking the pan often to turn them. Season them with the salt and pepper and serve them immediately.

Sautéed mushrooms are good escorts to omelets, scrambled eggs, fish and shellfish, chicken, and beef.

DEEP-FRIED ONION RING GARNISH

I was first served these crisp onion rings on chicken tandoori. Crunchy and delicate in flavor, they also complement many fish and seafood dishes.

> 1 medium onion, very thinly sliced
> 2 cups vegetable oil
> Salt and freshly ground pepper to taste

Heat the oil in a 1½-quart heavy saucepan. Break the onion slices into rings and gently add them to the hot oil. Stirring occasionally, watch the onions until they turn golden. Remove them with a fork or slotted spoon and drain them. Sprinkle them with the salt and pepper.

EXTRA SUGGESTION: For extra oil, see Arincini in the index.

FRIED ONION RINGS

> 1 large onion, cut into ½-inch slices
> 1 egg yolk
> ½ cup milk
> ½ cup flour
> ⅛ teaspoon salt
> 2 cups vegetable oil

Break the onion slices into rings. Use only the largest 6 or 7 rings. (Save the remaining onion for soups, salads, or other dishes.) Beat the egg yolk, milk, flour, and salt together until they are smooth. Heat the oil in 10- to 12-inch skillet. Dip each onion ring into the batter, letting extra batter drip off. Fry the rings in the hot oil until they are golden brown on each side. Drain them on absorbent paper. Season them with salt.

GRILLED ONION SLICES

Restaurant-grilled onions are usually practically raw or burned or soggy or chewy. Nevertheless, grilled onions are an excellent addition to a hamburger, steak, or pork chop, to a grilled or broiled fish, and to many sandwiches. I even like grilled onions served plain on buttered rye toast.

1 or 2 ¼-inch-thick slices of a large onion
1 tablespoon vegetable oil
Salt and freshly ground pepper to taste

Heat the oil in a 9-inch skillet. Add the onion slices, left intact. Sauté them over medium heat until they are browned. Carefully turn them with a spatula so that they keep their shape. Brown them on the other side over medium-low heat. Sprinkle them with the salt and pepper.

EXTRAS SUGGESTION: Wrap the remaining onion in clear plastic so that you won't forget it. Use it in sauté dishes, soups, or wherever onion is required, but use it within 3 days.

CUBAN FRIED PLANTAINS

1 green plantain
Peanut or vegetable oil
Salt and freshly ground pepper to taste

Peel the plantain and cut it into 1-inch lengths. Pour enough oil into a 12-inch skillet to reach ½ inch in depth. When it is hot but not smoking, add the plantain pieces on their ends. Cook them for 2 minutes, then turn them and fry them for 3 minutes on the other ends. Remove them and cool them slightly. Remove the skillet from the heat while you are doing the next step. Between two pieces of aluminum foil, place a plantain piece and press it down with the heel of your hand until it is about ¼-inch thick. Remove it to a plate and flatten the other pieces. Reheat the oil in the skillet and fry the plantain pieces again, on each side, a few at a time, until they are golden. Season them with the salt and pepper. Serve them immediately.

CURRIED RICE

    1¼ cups Chicken Broth or water (see index for recipe)
    ½ cup long-grain rice
    ⅛ teaspoon salt
    2 teaspoons butter
    ½ teaspoon curry powder or to taste
    2 tablespoons minced onion
    2 tablespoons minced green pepper

In a small saucepan bring the broth or water to a boil. Add the remaining ingredients. Bring the liquid back to a boil, reduce the heat, stir, cover the pan, and simmer the rice for approximately 20 minutes or until it is tender.

RISI BISI
(Rice and Green Peas)

    1 tablespoon butter
    ½ cup cooked rice
    ⅓ cup cooked fresh green peas or frozen green peas
    Pinch of oregano
    1 teaspoon fresh chopped parsley
    Salt and freshly ground pepper to taste

Heat the butter in a 9-inch skillet. Toss the rice and peas in it for 1 minute over medium heat. Sprinkle them with the oregano, parsley, salt, and pepper. Stir the mixture and cook it over low heat until it is heated through, about 3 minutes.

SAUTÉED WILD RICE

When there is cause for celebration, and I'm going to be by myself, wild rice is on the menu. Or, I could say, when wild rice is on the menu, it's cause for celebration, for wild rice is one of my favorite foods. Since a pound of wild rice costs more than a pound of filet mignon these days, I buy a pound a year. I cook it a quarter of a pound at a time, about once each season. It is excellent boiled plain with butter or mixed with herbs and mushrooms as a stuffing, but sautéing brings out its best qualities—the nutty flavor and rough texture.

½ cup wild rice
2 tablespoons butter
2 shallots, finely chopped
2 tablespoons heavy cream

Cover the wild rice with 1½ cups of water in a small heavy saucepan, cover the pan tightly, and simmer the rice for 30 minutes. Heat the butter in a 9-inch skillet and sauté the shallots for 4 minutes, stirring. Add the rice and heat it thoroughly. Pour in the heavy cream, stir, and cook the mixture over low heat for 10 minutes. Drain in colandar.

FRESH COOKED SPINACH

½ pound fresh spinach, cleaned and stemmed
Salt and freshly ground pepper to taste
Dash of nutmeg
2 teaspoons butter

Boil the spinach in 2 cups of rapidly boiling water for 4 minutes. Drain it well. Season it with the salt and pepper, add a dash of nutmeg, and toss it with the butter.

SAUTÉED CHERRY TOMATOES

1 tablespoon butter
6 to 8 cherry tomatoes
Salt and freshly ground pepper to taste
1 teaspoon fresh chopped parsley

Heat the butter in a 9-inch skillet. Add the tomatoes and cook them over high heat for 3 minutes, constantly shaking the pan. Season them with the salt and pepper and sprinkle them with the parsley. Shake the pan again.

STIR-FRIED FRESH VEGETABLES

1½ tablespoons peanut or vegetable oil
1 carrot, grated
1 small zucchini, cut into julienne strips
½ cucumber, peeled and cut into julienne strips
½ cup broccoli florets, broken into small pieces
1 small onion, thinly sliced and broken into rings
1½ teaspoons light soy sauce

Heat the oil in a small wok or skillet. Add the vegetables and stir-fry them for 3 minutes over medium-high heat. Add the soy sauce, toss, cover the pan, and cook the vegetables for 2 more minutes. Toss again and serve them immediately. (The vegetables should be crisp.)

ZUCCHINI AND RED PEPPER SAUTÉ

1½ tablespoons olive oil
1 small red pepper, seeded, cored, and cut into thin strips
1 small onion, cut into thin strips
1 small zucchini, thinly sliced
Salt and freshly ground pepper to taste
1 teaspoon fresh chopped parsley

Heat the oil in a 9-inch skillet. Sauté the red pepper and onion for 4 minutes, stirring occasionally. Add the zucchini, season it with the salt and pepper, and sprinkle it with parsley. Cover the pan and cook the zucchini for 3 minutes. Remove the cover, stir, and sauté the zucchini for 2 more minutes. Serve it at once.

ZUCCHINI AND TOMATOES

1 tablespoon butter
1 tablespoon olive or vegetable oil
1 tablespoon grated onion
1 small clove garlic, minced
2 small or 1 medium peeled fresh ripe tomato (canned may also be used)
1 tablespoon dry white wine or vermouth
1 small zucchini, thinly sliced
1 teaspoon fresh chopped parsley
Salt and freshly ground pepper to taste

Heat the butter and oil in a saucepan. Add the onion and garlic and cook them for 1 minute. Add the tomato and cook it, stirring, for 2 minutes. Add the wine and bring it to a boil. Reduce the heat and simmer the mixture for 4 minutes. Add the zucchini and parsley. Season them with the salt and pepper, cover the pan, and cook the vegetables for 5 more minutes.

ZUCCHINI IN CREAM SAUCE

1½ tablespoons butter
1 cup ¼-inch-thick slices zucchini
Salt
3 tablespoons heavy cream
1 teaspoon finely chopped fresh parsley
Freshly ground pepper to taste

Melt the butter in an 8-inch skillet. Add the zucchini and sprinkle it with salt. Cover the pan and simmer the zucchini for 8 minutes, stirring it once during the cooking time. Add the cream and sprinkle the parsley over the zucchini. Bring it to a boil and gently turn the zucchini. Season it with the pepper.

12. For Potato Eaters

The potato has a special place in the eating habits of people all over the world, so it is no surprise that potatoes are America's most popular vegetable. Statistics show that the average individual consumes about 60 pounds of potatoes a year—boiled, baked, fried, mashed, sautéed, and scalloped, cold and hot, in soups and in salads. Potatoes are not fattening. A medium-sized baking potato has only about 90 calories. It is the ingredients that are added to potatoes that produce a high calorie count, but these enhancers are temptingly delicious. Potatoes are great plain or complemented by butter, cheese, smoked fish, bacon, ham, ground beef, cream, sour cream, herbs, spices, or any number of sauces.

TULLY PLESSER'S BAKED POTATO LATKE

Tully Plesser heads a national market and public opinion research firm. He says:

"The baked potato has always been my ultimate symbol of security. At age seven, catching the flu meant staying home from school, listening to radio soap operas, and a baked potato served in bed. Sunday afternoon visits to Grandma's were invariably punctuated by a baked potato, prepared in a battered stove-top apparatus that was her version of a microwave oven. When military service brought with it a startling exposure to foods never seen on my family table, the sight of the familiar baked potato emerging from the ship's galley was a welcome reminder of civilization awaiting our return to port. Later, summer weekend dinners at Westhampton Beach always included charcoal-broiled steaks of unpredictable quality and a baked potato as the backup or fail-safe mechanism. Today, the baked potato is my most private dish, the great secret being that it is the jacket I really crave. Only with the cool objectivity that comes after years of disastrous bungling in the kitchen did it occur to me that the insides of a baked potato could be transformed into an infinitely more appetizing potato pancake by the addition of only a few basic ingredients and a frying pan—leaving the jacket to be consumed with the dignity and focus it was meant to enjoy."

> 1 large Idaho baking potato, well scrubbed
> 1 egg
> 1 tablespoon grated onion
> 1 tablespoon flour
> Salt and freshly ground pepper to taste
> 1 tablespoon vegetable oil

Pierce the potato in 2 places and bake it in preheated 400°F oven for 45 minutes or until it is done. Cut it in half lengthwise. Scoop out the insides without damaging the jacket and place them in a bowl. Add the egg, onion, and flour, season them with the salt and pepper, and mix the ingredients thoroughly. Heat the oil in a 9-inch frying pan (nonstick, if possible). Add the potato mixture, flattening it with a spatula into a pancake. Sauté the pancake about 4 minutes on each side over medium-high heat until it is brown. Add more oil after browning the first side, if necessary.

Garnish the pancake with apple sauce. Paint the potato jacket with butter, toast it under the broiler for 2 to 3 minutes, and serve it as is or filled with scrambled eggs topped with sour cream.

SAUTÉED POTATO PANCAKES WITH CAULIFLOWER PUREE

1 medium baking potato, peeled
3 tablespoons olive or vegetable oil
½ cup chopped cauliflower florets
1 tablespoon butter
1 tablespoon heavy cream or milk, as needed
Salt and freshly ground pepper to taste

With a vegetable peeler, pare the entire potato into ribbons. Heat the oil in a 9-inch skillet. Add the potato ribbons and flatten them over the entire surface of the pan. Cook them until they are browned. Turn them in one piece with a spatula and cook them until they are golden brown and crisp. Drain them. Meanwhile, add the cauliflower to a saucepan with 2 cups of lightly salted boiling water. Cook it for 6 minutes. Drain it. Combine the cauliflower, butter, and heavy cream in a food processor or blender until they form a smooth puree. Season it with salt and pepper. Scrape down the sides of the container occasionally with a spatula. The consistency should be smooth and fluffy, like mashed potatoes. Cut the potato pancake into quarters crosswise. Trim the pieces into 4 ovals. Spread equal amounts of the cauliflower puree over 2 of the pieces. Top these with the 2 remaining pancake pieces. Place these on an ovenproof dish and heat them in a preheated 325°F oven for 5 minutes. Serve them immediately.

CRISP FRIED INDIVIDUAL ROESTI POTATOES

3 tablespoons oil
2 teaspoons butter
1 medium-small baking potato, peeled
Salt and freshly ground pepper to taste

In a heavy 9-inch skillet heat the oil and butter. Grate the potato and form a mound of it in the center of the pan. With the back of a fork, spread the potato evenly over the bottom of the pan. Season it well with the salt and pepper. Fry it on medium heat until the edges underneath turn golden. Turn it with a large spatula, keeping it in one piece. Cook it for a few more minutes until it is golden brown. Transfer it to a sheet of absorbent paper. Turn it immediately and pat it with the back of the fork. Then serve it on a heated dinner plate.

BOILED POTATOES WITH PARSLEY

> 3 small potatoes, peeled
> 1 tablespoon butter
> 1 teaspoon fresh chopped parsley
> Salt and freshly ground pepper to taste

Drop the potatoes into boiling water and cook them for 12 minutes or until they are just tender. Drain them and put them in a small bowl. Add the butter and parsley and gently turn the potatoes until they are evenly coated. Season them with the salt and pepper.

ROASTED POTATOES

> 1 medium-large potato, peeled and cut into 8 pieces
> 2 tablespoons melted butter
> Salt and freshly ground pepper to taste

Place the potatoes in a small roasting pan with the butter. Season them with the salt and pepper and cook them in a preheated 375°F oven for 15 minutes. Turn them and cook them another 20 minutes or until they are tender and golden.

POTATOES À LA PARISIENNE

1 large potato, peeled
4 tablespoons Clarified Butter (see index for recipe)
Salt and freshly ground pepper to taste
½ teaspoon fresh chopped parsley

Cut the potato into small balls with a round vegetable scoop. Heat the butter in a medium-sized skillet. Sauté the potato balls for 5 minutes. Season them with the salt and pepper, turn them, and cook them until they are golden brown all over. Sprinkle them with the parsley.

BAKED STUFFED POTATO

1 large baking potato
1 teaspoon fresh chopped parsley
2 tablespoons shredded Cheddar or Swiss cheese
2 tablespoons light cream or milk
1½ tablespoons butter
Salt and freshly ground pepper to taste
2 teaspoons melted butter
2 teaspoons fresh grated Parmesan cheese

Pierce the potato in two places with the sharp point of a knife. Cook it in a preheated 400°F oven for 45 minutes or until it is tender. Cut off the top ⅓ and scoop out the potato pulp, reserving the shell. Force the pulp through a food mill or sieve. Combine it with the parsley, Cheddar cheese, light cream, butter, salt, and pepper. Fill the bottom of the potato shell with this mixture. Sprinkle the melted butter and Parmesan cheese over the top. Pass it under the broiler until the top is golden.

ELOUISE A. HETHERLY'S BAKED POTATO DISCOVERY

Elouise A. Hetherly is the owner of Ouisie's Table and the Traveling Brown Bag Lunch Company and Storeside in Houston, Texas. Here is her account of a recipe development or, as she puts it, the Potato Saga:

"I recently spent a quiet night at home with a fevered child who wanted only a baked potato for his dinner. By seven he was asleep, and by eight I removed the foiled potato, and by midnight it was a warm room temperature and I was just a little hungry. I cut a two-bite piece and drizzled sweet olive oil over it, and salt and freshly ground black pepper, lots. Before I knew what I had done, the entire potato had disappeared in an over-the-sink manner. I enjoyed every bite.

"The next night I was baking potatoes for the fevered one again. Several times during the course of the day I thought about the simplicity and goodness of the midnight supper and made a few mental notes for additional ingredients. A friend joined me and we took the potato a natural step further. We each took ½ of a baked potato at room temperature and gently broke it open, making little cracks in it like those in the earth. We drizzled sweet olive oil over the potato and into the cracks. Then we sprinkled it with fresh, coarsely ground black pepper and spooned 2 heaping tablespoons of sour cream over it end to end. Then we added finely chopped green onions and 2 heaping tablespoons of black lumpfish caviar and squeezed 2 wedges of lemon over the whole thing. My friend and I enjoyed this with a glass of very cold dry white wine.

"Then on the third night we and several others topped the above with several super-thin slices of raw garlic, a sprinkling of dill weed, and a parsley tuft to freshen the breath (after the garlic). We enjoyed it this time with ice-cold vodka, the best. But it's also good with champagne. It served that night as an appetizer to a roast chicken and sautéed squash, but that is another story.

"The lumpfish caviar, if excessively salty, that is to say, inexpensive, should be rinsed in cold water in a fine mesh strainer lined with cheesecloth and drained well.

"A week later I added The Potato to the menu at Ouisie's. It is served with the house salad and French bread and unsalted butter. A good coarse black bread would be excellent with it too. Our customers may have it with or without smoked salmon and capers, which I highly recommend. It has been an instant success."

BAKED POTATO WITH SOUR CREAM AND RED CAVIAR

Oddly enough, an ordinary baked potato topped with sour cream and salmon caviar, or black caviar as described in the previous recipe, is a splendid combination. I prefer the potato hot. For Sunday brunch it's a welcome change from Eggs Benedict, Quiche Lorraine, or an omelet. The dish is easily doubled. I treat myself to this simple and elegant dish with a Mini Caesar Salad and a split of iced champagne on nights when I want something special that won't take a lot of work. (See index for recipes.)

> 1 medium-large baking potato
> ⅓ cup sour cream
> 1 teaspoon chopped scallion
> ½ teaspoon lemon juice
> Salt and freshly ground pepper to taste
> 1½ to 2 ounces red caviar

Pierce a cleaned potato in 2 places with the sharp point of a knife and bake it in a preheated 400°F oven for 45 minutes or until it is tender. Cut the potato in half. Combine the sour cream with the scallion and lemon juice and season the mixture well with the salt and pepper (not too much salt, because the caviar has salt in it). Spoon the mixture over the hot potato and top it with the caviar.

FRIED POTATOES IN THEIR JACKETS

4 or 5 small potatoes
1½ cups vegetable oil
Salt and freshly ground pepper

Drop the potatoes in boiling water and cook them for 10 minutes. Remove them from the water and dry them on absorbent paper. Cool them to room temperature and cut them into quarters. Heat the oil in a medium-sized skillet and fry the potatoes until they are crisp and golden brown. Remove them with a spatula and season them with the salt and pepper.

MASHED POTATOES WITH MUSHROOMS AND ONIONS

1 medium boiling potato, peeled and cut into 8 pieces
3 tablespoons butter
3 or 4 medium fresh mushrooms, thinly sliced, then chopped
1 tablespoon finely chopped onion
2 tablespoons milk or as needed
Salt and freshly ground pepper to taste

Boil the potato in lightly salted boiling water for about 12 minutes or until it is tender. Meanwhile, heat 2 tablespoons of the butter in a 9-inch skillet and sauté the mushrooms and onion for 5 minutes, stirring them often. Remove the mushrooms and onion from the pan. Drain the potato and mash it well with the other tablespoon of the butter and the milk. Season it with the salt and pepper. Add a little more milk and butter if desired or necessary. Now add the mushroom and onion mixture and combine them thoroughly.

LYONNAISE POTATOES WITH BACON GARNISH

1 medium-large potato, peeled and thinly sliced
3 strips bacon
1 small onion, chopped
1 tablespoon butter
1 tablespoon vegetable oil
Salt and freshly ground pepper to taste
Paprika
1 teaspoon fresh chopped parsley

Drop the potato slices in lightly salted boiling water and blanch them for 3 minutes. Drain them. In a 12-inch skillet, cook bacon until it is crisp. Then remove it and drain it on absorbent paper. Sauté the onions in the bacon drippings for about 5 minutes, stirring often. Transfer the onions with a slotted spoon to a side dish. Add the butter and vegetable oil to the skillet. Cook the blanched potatoes over medium heat for about 8 minutes until they are browned; then turn them and cook them until they are browned on the other side. Season them with the salt, pepper, and paprika. Add the onions and gently turn the ingredients to combine them. Let them cook for 2 minutes. Crumble the bacon and garnish the potatoes with the bacon and the parsley.

SAUTÉED POTATOES WITH GARLIC

1 medium-large boiling potato
2 tablespoons vegetable oil
2 tablespoons Clarified Butter (see index for recipe)
4 cloves garlic, peeled and left whole
Salt and freshly ground pepper to taste
Paprika
½ teaspoon lemon juice

Cut the potato into 6 pieces and drop them into enough lightly salted boiling water to cover them. Boil them for 5 minutes. Drain them. Meanwhile, heat the oil and butter in a 9-inch skillet. Add the garlic and cook it over low heat for 10 minutes. Cut the potato into ¼-inch-thick slices and add them to the skillet. During the cooking time, make sure the garlic cloves are always touching the bottom of the pan. Cook the potato slices for 10 minutes, then turn them and season them with the salt and pepper. Cook them for 5 more minutes over medium-high heat until they are lightly browned on both sides. Sprinkle them with the paprika and lemon juice. Discard the garlic cloves.

FRESH POTATO CHIPS

2 medium potatoes, peeled
2½ cups vegetable oil
Salt

Slice the potatoes very thin and soak them in ice-cold water for 15 minutes. Pat them dry with a cloth towel. Heat the oil in a medium-sized frying pan until it is hot but not smoking. Fry the potatoes for a few minutes until they are crisp and golden. Carefully stir them to cook them evenly. Drain them and sprinkle them lightly with salt.

FRESH POTATO SALAD WITH SOUR CREAM

¼ cup sour cream
½ teaspoon Dijon-style mustard
1 tablespoon vinegar
¾ cup cooked cubed potatoes, warm
1 hard boiled egg, diced
1 tablespoon minced scallion
1 rib celery, diced
Salt and freshly ground pepper to taste
2 or 3 strips crisp cooked bacon, crumbled (optional)

Combine the sour cream, mustard, and vinegar. Put the remaining ingredients in a bowl and pour the sour cream mixture over them. Toss until the salad is well blended. Taste it for seasoning. Eat it at room temperature or refrigerate it for several hours until it is chilled.

MASHED SWEET POTATO WITH RUM

1 medium-sized sweet potato
1 tablespoon butter or margarine or to taste
2 tablespoons light cream
1 tablespoon rum
Salt and freshly ground pepper to taste

Bake the sweet potato in a preheated 400°F oven for about 40 minutes, until it is tender. Let it cool for 3 or 4 minutes until you are able to handle it and remove the skin. Mash the peeled potato in a bowl with a fork and add the butter, cream, and rum. Mix the ingredients thoroughly and season the mixture with the salt and pepper. If it is too dry, add a little more cream. Warm it in a small baking dish in the oven for 5 minutes.

BAKED YAM

    1 medium yam

Scrub the yam and pierce it with the sharp point of a knife in several places. Bake it in a preheated 400°F oven for about 40 minutes or until it is tender. When the sharp point of a knife pierces the yam without resistance, the yam is done.

YAMS À LA ST. THOMAS

One Thanksgiving on St. Thomas in the Virgin Islands, I was asked by my dinner companions to serve a brand-new yam dish with the turkey. Thus, the recipe and its name. I liked the dish so much that I immediately converted it to a recipe for one, and I serve it at many little Thanksgivings I make for myself all through the year.

    1 medium-large yam
    2 tablespoons pineapple preserves or orange marmalade
    1½ tablespoons brown sugar
    1½ tablespoons butter

Bake the yam in a 400°F oven for about 40 minutes, until it is tender. When it is cool enough to handle, remove the skin. Cut the yam into ¼-inch slices and arrange them overlapping in a lightly buttered individual au gratin dish. Spoon the pineapple preserves or marmalade evenly over the yam slices; then sprinkle them with the brown sugar and dot them with the butter. Place the dish under the broiler until the topping sizzles.

13. Stocks, Sauces, and Butters

Stocks

CHICKEN STOCK

A cook should have chicken stock on hand at all times to enhance the flavor of soups, stews, and other dishes. Because there is no canned product as good as homemade stock, and because it freezes well, I recommend making it regularly when time permits. You can store it in the freezer in quart-size or smaller containers. If you are cooking for one most of the time, you can freeze small quantities in ice cube trays and store them in refrigerator bags.

If you don't have any frozen stock on hand and time doesn't permit making any, you may substitute canned broth, but bouillon cubes and powder are poor substitutes.

> 3 pounds chicken wings, backs, necks, or parts (the carcass of a roasted chicken can also be used)
> 3 pounds veal shank and knuckle, split
> 1 large onion, chopped
> 3 celery stalks, chopped
> 3 carrots, chopped
> 1 clove garlic, coarsely chopped
> 1 parsnip or turnip, chopped
> 1 bouquet garni of several sprigs of parsley, 1 leek, 1 bay leaf, and 1 sprig of fresh thyme, if available, tied together with kitchen string

1 tablespoon salt
Several grates of fresh pepper
4½ quarts of cold water

Combine the ingredients in large pot and bring them to a boil. Reduce the heat and simmer the stock for about 2½ hours. Skim the top occasionally and spoon off the fat. Strain the stock and cool it. Cover and refrigerate it until it is cold (several hours). Remove the fat that will have risen to the top and solidified. Use the amount you need and freeze the rest in quantities that best suit your cooking requirements.

Makes about 2½ quarts.

ENRICHED ONE-HOUR CANNED CHICKEN BROTH

1 13¾-ounce can cold chicken broth
1 small onion, chopped
1 small carrot, chopped
½ bay leaf, crushed
3 sprigs parsley
1 chicken neck
1 chicken gizzard
1 chicken heart
4 peppercorns
1 cup cold water

Bring the ingredients to a boil in a medium-sized saucepan. Reduce the heat and simmer the broth slowly for 1 hour. Strain it and spoon off the fat.

Makes about 2 cups.

BEEF STOCK

2½ pounds beef bones (shank, shin, or shoulder)
1 veal knuckle, quartered
1 pound chicken wings, necks, and backs
2 stalks celery, coarsely chopped
2 carrots, coarsely chopped
1 turnip, quartered
1 large leek, quartered
1 bay leaf, crushed
4 sprigs parsley
½ teaspoon dried thyme
8 peppercorns
1 tablespoon salt
3½ quarts cold water

Place the bones, knuckle, and chicken in a roasting pan with celery, carrots, turnip, and leek. Roast them in a preheated 425°F oven for 15 minutes. Turn them with a wooden spoon and roast them another 15 minutes. Drain off any fat and transfer the ingredients to a stock pot. Add the remaining ingredients and bring the liquid to a boil. Reduce the heat and simmer the stock for 2½ hours, stirring occasionally. Strain the stock and cool it. Spoon off as much fat as possible. Refrigerate the stock. When it is cold, remove any solidified fat that has risen to the top.

Makes about 2½ quarts.

ENRICHED ONE-HOUR CANNED BEEF BROTH

1 onion, cut in half crosswise
1 pound beef bones, chopped
1 13¾-ounce can cold beef broth
1 stalk celery, chopped

1 carrot, chopped
1 turnip, chopped (optional)
½ bay leaf, crushed
4 sprigs parsley
4 peppercorns
1 cup cold water

Place the onion under a heated broiler until it turns black on the cut sides. Transfer it to a medium-sized saucepan. Place the beef bones under the broiler in a roasting pan until they are browned, turning them a few times. Transfer them to the saucepan and add the remaining ingredients. The ingredients should be just covered with liquid. Add a little more water if necessary. Bring the liquid to a boil, reduce the heat, and simmer the stock for 45 minutes. Strain it and spoon off the fat.

Makes about 2 cups.

FISH STOCK

1½ pounds fish heads, bones, and tails
1 bay leaf
1 leek or medium onion, quartered
¼ cup cold dry white wine
1 quart cold water

Bring the ingredients to a boil in a medium-sized saucepan. Reduce the heat and simmer the stock for 45 minutes. Strain it.

Makes approximately 3 cups.

Hot and Cold Sauces

BÉCHAMEL SAUCE

Béchamel sauce is a simple white sauce that is used to make creamed vegetables and au gratin dishes or to serve as a binding agent. With the addition of cheese it becomes a Mornay Sauce. With the addition of cream it becomes a Velouté Sauce. A Fish Velouté Sauce is made with equal amounts of fish stock and cream instead of milk. The recipes that follow make about ½ cup each for the single diner.

> 1 tablespoon butter
> 1 tablespoon flour
> ½ cup milk
> Salt and white pepper to taste

Melt the butter in a small saucepan, the heavier the better. Whisk in the flour and cook the mixture, stirring it constantly, over medium heat for 1 minute. Slowly pour in the milk, whisking it until the sauce thickens and is smooth. Season it with the salt and pepper.

MORNAY SAUCE

Add 2 tablespoons of shredded Gruyère, Swiss, or Cheddar cheese to the Béchamel Sauce above after it has thickened. Stir until the cheese is melted and incorporated into the sauce.

VELOUTÉ SAUCE

> 1 tablespoon butter
> 1 tablespoon flour

½ cup light cream
Salt and freshly ground white pepper to taste

Melt the butter in a small, heavy saucepan and whisk in the flour. Cook the mixture for 1 minute. Slowly pour in the cream, whisking constantly until it is thickened. Season the sauce with the salt and pepper. If it is too thick, add extra cream.

FISH VELOUTÉ SAUCE

Follow the Velouté Sauce recipe above, only replace the light cream with ¼ cup of fish stock or bottled clam juice and ¼ cup of light cream. For richer flavor, add extra butter to the sauce after it has thickened.

HOLLANDAISE SAUCE

2 egg yolks
1 tablespoon cold water
4 tablespoons butter
1 teaspoon lemon juice
Salt to taste

Place the egg yolks in the top pan of a double boiler over water that is just barely simmering and beat them vigorously for 30 seconds. Add the cold water and heat the mixture until it is slightly thickened, still beating. Add the butter, beating, 1 tablespoon at a time. When all the butter has been added, whisk in the lemon juice and beat the sauce for a few more seconds. Remove it from the heat and season it with the salt.

Makes about ½ cup.

BÉARNAISE SAUCE

½ teaspoon dried tarragon
1 shallot, minced
2 tablespoons white wine vinegar
1 tablespoon dry white wine
½ cup hot Hollandaise Sauce (see page 337)

Cook the tarragon, shallot, wine vinegar, and wine in a small saucepan over medium-high heat until the mixture is reduced to about 1 tablespoon. Stir it into the hot Hollandaise Sauce.

Makes a little over ½ cup.

Béarnaise sauce is excellent spooned over fresh cooked broccoli, asparagus, or cauliflower instead of hollandaise sauce, but it is more often served with steak. I think it is a fine companion for hamburger steak.

CURRIED LEMON MAYONNAISE

¼ cup Mayonnaise (see index for recipe)
½ teaspoon curry powder
2 teaspoons lemon juice
2 teaspoons minced scallion or chives (optional)

Combine the ingredients well. Refrigerating the mayonnaise for several hours brings out the flavors.

GREEN GODDESS MAYONNAISE

¼ cup Mayonnaise (see index for recipe)
2 teaspoons white wine vinegar
1 teaspoon tarragon
1 teaspoon fresh chopped chives or scallion

1 teaspoon fresh chopped parsley
Freshly ground pepper to taste

Combine the ingredients in a bowl. To bring out the tarragon flavor, cover the mayonnaise and refrigerate it for 1 hour.

APRICOT SAUCE

¼ cup apricot preserves
2 teaspoons minced scallion
1 tablespoon chili sauce
1 teaspoon lemon juice
1 teaspoon soy sauce
1 teaspoon fresh grated ginger (optional)

Combine the ingredients well. For better flavor, refrigerate the sauce for 1 hour. Serve with Beer Batter Shrimp. (See index for recipe.)

CREAMY TARTAR SAUCE

⅓ cup Mayonnaise (see index for recipe)
2 tablespoons sour cream
1 teaspoon white vinegar
½ teaspoon Dijon-style mustard
3 small gherkins, minced
1 teaspoon capers
1 teaspoon minced scallion or onion
1 teaspoon fresh chopped parsley

Combine the ingredients well in a small bowl. Cover the sauce and refrigerate it for several hours.

DILL CREAM SAUCE

> 1 teaspoon horseradish
> ¼ cup sour cream
> 2 tablespoons heavy cream, whipped
> 1 teaspoon fresh chopped dill weed or ½ teaspoon dried dill
>   weed
> ½ teaspoon fresh chopped chives
> Salt and freshly ground pepper to taste

Combine the ingredients well.

Dill cream sauce makes an excellent escort for cold poached fish. It is also good as a dip with fresh raw vegetables.

Butters

CLARIFIED BUTTER

Clarified butter burns less easily than unclarified butter. Make it often and use it in all sauté cooking, for it always produces a better result.

Cut up 1 stick or up to a pound of butter into 1-tablespoon-sized pieces. Heat them very slowly in a saucepan or double boiler. Skim off the white substance that rises to the surface. A white sediment will settle on the bottom of the pan. Slowly pour the clear butter into a clean jar through two thicknesses of cheesecloth or a fine mesh strainer, leaving the white residue in the pan. Tightly covered, clarified butter lasts for several weeks in the refrigerator. You can also freeze it.

HERB BUTTER

> 3 tablespoons butter, at room temperature
> 2 teaspoons fresh chopped parsley
> ½ teaspoon tarragon
> ⅛ teaspoon basil
> ⅛ teaspoon thyme
> ⅛ teaspoon freshly grated pepper

Mix the ingredients well in a tiny bowl. Cover the butter and refrigerate it until it is cold.

Makes about 4 tablespoons.

Use herb butter on sandwiches or with broiled chops, steak, fish, or seafood.

GARLIC BUTTER

> 3 tablespoons butter, at room temperature
> 1 clove garlic, crushed

Mix the butter and garlic well in a tiny bowl. Cover the butter and refrigerate it until it is cold.

Makes about 3 tablespoons

STRAWBERRY BUTTER

> 1 stick butter, softened
> ¼ cup coarsely chopped ripe strawberries
> 1 teaspoon superfine or granulated sugar

Puree the ingredients in a food processor for about 30 seconds or in a blender. Transfer the butter to a small dish. Smooth the top and cover it with plastic wrap. Refrigerate it for several hours.

Strawberry butter is superb on toast, English muffins, and croissants. It is also surprisingly delicious on cooked hot green vegetables or as a sandwich spread. A favorite sandwich of mine is sliced chicken, watercress, and strawberry butter on whole wheat toast.

VARIATION: You can substitute raspberries for the strawberries.

Crème Fraîche

One of the blessings of cooking for yourself is knowing exactly what quantity of something you love to eat remains in the refrigerator when you are ready to use it. In my case, I am referring to crème fraîche, the heavenly, nutty-flavored, double-thick cream that enhances sauces, soups, and, particularly, fresh fruit desserts.

Some companies are now importing European crème fraîche, but it costs more than Brie. You can make your own respectable crème fraîche with either of two simple recipes at about one-fifth the price of the imported brands. Of the two recipes, I prefer the flavor of the first.

The crème fraîche is worth learning to make and keeping handy in the refrigerator.

Crème fraîche will keep in the refrigerator, tightly covered, for at least 1 week.

BUTTERMILK CRÈME FRAÎCHE

1 cup heavy cream
2 tablespoons buttermilk

Combine the two ingredients in a jar with a tightly fitting lid. Shake the jar vigorously and leave it at room temperature for 8 to 10 hours or overnight, until the cream thickens. Shake it again and refrigerate it.

Makes a little over 1 cup.

SOUR CREAM CRÈME FRAÎCHE

1 cup heavy cream
1 cup sour cream

Follow the directions for Buttermilk Crème Fraîche above.

Makes about 2 cups.

Mustards

Combine ¼ cup of Dijon-style mustard with any of the desired ingredients listed below.

Red Pepper

1 tablespoon minced roasted red pepper
1 minced shallot
¼ teaspoon paprika

Herb

    ¼ teaspoon tarragon
    ¼ teaspoon thyme
    1 teaspoon fresh chopped parsley

Lemon and Pepper

    1½ teaspoons fresh lemon juice
    ½ teaspoon grated lemon rind
    ¼ teaspoon freshly grated pepper or to taste

Garden-Style

    1 tablespoon minced gherkins
    1 teaspoon finely chopped scallion
    1 teaspoon fresh chopped parsley

Seasoned Salt

    ½ cup salt
    2 teaspoons paprika
    1 tablespoon dried shallots
    1 teaspoon dried garlic slivers
    2 tablespoons dried parsley
    1 tablespoon dried celery flakes
    ½ teaspoon freshly ground pepper
    ½ teaspoon oregano
    ½ teaspoon thyme

Place the ingredients in a food processor or blender and run the motor until the mixture is smooth. Store the salt in a jar with a tightly fitting lid.

Makes a little over 1 cup.

14. Desserts

Thirteen Fruit Desserts

A wonderful dessert doesn't have to be a rich, fattening, complicated production. Nutritious, succulent, attractive, and inexpensive fruits provide a sensible answer for the single cook's dessert. Here are thirteen recipes focusing on fresh fruits.

For those with sweeter teeth, here, too, are diverse dessert recipes for hot and cold cakes, tarts, pie, candy, cookies, custards, a cobbler, a soufflé, and ice cream developed specifically for single servings.

ELIZABETH ANN McGINN'S GEORGIA PEACHES

Elizabeth Ann McGinn, my home economics teacher in high school, was responsible for the first formal dinner I ever cooked. It was an exam. Half a semester was cooking and the other half, sewing. I did not excel in the latter class. The less said about my unusual apron, the better. When I graduated from high school, Mrs. McGinn gave me a silver pincushion as a lovely encouraging gesture. Designing was her dream, and today she is a successful clothes designer in Atlanta, Georgia. Elizabeth McGinn's talents, guidance, and cheerful manner, to a large extent, stimulated my early serious interest in food.

1 macaroon, crumbled
1 fresh ripe peach, peeled, pitted, and sliced
2 heaping tablespoons sour cream
2 tablespoons chopped pecans
2 teaspoons brown sugar or to taste

Arrange the peach slices in a stemmed goblet and sprinkle on the macaroon crumbs. Combine the sour cream, pecans, and brown sugar and spoon the mixture over the macaroon and peach.

PARFAIT OF FRESH PAPAYA AND BLUEBERRIES

  1 small ripe papaya
  ½ cup blueberries
  1 teaspoon fresh lime juice
  ½ cup Crème Fraîche sweetened with 2 teaspoons sugar or
      sweetened whipped cream (see index for recipe)
  2 tablespoons toasted pine nuts

Cut the papaya in half, remove the seeds, and peel it. Cut it into ½-inch cubes and place it in a bowl with the blueberries. Sprinkle the lime juice over the fruit and toss it. Spoon half of the mixture into a parfait or balloon-shaped wine glass. Spoon half of the crème fraîche over the fruit. Repeat the process, ending with the crème fraîche. Sprinkle the pine nuts over the top.

GRILLED APRICOTS WITH PECAN FILLING

  2 whole apricots, fresh if possible
  2 tablespoons chopped pecans
  2 tablespoons brown sugar
  2 tablespoons honey
  2 teaspoons butter

Halve and pit the apricots. Combine the pecans and brown sugar in a bowl and spoon the mixture into the apricot centers. Drizzle the honey over the filling and the apricot edges. Dot with butter. Place the apricots under a heated broiler on a baking sheet until the filling sizzles and the apricots are golden.

CANTALOUPE WITH PORT

½ small cantaloupe
¼ cup port or sweet sherry

Peel the cantaloupe and cut it into thin slices. Spoon the port over the slices and let the melon stand for 15 minutes before serving it.

FRESH FIGS WITH DATES AND CRÈME FRAÎCHE

¼ cup finely chopped pitted dates
¼ cup Crème Fraîche (see index for recipe)
2 fresh ripe figs, skinned and quartered
4 whole dates

Combine the chopped dates and the crème fraîche. Spread the mixture over the bottom of a dessert plate. Top it with the figs and the whole dates.

BAKED APPLE

1 slice toast, crusts trimmed
Butter
1 large baking apple
1½ tablespoons chopped walnuts
1 tablespoon butter
1 tablespoon sugar or brown sugar
⅛ teaspoon cinnamon

Spread the toast with a little butter and place it in a small, shallow baking dish. Core the apple and pare away about 1 inch of the top of the peel. Place it on the middle of the toast. Combine the walnuts, butter, sugar, and cinnamon. Fill the center of the apple with the mixture. Bake it in a preheated 375°F oven for 30 minutes or until it is tender. Don't overcook it or it will be mushy. Serve the apple warm or refrigerated.

YOGURT WITH GOLDEN RAISINS, FRESH FRUIT, AND HONEY

    1 cup plain yogurt
    3 tablespoons golden raisins
    4 fresh strawberries, sliced
    ½ banana, cubed
    1 fresh peach, pitted, peeled, and sliced
    2 tablespoons chopped walnuts
    2 tablespoons honey

Combine the yogurt with the raisins, strawberries, banana, and peach. Sprinkle the mixture with the walnuts and honey.

EXTRAS SUGGESTIONS: Any combination of approximately 1 cup of fresh fruit can be used with yogurt, raisins, walnuts, and honey—for example, blueberries, pineapple, and melon balls. The extra banana half in this recipe also goes into a Banana Daiquiri. (See index for recipe.)

BANANA CROWN

    1 banana, peeled and sliced
    1 Coconut Macaroon, crumbled (see index for recipe)
    2 heaping tablespoons Crème Fraîche (see index for recipe)
    2 tablespoons toasted almond slivers

Combine the banana slices and macaroon in a dessert bowl. Spoon the crème fraîche over them and sprinkle it with a circle of almonds.

SAUTÉED BANANA WITH BROWN SUGAR

    1 banana, peeled
    1½ tablespoons butter
    2 tablespoons brown sugar

Cut the banana in half lengthwise. Heat the butter in a 9-inch skillet
and sauté the banana halves until they are lightly browned on both
sides. Sprinkle them with the brown sugar, carefully turn them, and
cook them over high heat for 1 minute.

FRESH STRAWBERRIES WITH CRÈME FRAÎCHE AND
BROWN SUGAR

This recipe is so simple that you might wonder why it needs explain-
ing in a cookbook. I've never been served this dish in people's homes,
but it is always available in better restaurants when the berries are in
season. Therefore, this is merely a reminder for the single cook on
how to have an exquisite ending to a meal.

    1 cup fresh ripe strawberries (or any fresh berries, such as
        raspberries or blueberries)
    2 heaping tablespoons Crème Fraîche (see index for recipe)
    1 tablespoon brown sugar

Heap the strawberries in a bulb-shaped Burgundy wine glass. Top
them with the crème fraîche and brown sugar.

INDEPENDENCE DAY FRUIT SUNDAE

    ½ cup sliced strawberries
    ½ cup blueberries

6 canned litchi nuts in syrup, drained and halved
2 heaping tablespoons Crème Fraîche (see index for recipe) or
    whipped cream
2 tablespoons toasted chopped hazelnuts or chopped almonds

Combine the strawberries, blueberries, and litchi nuts in a glass dessert bowl. Top them with the crème fraîche or whipped cream and the toasted nuts.

POACHED PEAR WITH CRANBERRY AND
APRICOT SAUCE

1 fresh pear
3 tablespoons vanilla sugar (see below)
⅓ cup cranberry sauce
1 heaping tablespoon apricot preserves

Peel the pear, leaving the stem on, and set it aside. Bring 3 cups of water to a boil in a medium-sized saucepan. Add the vanilla sugar and stir until it is dissolved. Simmer the pear in the boiling water for 10 minutes or until it is tender. Remove it with a slotted spoon. Combine the cranberry sauce and apricot preserves. Spoon the sauce over the warm pear.

How to Make Vanilla Sugar

Put 4 whole vanilla beans into a 1-quart mason jar full of sugar. Seal the jar tightly. You can use the sugar after one week.

FRESH PEAR WITH CREAMY GORGONZOLA

  1½ ounces Gorgonzola cheese
  1 teaspoon pear or other brandy
  ¼ cup Crème Fraîche (see index for recipe)
  1 fresh ripe pear
  2 tablespoons golden raisins

Pour the brandy over the cheese and let it sit for 30 minutes. Mash it with the back of a fork. Add the crème fraîche and beat the mixture until it is smooth. Peel and core the pear and quarter it. Arrange the quarters in the center of a dessert plate with the stem ends pointing towards the center. Spoon the cheese mixture onto the center of the plate and sprinkle it with the raisins.

Other Favorite Delicious Desserts

PEACH WAFFLE CAKE

  2 small frozen waffles
  2 teaspoons butter
  1 large fresh ripe peach, peeled and thinly sliced
  2 tablespoons peach preserves, at room temperature
  ¼ teaspoon cinnamon
  ⅓ cup Crème Fraîche (see index for recipe) or sweetened
      whipped cream

Toast the waffles and spread 1 teaspoon of butter over each. Combine the peach slices with the peach preserves and cinnamon. Spoon the mixture on top of one waffle. Place the other waffle over the peach mixture and top it with the crème fraîche.

VARIATION: Use 8 fresh strawberries in place of the peach and strawberry preserves instead of peach preserves. Eliminate the cinnamon.

ZUCCHINI CAKE

¼ cup vegetable oil
1 egg
⅓ cup brown sugar, packed
¼ teaspoon vanilla
½ cup flour
½ teaspoon baking soda
¼ teaspoon salt
¼ teaspoon cinnamon
¼ teaspoon fresh grated nutmeg
Pinch of ground cloves (optional)
1 cup grated zucchini
¼ cup chopped walnuts
¼ cup chopped dates or raisins

Beat together the vegetable oil, egg, and brown sugar. Add the vanilla. Combine the flour, baking soda, salt, cinnamon, nutmeg, and cloves in a separate bowl. Add this mixture to the oil, egg, and sugar mixture. Beat them until they are well combined. Stir in the zucchini, walnuts, and dates. Grease a 3¾-by-7½-inch bread loaf pan lightly with butter. Add 1 teaspoon of flour and tilt the pan until it is coated with flour. Tip out the loose flour. Turn the cake batter into the pan and bake it in a preheated 350°F oven for 35 to 40 minutes, until an inserted toothpick comes out clean. Wait 5 minutes before turning the cake out of the pan.

Eat the cake as is or frost it with cream cheese frosting (see page 354).

VARIATION: You can substitute the same amount of grated carrots for the zucchini.

Cream Cheese Frosting:

> 3 ounces cream cheese, at room temperature
> ¼ pound confectioners' sugar
> 1½ tablespoons softened butter
> ½ teaspoon vanilla
> 2 tablespoons chopped walnuts (optional)

Whip the cream cheese in an electric mixer or by hand until it is light and fluffy. Beat in the confectioners' sugar and beat until the mixture is well blended and smooth. Stir in the vanilla and walnuts. Spread the frosting on the cooled cake.

PINEAPPLE MERINGUE CAKE

> 1 slice pound cake
> ⅓ cup crushed pineapple
> 2 tablespoons orange marmalade
> 1 egg white
> 1½ tablespoons sugar or to taste

Toast the pound cake, cut it in half, and spread one half with the combined pineapple and marmalade. Place the other half on top of the mixture. Beat the egg white until soft peaks form; then add the sugar and beat until the mixture is stiff but not dry. Cover the top and sides of the cake with the meringue and pass it under the broiler until it is lightly browned.

EXTRAS SUGGESTIONS: Add any remaining pineapple to a fruit salad or to orange marmalade to be used as a spread.

PEACH COBBLER

2 tablespoons melted butter
¼ cup sugar
⅓ cup flour
¼ cup milk
½ teaspoon baking powder
⅛ teaspoon salt
1 large fresh ripe peach, peeled, pitted, and chopped
1 tablespoon brown sugar
⅛ teaspoon cinnamon
2 teaspoons butter

Combine the melted butter, sugar, flour, milk, baking powder, and salt. Pour the batter into a greased 4-inch soufflé dish or something of a similar shape. Top it with the chopped peach and sprinkle the peach with the combined brown sugar and cinnamon. Dot the top with the butter. Bake the cobbler in a preheated 350°F oven for 45 minutes or until it is golden brown on top.

MARTIN RAPP'S SQUARE APPLE TART WITH INSTANT PUFF PASTRY

Martin Rapp, director of publications for the Museum of Modern Art in New York, created this divine pastry when his wife, Samantha, was away working in California.

> 1 frozen patty shell
> Flour
> 1 Delicious apple, peeled, cored, and thinly sliced
> 1 teaspoon melted butter
> 2 teaspoons sugar
> 2 heaping tablespoons apricot preserves

Dust a pastry board and a rolling pin with flour. Roll out the frozen patty shell to a 6-inch circle. With a chopping knife cut it into a 5-inch square. Place it on an ungreased baking sheet. Line apple slices in two rows across pastry. Drizzle the butter over the apples and sprinkle them with the sugar. Bake the tart in a preheated 400°F oven for 20 minutes or until the pastry is golden and the apples are beginning to color. About 3 minutes before the tart is cooked, put the apricot preserves in a small saucepan with 1 tablespoon of water and boil them, stirring, for 2 minutes. Strain the sauce. Remove the tart from the oven and brush it with the apricot glaze.

VARIATIONS: This tart can also be made with a pear, a peach, or 3 plums.

FRESH STRAWBERRY TART

> 6 to 8 fresh strawberries, hulled
> 1 tablespoon shelled chopped pistachio nuts

PASTRY:

¾ cup flour
3 tablespoons cold butter
⅛ teaspoon salt
1½ tablespoons ice water

STRAWBERRY GLAZE:

⅓ cup strawberry preserves
½ teaspoon sugar
1 tablespoon water

First, make the pastry. With a pastry blender or knife, cut together the flour and butter until they form a crumblike mixture. Sprinkle it with the salt and add the water. Stir it until it forms into a ball. Roll it on a lightly floured board to a little more than a ⅛-inch thickness. Fit it into an individual tart pan, covering the bottom and the sides, and cut off any extra pastry. Line the pastry with a small circle of foil and fill it with uncooked beans or rice. (This is called baking blind. It prevents the pastry from bubbling while it is cooking.) Place it on a baking sheet in a preheated 400°F oven and bake it for 10 minutes. Remove the foil with the beans or rice and continue cooking the tart for 6 to 8 minutes or until the pastry is golden brown. Remove it from the oven and let it cool. Prepare the strawberry glaze. Place the ingredients in a small saucepan and bring them to a boil. Stir the glaze and cook it over low heat for 3 minutes. Strain it. Brush the bottom and sides of the pastry shell with the glaze and place the strawberries, stem side down, in the shell. Brush the strawberries with the glaze. Sprinkle the pistachio nuts over the top. Serve the tart immediately or refrigerate it for several hours.

FOUR INDIVIDUAL LIME PIES

    1 14-ounce can sweetened condensed milk
    ¼ cup fresh lime juice
    1 egg yolk, beaten
    2 teaspoons fresh grated lime rind
    1 cup heavy cream, whipped
    4 individual graham cracker crusts

Individual graham cracker crusts can be bought prepared or can be made by following the directions on a package of graham crackers for a 9-inch pie crust. Just divide the recipe into 4 parts and line 4 individual pie pans. Bake the crusts a few minutes less than the package recipe recommends.

Combine the sweetened condensed milk with the lime juice and stir it until it thickens. Add the egg yolk and 1 teaspoon of the grated lime rind, mixing well. Fold in the whipped cream. Turn the filling into the pie shells in equal portions. Sprinkle them evenly with the remaining teaspoon of grated lime rind. Cover one pie and refrigerate it at least 2 hours before serving it. Cover the remaining pies and freeze them. Use them as needed. Before using the frozen pies, transfer them to the refrigerator for 8 hours before serving them so that they can thaw.

Lime pies can be garnished with toasted grated coconut or fresh fruit such as strawberries or seedless green grapes.

HELEN ABBOTT'S HIGHLAND TOFFEE

Helen Abbott, who lives in Pollensa on Majorca, has been sharing recipes with me for years. I greedily wait for her letters, and I was not disappointed with her latest treasure, called highland toffee. Helen says, "This recipe is easy and stores well if kept covered tightly in a covered dish to have as a healthy sweet treat. It doesn't last very long whether it's made for one or many."

⅓ cup melted margarine
2 cups quick-cooking oatmeal
½ cup brown sugar
¼ cup light corn syrup
¼ teaspoon salt
1½ teaspoons vanilla
1 cup semisweet chocolate, melted
¼ cup chopped walnuts

Combine the margarine with the oatmeal and mix them well. Add the brown sugar, corn syrup, salt, and vanilla and again mix well. Grease foil and line an 8-inch-square cake pan. Spread the mixture evenly in the pan. (It should be on the dry side.) Bake it in a preheated 375°F oven for about 15 minutes, until it is lightly browned. When it cools, remove the foil from the pan; then remove the foil from the toffee. While the toffee is cooling, place the chocolate in an ovenproof bowl in the turned-off warm oven. By the time the toffee is cool enough to coat, the chocolate has melted. Coat the toffee with the melted chocolate and sprinkle it with the nuts. Cut it into 36 squares and let it cool.

CRISP MOLASSES COOKIES

¼ cup sugar
3 tablespoons butter
1 egg
¾ cup flour
1 teaspoon baking soda
¼ teaspoon salt
¼ cup molasses

Cream together the sugar and butter. Add the egg, flour, baking soda, and salt. Mix the ingredients well and stir in the molasses. Drop the dough on a greased baking sheet by teaspoonfuls, 2 inches apart. Bake the cookies in a preheated 350°F oven for about 12 minutes.

Makes about 2½ dozen cookies.

COCONUT MACAROONS

2 egg whites
½ cup confectioners' sugar
½ teaspoon vanilla
¼ cup flour
1 scant cup shredded coconut

Beat the egg whites until they are stiff. Gradually add the sugar and vanilla. Beat in the flour and fold in the coconut. Drop the dough by teaspoonfuls onto a greased baking sheet, 2 inches apart. Bake the cookies in a preheated 350°F oven for about 12 minutes.

Makes about 1½ dozen cookies.

CRÈME BRÛLÉE WITH FRUIT

½ cup heavy cream
1 large egg yolk
1 tablespoon sugar
½ scant teaspoon vanilla
12 fresh raspberries or blueberries
1 tablespoon brown sugar

Heat the cream in a small saucepan over low heat until it begins to bubble. Immediately remove it from the heat. Beat the egg yolk and sugar with a wire whisk until the mixture is lemon-colored. Add the vanilla and the heated cream and mix them well. Place the fruit in a custard cup or a 1-cup soufflé dish and pour the sauce over it. Set the cup in a pan containing ¾ of an inch of hot water. Bake it in a preheated 350°F oven for 30 minutes. Sprinkle the crème with the brown sugar and pass it under the broiler for 2 minutes. Remove the dish and cool it at room temperature for 30 minutes. Refrigerate it for 2 more hours before serving it.

WHOLE WHEAT BREAD PUDDING WITH BLUEBERRIES

2 slices day-old whole wheat bread, cut into ½-inch cubes
1½ tablespoons sugar
¼ teaspoon cinnamon
3 tablespoons melted butter
½ cup fresh or frozen (drained) blueberries
1 teaspoon lemon juice
2 tablespoons brown sugar

Place the bread cubes in a bowl. Sprinkle the combined sugar and cinnamon over them and toss. Pour the butter over the mixture and turn it with a fork until the cubes are evenly coated. In a small bowl combine the blueberries with the lemon juice and brown sugar. Place half of the bread cube mixture in a buttered individual soufflé dish or a small, deep, ovenproof dish. Spoon the blueberry mixture over the bread cubes and top it with the rest of the bread cubes. Bake the pudding in a preheated 350°F oven for 20 minutes.

Serve it with heavy cream or a scoop of vanilla ice cream.

ZABAGLIONE

Zabaglione, the hot, airy, mousselike Italian dessert, is sheer perfection for the solo cook. It stands alone, but spooned over a ball of vanilla ice cream and topped with sliced ripe strawberries, zabaglione is my personal favorite dessert, the dessert I want for the last meal. This I wholeheartedly admitted to only minutes after the final testing and tasting of the following recipe.

> 2 egg yolks
> 1 tablespoon sugar
> ¼ cup dry Marsala

Beat the egg yolks and sugar in the top pan of a double boiler (the heavier the better) until the mixture is pale yellow and thickened to a creamy consistency. Place the pan over the bottom double boiler pan holding simmering, but not boiling, water. Add the Marsala and beat the mixture continuously until it is foamy and smooth. Spoon it into a tall bulb wine glass and serve it at once.

DESSERT CREPES

Add 2 teaspoons of sugar and substitute melted butter for the oil in the Basic Crepes recipe. (See index for recipe.)

Whipped Cream and Strawberry Dessert Crepes

Spread whipped cream over each crepe and top it with sliced fresh strawberries. Roll up the crepe and sprinkle it with confectioners' sugar.

Easy Fruit Preserves Crepes

Spread fruit preserves of your choice over each crepe and roll it up. Sprinkle it with confectioners' sugar.

Grand Marnier Crepes

Fold 4 crepes in half and then in half again. Heat 2 tablespoons of butter in a medium skillet and add the crepes. Pour ¼ cup of Grand Marnier into the skillet and ignite it. When the flame goes out, sprinkle the crepes with confectioners' sugar and serve them immediately.

CHOCOLATE SOUFFLÉ

> 1 tablespoon butter
> 1 tablespoon flour
> ⅔ cup milk, heated
> 1½ egg yolks
> ⅓ cup sugar
> 1½ ounces unsweetened chocolate
> 2 tablespoons sugar
> 1 teaspoon butter
> 1 tablespoon sugar
> 3 egg whites

Melt the butter in a small saucepan. Whisk in the flour and cook the sauce over medium heat for 1 minute, stirring. Slowly pour in the hot milk, whisking constantly, until the sauce is smooth and thickened. Remove it from the heat. Beat together the egg yolks and the ⅓ cup of sugar until they are light yellow. Pour them into the sauce and stir well. Melt the chocolate with the 2 tablespoons of sugar in the top of a double boiler over simmering water in the lower pan. Cool the chocolate slightly and stir it into the sauce. Fit a piece of doubled aluminum foil around a 1½-cup soufflé dish, forming a collar. Tie it with string. Carefully butter the dish and the inside of the foil. Place the 1 tablespoon of sugar in the dish and tilt it to coat the buttered surface of the dish and foil. Beat the egg whites until they are stiff and fold them into the chocolate sauce. Pour the sauce into the prepared soufflé dish. Bake it in a preheated 350°F oven for 30 minutes. Remove the foil collar and serve the soufflé immediately.

COINTREAU DESSERT OMELET WITH
FRESH STRAWBERRIES

2 eggs
Dash of salt
1 tablespoon Cointreau
1 teaspoon sugar
1 tablespoon butter
4 fresh strawberries, at room temperature, thinly sliced
Confectioners' sugar

Beat together the eggs, salt, Cointreau, and sugar. Heat the butter in an omelet pan and add the egg mixture. With a tablespoon, stir it in a circle over medium heat until the eggs begin to set. Smooth the eggs evenly over the bottom of the pan. Remove the pan from the heat. Quickly place the sliced strawberries across the center of the eggs. Return the pan to the heat. Tilt the pan and begin folding the eggs over with the tablespoon until the strawberries are covered. Turn the omelet out onto a plate and sprinkle it with the confectioners' sugar.

The omelet can also be garnished with a dollop of Crème Fraîche (see index for recipe).

CINNAMON ICE CREAM

Sprinkle ½ teaspoon of cinnamon over ½ pint of softened vanilla ice cream and mix them thoroughly. Freeze the ice cream again.

Serve it with fresh blueberries, peaches, or cherries. It is also very good with toasted almond slivers or coconut.

CHERRY VANILLA ICE CREAM

¼ cup chopped roasted almonds
1 pint vanilla ice cream, softened
¾ cup fresh bing cherries, pitted and halved

Roast the almonds on a baking sheet under the broiler for 3 or 4 minutes. Turn them and cook them until they are golden brown, another minute or two.

In a bowl blend together the softened ice cream, cherries, and roasted almonds. Transfer the mixture to a 3-cup freezer container and freeze it.

Since ice cream must be kept frozen, it's both easy and sensible to make a large enough quantity for several future servings.

CREAM PUFF

¼ cup water
2 tablespoons butter
Pinch of salt
¼ cup flour
1 medium-sized egg

Bring the water to a boil in a saucepan. Add the butter and salt. When the butter has melted, remove the saucepan from the heat and add the flour immediately. Beat the mixture vigorously until it rolls off the sides of the pan. Beat in the egg until the mixture is smooth. Lightly butter a baking sheet. Spoon the mixture onto the sheet in one or two mounds. Bake it in a preheated 400°F oven for 35 minutes or until it is puffed up and golden. Take it out of oven and immediately pierce it with the sharp point of a knife in two places. Turn off the oven. Return the puff to the oven, leaving the door open, for 1 minute. (This will help release the moisture from inside.)

I like to serve myself a cream puff with butter and preserves for Sunday breakfast. To serve as a dessert, cut open the cream puff and fill it with a scoop of ice cream; replace the top and spoon Chocolate Sauce or ½ cup of pureed strawberries or raspberries over it.

STRAWBERRY ICE

  1 cup sliced fresh strawberries
  1 tablespoon sugar
  1 tablespoon kirsch

Puree the ingredients in a food processor or blender. Pour the mixture into a small soufflé dish and freeze it.

RASPBERRY FOOL

  ½ cup raspberries
  2 teaspoons sugar
  1 tablespoon framboise
  ½ cup heavy cream
  1 teaspoon sugar

Puree the raspberries with 2 teaspoons of sugar and the framboise in a food processor or blender. Cover the mixture and refrigerate it for 30 minutes. Whip the heavy cream and add the 1 teaspoon of sugar. Cover it and refrigerate it for 30 minutes. Fold the raspberry mixture into the whipped cream and serve it in a chilled glass bowl.

SUGAR-AND-ALMOND-TOASTED BRIOCHE

  1 brioche
  2 teaspoons almond-flavored liqueur
  1 tablespoon butter
  2 tablespoons sliced almonds
  1 tablespoon sugar
  Cinnamon

Cut the brioche into 3 slices crosswise. Sprinkle with the almond-flavored liqueur. Spread an equal amount of butter on each slice. Sprinkle the slices with equal amounts of almonds, sugar, and cinnamon. (Go easy on the cinnamon.) Place the prepared brioche slices on a baking sheet and toast them under the heated broiler until they are golden. This dessert can be prepared an hour or two before dinner.

CARIBBEAN RUM-FLAVORED FRUIT

¼ cup crushed pineapple
1 small banana, thinly sliced
1 small orange, peeled and separated into sections
1½ tablespoons dark rum
1 tablespoon brown sugar

Place the fruit in a bowl. Add the rum and sugar. Mix the ingredients gently, then cover and refrigerate them for 30 minutes.

FOUR-FRUIT COMPOTE

½ cup halved and pitted bing cherries
½ cup seedless green grapes
1 plum, pitted and cut into wedges
1 apricot, skinned, pitted, and cut into wedges
1 tablespoon confectioners' sugar
2 tablespoons Cointreau

Combine the ingredients and refrigerate the compote for 30 minutes.

BROILED GRAPEFRUIT WITH MAPLE SYRUP

½ grapefruit, cut into sections in the skin
1 tablespoon maple syrup
2 teaspoons butter

Sprinkle the maple syrup over the grapefruit and dot it with the butter. Cook it under the heated broiler for about 5 minutes, until it is golden.

VANILLA ICE CREAM WITH CRÈME DE MENTHE AND CHOCOLATE MORSELS

  2 scoops vanilla ice cream
  2 tablespoons crème de menthe
  2 tablespoons chocolate morsels

Place the ice cream in a bowl. Pour the crème de menthe over it and sprinkle it with the chocolate morsels.

DATES STUFFED WITH PECANS AND CREAM CHEESE

  4 pitted dates
  4 whole pecans
  8 teaspoons cream cheese
  Confectioners' sugar

Place 1 pecan and 2 teaspoons of cream cheese in the center of each date. Dust the dates with confectioners' sugar.

SLICED BANANAS WITH CREAM

  1 banana
  2 tablespoons heavy cream
  Fresh grated nutmeg

Slice the banana into a glass bowl. Pour the heavy cream over it and sprinkle it with nutmeg.

15. Spirited Drinks

Alcoholic

ANN URBAN'S APRICOT BRANDY

New Jerseyite Ann Urban has a grown family, which she raised on interesting and varied foods. Her daughter, Amanda, let me sample her mother's homemade apricot brandy one evening after dinner as an example of her mother's recent wizardry. The smooth, sweet, apricot-flavored brew was outstandingly good. Amanda shared the recipe with me, and by gracious permission of Mrs. Urban I print it here. Homemade apricot brandy is an example of unusual things the single cook can achieve if he or she is inspired. The brandy, once made, can serve one or many. I use it sparingly. It's a great holiday food gift. If you are making it for that purpose, keep in mind that nearly 4 months are required for the final product. A friend who tasted the golden brandy asked for the recipe, and he tells me he turns the bottle at the same time each week: before reading Wednesday morning's food section of *The New York Times.*

   4½ cups sugar
   2 pounds dried apricots
   2 quarts vodka

Place the ingredients in a glass container with a tight-fitting lid. Invert the container and shake it once a week for 15 weeks. Drain the brandy into a bowl through a fine sieve, pressing down on the apricots with the back of a spoon to extract as much liquid and flavor as possible. Pour the brandy into a bottle or decanter.

EXTRAS SUGGESTIONS: Remaining apricots can be pureed and used as ice cream topping or in fruit bread.

ROGER

Venice's great restaurant, Harry's Bar, serves a spectacular drink called a Roger. It was named after and invented by Harry's resident alchemist and bartender. Making a Roger successfully depends on the seasonal availability of flavorful ripe and juicy peaches. Italy's peaches are the world's tastiest. Several years ago, Roger gave me the recipe for his potion with the apology that since he mixes the drink in huge quantities, I'd have to work out the exact formula for one.

    1 large fresh ripe peach, pitted, peeled, and chopped
    2 ounces vodka
    ½ cup fresh orange juice
    1 teaspoon lemon juice
    ¼ teaspoon grenadine
    ½ teaspoon sugar or to taste
    1 cup crushed ice

Puree the ingredients in a blender and serve the Roger in a tall highball glass, as Harry's does, or in a goblet.

BLOODY MARY

A Bloody Mary is a satisfying drink worth learning to make well. The secret is lemon juice, whether you prefer a regular Bloody Mary, the more exotic Rum Bloody Mary, or the exquisite Danish Mary.

Basic Bloody Mary

> 1 cup tomato juice
> 1 teaspoon Worcestershire sauce
> 2 dashes of Tabasco sauce
> 1 tablespoon lemon juice
> ¼ cup vodka

Mix the ingredients well and pour them into an ice-filled glass. Use a celery stick as a stirrer.

Rum Bloody Mary

Use the basic Bloody Mary recipe, substituting dark rum for the vodka.

Danish Mary

Use the basic Bloody Mary recipe, substituting aquavit for the vodka.

FROZEN BANANA DAIQUIRI

> 1 small banana
> 2 teaspoons lime juice
> 1 teaspoon lemon juice
> 1 teaspoon sugar
> ⅓ cup rum
> 6 crushed ice cubes

Puree the ingredients in a blender until the ice is smoothly incorporated into the mixture.

WHITE SANGRIA

    1 cup dry white wine
    1 cup soda water
    1 teaspoon sugar or to taste
    1 tablespoon vodka
    1 strawberry
    1 slice orange
    1 slice apple

Combine the wine, soda water, sugar, and vodka in a pitcher with several ice cubes. Add the fruit and stir.

PIMM'S CUP

    8 ounces 7-Up
    1½ ounces Pimm's Cup No. 1
    1 slice cucumber
    1 strawberry

Fill a large glass with ice. Add the ingredients and stir.

Nonalcoholic

PATRICIA BRILL'S MEAL-IN-A-DRINK

Patricia Brill is a personnel consultant. She says, "One weekend following a period when junk food served as fuel to keep me juggling work and social events, I decided my 'fuel habits' had to change. For me, this meant getting a better 'return' for what I shoved into my body—better to replace candy bars and chips with fruits and nuts for sources of energy! Out of this, my own 'energy crisis,' was born a drink which not only serves as a meal substitute but is tasty as well. Here's the brief background. In an effort to banish fantasies of an ice cream sundae smorgasbord, I decided one Saturday to combine in my blender all the healthy ingredients I liked. The result follows and has literally converted me to healthier eating habits. In a thermos it serves as my lunch or dinner when time doesn't permit dining in style. I may miss the ambiance of a fine restaurant, but who can argue with a nutritious drink that gives me pep, aids in weight loss, and beats the Reese peanut butter cup in the race to my mouth?"

1 cup vanilla yogurt
¼ cup wheat germ
1 banana, cut into 2-inch lengths
3 tablespoons sunflower seeds (I prefer the dry roasted variety)
½ teaspoon ground cardamom
Apple juice to bring the level in a blender up to 3 cups

Combine the ingredients in the blender. Turn the blender on and slowly count to 10. This gives the drink a "texture"—small bits of banana and crunchy seeds. You can blend it longer to suit your own taste.

AYRAN
(A Turkish Cold Yogurt Drink)

On a hot, crowded ferryboat going from Istanbul to the Princes' Islands, I thirstily spotted a man selling Cokes, hot tea, and a mysterious-looking thick white drink from his large brass tray. When he finally made his way to the row I was seated in, I learned the name of the drink—Ayran—and bought one. Delectable and smooth, it was the first of many Ayrans I sipped while in Turkey. The maitre d'hôtel at the excellent Istanbul Hilton Grill Room Restaurant gave me the uncomplicated recipe.

> 1 cup cold plain yogurt
> ¾ cup cold club soda

Combine the ingredients thoroughly and drink the Ayran immediately.

VARIATIONS: Add 6 or 7 strawberries or ½ cup of blueberries—or the equivalent amount of the fruit of your choice—to the mixture and puree it in a blender.

INSTANT CAPPUCCINO

> 1 demitasse cup hot espresso
> 1 demitasse cup hot milk
> ½ teaspoon grated unsweetened chocolate

Combine the ingredients with a wire whisk in a saucepan until the mixture is frothy. Pour it into a cup. Add sugar if you prefer it sweet.

Index

acorn squash, baked, 300
anchovy
  chicken, caper and, salad, 99
  fete dishes, Harry Baron's, 289–90
  onion and, canapés, 43
  vinaigrette sauce, 107
Alsatian pork chop, 212
antipasto plate, dieter's, 294
appetizers and first courses, 42–57
  canapés, 43, 60–61
  quick and easy, 55–57
  spreads and dips, 58–59
apple
  baked, 348–59
  pancake, Dutch, 290–91
  tart, square, with instant puff pastry,
    Martin Rapp's, and variations, 356
apricot(s)
  brandy, Ann Urban's, 370–71
  grilled, with pecan filling, 347
  sauce, 339
artichoke
  boiled, with herbed pepper sour
    cream sauce, 47
  hearts, marinated, in curry sauce, 58
  soup, 63
arugula and endive salad, 89
asparagus
  cold vinaigrette, 301
  fresh cooked, 300–1
avocado
  and bean sprouts burger, 192
  grilled cheese sandwich, 275
  guacamole, 53
  leftovers, in salads, 54

bacon
  cubes, chicken fried with, 152
  pimiento cheese and, spread, 58–59
baked beans, improved canned, 295
banana
  crown, 349–50
  Daiquiri, frozen, 372–73
  sautéed with brown sugar, 350
  sliced, with cream, 368
bean sprouts and avocado burger, 192
beef (see also beef, ground)
  broth, canned, enriched one-hour,
    334–35
  and carrot ragout, 269
  cold beef vinaigrette, 105
  flank steak, broiled, with mustard
    pepper crust, 182
  liver, calf's sautéed, 201
  ressac et gazon, John Bunge's, 180–81
  roast, and watercress croissant
    sandwich, 277
  shell steak, broiled, marinated, 183
  steak, sliced, sandwich, 279
  steak, chicken fried, 185
  steak, flank, broiled with mustard
    pepper crust, 182
  steak, shell, broiled wine-marinated,
    183

stew, 267
stock, 334
stir-fried Chinese, with black bean
	sauce, 130–31
tournedos, sautéed, with Madeira,
	184
beef, ground
	burger, Pablo, 191
	burger, avocado and bean sprouts,
		194
	hamburger, crusty, 192–93
	hamburger, German, 192
	hamburger, herb, 193
	hamburger, master recipe, and
		variations, 189–90
	hamburger, pepper, 193
	hamburger with sour cream and red
		caviar, 195
	meatballs, spicy, 188–89
	meat loaf, 187–88
	patty, encroûte, 196
	omelet, Spanish-style, 29
	stuffed cabbage, Marion Newberg's,
		186–187
beverages
	aryan, and variations, 375
	cappucino, instant, 375
	meal-in-a-drink, Patricia Brill's, 374
beverages, alcoholic
	apricot brandy, Ann Urban's, 370–71
	banana Daiquiri, frozen, 372–73
	bloody Mary, and variations, 371
	Pimm's Cup, 373
	Roger, 371
	sangria, white, 373
biscuits, ham-filled, 43
black bean(s), 128
	basic recipe, 128–29
	chili, 131
	and green pepper with rice, 296
	salad, 132
	sauce, stir-fried Chinese beef with,
		130–31
	shrimp with, 244
	soup with curried tomatoes, 130

blueberries and papaya, fresh, parfait
	of, 347
blue cheese vinaigrette sauce, 107
bread(s)
	biscuits, ham-filled, 43
	bread stick rolls, ham and, 56
	brioche filled with sour cream and
		lumpfish caviar, 56–57
	brioche, sugar-and-almond-toasted,
		366–67
	crumbs, sautéed, 61
	English muffins, fresh, 298
	French, 297
	for hamburgers, 190–91
	pain grillé, 60
bread pudding, whole wheat, with
	blueberries, 361
brioche
	filled with sour cream and lumpfish
		caviar, 56–57
	sugar-and-almond-toasted, 366–67
broccoli
	creamed, 301
	creamed, and red caviar crepe filling,
		286
	salad, 94
	sautéed, with garlic and basil, 302
butter
	clarified, 340
	garlic, 341
	herb, 341
	mustard, 229
	strawberry, and variations, 342

cabbage, stuffed, Marion Newberry's,
	186–87
Caesar salad, mini, 89
	sandwich, 274
cake
	peach cobbler, 355
	peach waffle, and variations, 352–53
	pineapple meringue, 354
	zucchini, and variation, 353–54
calf's liver, sautéed, 201

canapés
  onion and anchovy, 43
  topping suggestions, 60–61
cantaloupe with port, 348
caponata, 56
cappuccino, instant, 375
carrot(s)
  beef and, ragout, 269
  celery and, herb soup, 262
  cooked in chicken broth, 302
  lemon-glazed, 303
  and potato salad, 95
  and raisin salad, 95
  Vichy, 303
cauliflower au gratin, 304
celery
  and carrot herb soup, 262
  slaw, piquant, 90
celery root rémoulade, 52–53
cheese
  arancini, 283
  blue cheese vinaigrette sauce, 107
  cottage cheese dressing, diet, 109
  cream cheese dips and spreads, 58–59
  crepes with sausage and, 284–85
  fondue, 293
  melon cubes wrapped in, and
    prosciutto, 45
  Parmesan cheese, crouton, and
    prosciutto omelet, 78
  pizza, basic, 287
  and rice omelet, 78
  Roquefort vinaigrette sauce, 108
  and tuna salad, 103–4
  storing, 29
cheese sandwiches
  cream cheese and mushroom, with
    bacon, 276
  mozzarella, prosciutto, and basil,
    grilled, 276–77
cherry tomato(es)
  mushroom and cucumber salad, 96
  sautéed, 314
chicken (*see also* chicken breasts, chicken
  salad)

broiled, crisp, 159
broth, canned, enriched one-hour,
  333
butter-fried, 153
fried, crisp, 151
fried with bacon cubes, 152
leg, Coki Beach fried, 150
liver pâté, 44
poulet Muguet, 154
roast, Angela Pagliaroli's, 160–61
roast half, 160
soup, noodle au gratin, thick, 260–61
soup, Pennsylvania Dutch corn and,
  260
stock, 332–33
sweet and sour, Sheilah Rae Gross's,
  154–55
tarragon, 156
thighs, sautéed, with mushrooms, 158
whole (or half) recipes for, 159–61
wings, deviled, 157
chicken breasts
  baked, in sherried tomato sauce with
    crisp cheese topping, 142
  bites, fried sesame, 55
  boned, Florentine, 145
  boned, in shallot sauce, 146
  with Brie filling, Kiev style, 147
  chunks, with mushrooms and lemon,
    Frank Perdue's, 134–35
  fried, lemon-flavored, 148
  loaf, 149
  peri-peri, Joy Rossi, 140–41
  poached, cold, with salmon sauce,
    139–40
  poached, low-calorie, with mustard
    and capers, 143
  pot pie with instant puff pastry, 136–
    137
  sate with peanut sauce, 138
  sautéed, with walnuts and sesame oil,
    136
  stuffed, 144
chicken salad
  caper and anchovy, 99

Chinese style, 98–99
cocktail, Italian, 56
  orange and, 99
chili
  black bean, 131
  gringo, 270
chilies rellenos, George Willig's, 270–271
chocolate soufflé, 363
chowder
  clam, creamy New England, 264
  swordfish, 266
chutney, mint, 207
clam chowder, creamy New England, 267
clams oreganato, 48
cod, sautéed, tidbits, 223
coconut
  macaroons, 360
  shrimp, 242
coleslaw, creamy, 90
condiments
  basic, 22–25
  chutney, mint, 207
  for hamburgers, 191
  mustards, 343–44
  salt, seasoned, 344
  storing, 30
cookies
  coconut macaroons, 360
  molasses, crisp, 359
  toffee, Helen Abbott's highland, 358–359
corn
  chicken and, soup, Pennsylvania Dutch, 260
  on the cob, 304
  sautéed cream of fresh, 305
Cornish game hens, 161–62
  butterflied with Parmesan cheese and butter crumbs, 171
  butter-roasted, 164–65
  Chinese barbecued, 173
  escabeche, Vera Kock's, 162–63
  fried pieces, 170

poached, with vegetables and creamy horseradish sauce, 169
roast, diet lemon-flavored, 167
roast, Frenchwoman's stuffed with spinach, 168–69
roast with honey glaze, 166
roast, with sherry, 165
roasted almond-coated, 164
tandoori style, 172
cottage cheese dressing, diet, 109
crabmeat
  with Cointreau, 246
  sautéed, with snow pea pods and water chestnuts, 247
crabs, soft-shell, sautéed, 254
cranberry
  and crème fraîche omelet, 81
  dressing, 112
cream cheese
  mushroom and, sandwich with bacon, 276
  orange-flavored, 59
  peach-flavored, 59
  pepper, and red salmon, 58
  pimiento, and bacon spread, 58
cream puff, 365
crème brûlée with fruit, 360
crème fraîche, 342
  buttermilk, 343
  sour cream, 343
Creole shrimp, 242–43
crepes (*see also* pancakes)
  basic, and variations, 284
  broccoli, creamed, and ham filling for, 286
  dessert, 362–63
  fillings for, 285–86
  fried, with honey butter, 62
  fruit preserves, easy, 362
  Grand Marnier, 363
  herb, 284
  with sausage and cheese, 284–85
  with shrimp and mushrooms, 285
  sour cream and red caviar filling for, 286

crepes (*see also* pancakes) (*cont.*)
   tuna and green peas filling for, 285
   tuna, sandwich tort, Maria Urtubey's,
     278–79
   whipped cream and strawberry, 362
crouton(s)
   fried butter, 59
   prosciutto and Parmesan cheese
     omelet, 78
cucumber(s)
   cherry tomato, mushroom and, salad,
     96
   sautéed, and variation, 305–6
   tea sandwiches, English-style, 45
   and yogurt soup, cold, 62
curried (curry)
   artichoke hearts, marinated, in curry
     sauce, 57
   deviled-egg salad, 100
   lamb strips in cream sauce, 206
   lemon mayonnaise, 338
   rice, 312
   tomato sauce, steamed mussels with,
     253
   tuna salad, 104

dates stuffed with pecans and cream
   cheese, 268
desserts
   cakes, 352–54
   crepes, 362–63
   fruit (*see also* names), 346–52
   ice cream and ice, 364–66, 368
   omelet, Cointreau, with fresh
     strawberries, 364
dip (*see* spreads and dips)
dos and don'ts, 39–40
duck, 174
   and orange salad, 100
   roast, glazed, 175
   sliced, bacon and mushroom open-
     faced sandwich, 275

eggdrop soup, pasta and spinach, 261
eggplant and ham tart, 288–89

eggs and egg dishes, 70
   anchovy omelet, Harry Baron's, 289–
     290
   baked eggs in cream, 73
   curried deviled-egg salad, 100
   egg-white omelet, 83
   French toast, 75
   heuvos rancheros, Vance Muse's, 76
   omelet, basic, and variations (*see also*
     omelets), 77–83
   one-egg-yolk omelet, 83
   poached eggs, 72
   quiche Lorraine, and variations (*see
     also* quiche Lorraine), 84–86
   Scotch eggs, Valerie Anderson's, 70–
     71
   scrambled eggs, Cecilia Goodman's
     Sunday, 74
   scrambled eggs, Prince Charles's, 72–
     73
   storing eggs, 30
endive
   and arugula salad, 89
   and pimiento salad, 91
English muffins, fresh, 298
equipment, 18–21
escarole, sautéed and braised, 306–7

fettucine
   buttered, with herbs, 122
   buttered Parmesan, 122
   buttered poppy seed, 122
figs, fresh, with dates and crème fraîche,
   348
fish and seafoods (*see also* names), 222–56
   and chips, 226–27
   chowders, 264, 266
   salads, 101–5
   soups, 264–65
   stock, 335
   storing, 29
   velouté sauce, 336–37
flounder fillet, fried, with sautéed
   almonds, 224–25
fondue, cheese, 293

French toast, 75
frozen foods, storing, 31
fruit (*see also* names)
  appetizers, 45, 52
  Caribbean rum-flavored, 367
  compote, four-fruit, 367
  desserts, 346–52
  preserves crepes, easy, 362
  storing, 29
  sundae, Independence Day, 350–51
fusilli with fresh marinara sauce, 125–126

garlic
  butter, 341
  vinaigrette sauce, 107
garnish
  bread crumbs, sautéed, 61
  onion rings, deep-fried, 310
German hamburger, 194
grapefruit, broiled, with maple syrup, 367–68
Greek salad, 98
green beans
  Cap Cruz, 307
  fresh, with parsley butter, 307
  sautéed, 308
green liquid salad, Melissa Avildsen's, 294–95
green pea(s), fresh
  soup, 63
  risi bisi, 312–13
  tuna and, crepe filling, 285
green pepper
  black beans and, with rice, 296
  and onion pizza, 287
greens, fresh, soup, 64
guacamole, 53–54

haddock, fresh, and rice soup with Parmesan cheese, 264–65
halibut steak, lemon-baked, 226
ham
  and bread stick rolls, 56
  and broccoli, creamed, crepe filling, 286
  caper and anchovy pizza, 288
  chutney and, omelet, 82
  eggplant and, tart, 288–89
  -filled biscuits, 43
  prosciutto, crouton, and Parmesan cheese omelet, 78
  prosciutto, melon cubes wrapped in cheese and, 45
  prosciutto, mozzarella, and basil sandwich, grilled, 276–77
  steak, broiled, with mustard and red currant jelly, 219
hamburger
  avocado and bean sprouts, 192
  bread for, 190–91
  cheeseburger, 190
  condiments for, 191
  crusty, 192–93
  German, 194
  herb, 193
  master recipe, good homemade, 189
  mushroom, 190
  Pablo burger, 191
  pepper, 195
  with sour cream and red caviar, 195
  soy-sauce-and-onion-flavored, 190
  Worcestershire-flavored, 190
herb(s)
  butter, 341
  hamburger, 193
  mustard, 343, 344
  omelet aux fines herbes, 78
  soup, celery and carrot, 262
  -stuffed, veal birds sautéed, 197
  vinaigrette sauce, fresh, 107
  vinaigrette sauce, with dill, 110–11
  vinaigrette with, one pint of, 111
horseradish dressing, creamy, 111
herring in cream sauce with mustard and capers, 56

ice cream
  cherry vanilla, 364–65

ice cream (*cont.*)
  cinnamon, 364
  vanilla, with crème de menthe and
    chocolate morsels, 368
ice, strawberry, 366
Irish stew, 268
Italian vinaigrette sauce, 107

kraut salad, sweet and sour, 96

lamb
  chops, broiled, Susan Angel's, 203
  ground, patty à la Lindstrom, 208
  hash, 209
  kebabs, marinated, 204
  shank, broiled, 205
  steak, broiled, with mint chutney,
    207
  stew, Irish, 268
  strips, curried, in cream sauce, 206
latke, baked potato, Tully Plesser's,
  318–19
leek quiche Lorraine, 85
leftovers, 28–29
lemon
  -baked halibut steak, 226
  -flavored fried chicken breast, 148
  -flavored roast Cornish game hen,
    diet, 167
  and pepper mustard, 343, 344
  vinaigrette sauce, 108
lentil, red, red pepper, and tomato
  soup, 66
lentil soup, and variations, 263
lettuce
  coleslaw, 95
  romaine, and orange salad, 91
lima beans, baby, in cheese and cream
  sauce, 308
lime pies, four individual, 358
linguini primavera, 120
liver, calf's, sautéed, 201
lobster
  boiled, 255

brochette basted with Pernod and
  butter, 256
salad, 101
salad, Caribbean style, 102
low-calorie dishes
  antipasto plate, 294
  Cornish game hen, lemon-flavored,
    167
  cottage cheese dressing, 109
  eggs, 170
  tomato yogurt dressing with mint,
    109

macaroons, coconut, 360
marketing, 26–27
mayonnaise, 110
  curried lemon, 338
  green, 46
  green goddess, 338–39
meal-in-a-drink, Patricia Brill's, 374
measurements, 25–27
meatballs, spicy, 188–89
meat loaf, 187–88
meats (*see also* names)
  beef, 180–96
  lamb, 203–9
  leftovers, using, 29
  pork, 210–18
  storing, 29
  veal, 197–202
melon
  cantaloupe with port, 348
  cubes wrapped in cheese and
    prosciutto, 45
  honeydew, with curried shrimp,
    walnuts, and apples, 52
minestrone, 262–63
molasses cookies, crisp, 359
mold
  mixed vegetable terrine, 51
  tomato, with vegetables and fresh
    basil, 50–51
mozzarella, prosciutto, and basil
  sandwich, grilled, 276–77

mushroom(s)
  brochettes, 309
  cherry tomato, and cucumber salad, 96
  creamed, on fried toast, 48–49
  crepes with shrimp and, 285
  hamburger, 190
  marinated, 57
  pizza, 287
  quiche Lorraine, 86
  sausage and, omelet, 80
  sautéed, 309
mussels
  marinated, 55–56
  sautéed breaded, 252
  steamed, and curried with tomato sauce, 253
mustard
  butter, 229
  herb, 343, 344
  garden-style, 343, 344
  lemon and pepper, 343, 344
  red pepper, 343
  sauce, 53
  vinaigrette sauce, 108

New Orleans shrimp salad, 103
Niçoise salade, 102–3

omelets (*see also* eggs and egg dishes)
  anchovy, Harry Baron's, 289–90
  aux fines herbes, 78
  basic, 77
  caviar, red salmon, sour cream and chives, 82
  cheese and rice, 78
  Cointreau, with fresh strawberries, 364
  cranberry and crème fraîche, 81
  crouton, prosciutto, and Parmesan cheese, 78
  egg-white, 83
  ham and chutney, 82
  mushroom and sausage, 80
  one-egg-yolk, 83

  potatoes, sautéed, and spinach, 82–83
  red salmon caviar, sour cream and chives, 82
  salami, green olives, and onion, 80–81
  shrimp and tomato, 80–81
  Spanish-style ground beef, 79
  vegetables, mixed julienne of, with dill, 80
onion
  and anchovy canapés, 43
  caper and red onion vinaigrette sauce, 107
  cornichon and, vinaigrette sauce, 107
  and green pepper pizza, 287
  rings, deep-fried, 310
  rings, fried, 310
  slices, grilled, 311
  tomato and, fresh hot soup, 64–65
  tomato and red onion salad, 96
orange
  chicken and, salad, 99
  -flavored cream cheese, 59
  romaine lettuce and, salad, 91
Oriental vinaigrette sauce, 100
oyster sandwich, poor boy's, 229

paella-style open rice casserole, 272
pain grillé, 60
pancake(s) (*see also* crepes)
  baked potato latke, Tully Plesser's, 318–19
  Dutch apple, 290–91
  potato, sautéed, with cauliflower purée, 320
panninis, fresh tomato and basil, Cristin Torbert's, 273–74
papaya and blueberries, fresh, parfait of, 347
pasta
  cooking, 114–15
  fettucine, buttered, with herbs, and variations, 122
  fettucine with ground veal, proscuitto, and cream sauce, 121

pasta (*cont.*)
   fusilli with fresh marinara sauce, 125–126
   linquini primavera, 120
   quick, Constance M. Madina's, with Sicilian-style tomato sauce, 124–25
   rigatoni with sardines, tomatoes, and basil, 126
   spaghetti, Bursa, 118
   spaghetti with butter, 116
   spaghetti carbonara, 117
   spaghetti with leek, fresh, and Parmesan cheese, 116–17
   spaghetti puttanesca, 119
   spaghetti with Roquefort, Madame Clair's, 115–16
   and spinach eggdrop soup, 261
   vermicelli with anchovy, tomato, and onion sauce, 122–23
   ziti, baked, with sausage, 126
pastries
   apple tart, square, with instant puff pastry, Martin Rapp's, and variation, 356
   cream puff, 365
   lime pies, four individual, 358
   strawberry tart, fresh, 356–57
pâté, chicken liver, 44
peach(es)
   cobbler, 355
   Elizabeth Ann McGinn's Georgia, 346–47
   -flavored cream cheese, 59
   waffle cake, and variation, 352–53
pear
   fresh, with creamy Gorgonzola, 352
   poached, with cranberry and apricot sauce, 357
   pies, lime, four individual, 358
pimiento
   endive and, salad, 91
   cheese and bacon spread, 58
pineapple meringue cake, 354
pizza, homemade, 386–87
   cheese, basic, 287

   ham, caper, and anchovy, 288
   mushroom, 287
   onion and green pepper, 287
   sausage, 288
plantains, Cuban fried, 311
pork (*see also* ham; pork chops)
   gingered, Sabine Sugarman's, 210
   roast, boneless, 211
   spareribs, barbecued, 218
pork chops
   Alsatian, 212
   baked, pizzaola, 217
   oven-baked, 213
   sautéed, with red currant sweet and sour sauce, 216
   smoked, 215
   thick, braised in red wine, 214
potato(es)
   baked, Elouise A. Hetherly's discovery, 323–24
   baked, with sour cream and red caviar, 324
   baked, stuffed, 322
   boiled, with parsley, 321
   chips, fresh, 327
   fried, crisp individual, Roesti, 320–321
   fried, in their jackets, 325
   latke, Tully Plesser's baked potato, 318–19
   Lyonnaise, with bacon garnish, 326
   mashed, with mushrooms and onions, 325
   omelet, spinach and sautéed potato, 82–83
   pancakes, sautéed, with cauliflower purée, 320
   à la Parisienne, 322
   roasted, 321
   salad, *see* Potato salad
   sautéed, with garlic, 327
   sweet, mashed, with rum, 328
   yams baked, 329
   yams, à la St. Thomas, 329

potato salad
  carrot and, 94–95
  fresh, with sour cream, 328
pot pie, chicken, with instant puff
    pastry, 136–37
poultry (*see also* names)
  chicken, 134–61
  Cornish game hens, 161–73
  duck, 174–75
  salads, 98–100
  storing, 30
  turkey breast, 176–77
prosciutto, *see* ham
puddings
  bread pudding, whole wheat, with
    blueberries, 361
  chocolate soufflé, 363
  crème brûlée with fruit, 360

quiche Lorraine, 84–85
  leek, 85
  mushroom, 86
  salmon and dill, 86
  sausage, 85
  spinach, 86

raspberry fool, 366
red pepper
  mustard, 343
  red lentil, and tomato soup, 66
  zucchini and, sauté, 315
rice
  arancini, 283
  casserole, paella-style open, 272
  cheese and, omelet, 78
  curried, 312
  fried, with shrimp, 282
  and mint salad, tomato stuffed with,
    97
  risi bisi, 312–13
  risotto primavera, 235
  salad, 100–1
  wild, sautéed, 313
rigatoni with sardines, tomatoes and
    basil, 126

romaine lettuce and orange salad, 91
Roquefort vinaigrette sauce, 108
Russian dressing, 108–9

salad dressings
  cottage cheese, diet, 109
  horseradish, creamy, 111
  mayonnaise (*see also* mayonnaise), 110
  Russian, 108
  tomato yogurt, with mint, low-
    calorie, 109
  vinaigrette, basic, and variations (*see
    also* vinaigrette), 107–8
  vinaigrette, herb, with dill, 110–11
  vinaigrette, herb, one pint of, 111
  vinaigrette, onion, 108
  vinaigrette, safflower, 93
Salade Niçoise, 102–3
salads
  beef, 105
  egg, 100
  fish and seafood, 101–5
  poultry, 98–100
  rice, 97, 100–1
  salade Niçoise, 102–3
  tossed and mixed green, 88–93
  vegetable, 94–98
salami omelet, 81
salmon
  and dill quiche Lorraine, 86
  patties, 230
  sauce for poached chicken breast, 139
  steak with mustard butter, 229
salt, seasoned, 344
sandwich
  avocado grilled cheese, 275
  Caesar salad, 274
  cream cheese and mushroom, with
    bacon, 276
  cucumber tea, English-style, 45
  duck, sliced, bacon, and mushroom,
    open-faced, 275
  hero, Nero's, 280
  Mozzarella, prosciutto, and basil,
    grilled, 276–77

sandwich (*cont.*)
  poor boy, 279
  panninis, fresh tomato and basil,
    Cristin Torbert's, 273–74
  roast beef and watercress croissant,
    277
  sole fillet, goujonnettes of, and
    variations, 281
  steak, sliced, 278
  tuna crepe tort, Maria Urtubey's,
    278–79
sardines
  with red onion rings and bacon, 56
  rigatoni with tomatoes, basil and,
    126
sauces, hot and cold
  apricot, 339
  Béarnaise, 338
  Béchamel, 336
  buttermilk crème fraîche, 343
  crème fraîche, 342–43
  curried lemon mayonnaise, 338
  dill cream, 340
  fish velouté, 181
  green herb, quick, 181
  green goddess mayonnaise, 338–39
  green mayonnaise, 46
  Gribiche, 105
  Hollandaise, 337
  marinara, 125
  mornay, 336
  mustard, 53
  peanut, 138
  salmon, 139
  sour cream crème fraîche, 343
  sour cream, herbed pepper, 47
  tartar, creamy, 339
  velouté, 336–37
sausage
  and cheese, crepes with, 284-85
  pizza, 288
  quiche Lorraine, 85
  tiny smoked, sautéed, with mustard,
    50
  zita, baked with, 126

scallops, bay
  sautéed, in cream sauce, 250
  sautéed, with lemon butter, 251
  Sebonac, 248–49
  and shrimp with rice, Marian Faux's,
    247–48
seafoods (*see* fish and seafoods; names)
Senegalese soup, 67
serving suggestions, 31–32
shellfish (*see* fish and seafoods; names)
shrimp
  with black beans, 244
  with bok choy, snow pea pods, and
    water chestnuts, 244–45
  coconut, 242
  Creole, 242–43
  crepes with, and mushrooms, 283
  curly, with lemon caper sauce, 49
  fried in beer batter, 241
  fried rice with, 282
  Mario, 240
  meunière, 239
  risotto, and variation, 234–35
  salad, New Orleans, 103
  and scallops, with rice, Marian
    Faux's, 247–48
  scampi, 238
  six-minute, in Marsala and butter
    sauce, 234
  tart, 237
  with tomato and lemon sauce and
    rice, 236
  and tomato omelet, 80–81
  wrapped with snow pea pods, 50
snapper baked in foil, Betty Pappas's,
  224
sole
  amandine, 228
  goujonettes of, sandwich, 281
spaghetti
  Bursa, 118
  with butter, 116
  carbonara, 117
  with leek, fresh, and Parmesan
    cheese, 116–17

puttanesca, 119
with Roquefort, Madame Clair's,
115–16
soufflé, chocolate, 363
soups
cold cucumber and yogurt, 62
hearty, 65, 130, 258–66
hot and sour, Andrew Bergman's,
258–59
sour cream
and black lumpfish caviar, brioche
filled with, 56–57
herbed pepper sauce, 47
potato salad, fresh, with, 328
and red caviar, baked potato with,
324
and red caviar crepe filling, 286
and red caviar, hamburger with, 195
red salmon caviar, and chives omelet,
82
spinach
fresh cooked, 314
and pasta eggdrop soup, 261
potatoes, sautéed, and spinach
omelet, 82–83
quiche Lorraine, 86
salad and strawberry yogurt
luncheon, Suzanne Evans Levi's,
92–93
salad, fresh, 91, 93
spreads and dips
dill cream sauce, 340
orange-flavored, 59
peach-flavored, 59
pepper and red salmon caviar,
58
pimiento and bacon, 58
stew
Irish, 268
beef, 267
stock
beef, 334
beef broth, canned, enriched one-
hour, 334–35
chicken, 332–33

chicken broth, canned, enriched one-
hour, 333
fish, 335
storing foods, 29–31
strawberry (strawberries)
butter, and variation, 342
fresh, with crème fraîche and brown
sugar, 350
ice, 366
tart, fresh, 356–57
striped bass soup, quick, 265
supplies, basic, 22–25
sweet and sour
chicken, Sheilah Rae Gross's, 154–55
kraut salad, 96
sweet potato, mashed, with rum, 328
swordfish
baked, with lemon broth and bacon,
233
chowder, 266

tabouleh, 291
tart(s)
dessert, *see* pastries
eggplant and ham, 288–89
shrimp, 237
tartar sauce, creamy, 339
temperatures
conversions, 39
oven, 39
terms, important, 32–38
tips on cooking, 27–28
toffee, Helen Abbott's highland, 358–59
terrine, mixed vegetable, 51
tomato(es)
and basil salad, Ross McClennan's, 92
cherry tomato, mushroom, and
cucumber salad, 96
cherry tomatoes, sautéed, 314
fresh, how to peel and seed, 54
mold with vegetables and fresh basil,
50
onion and, soup, fresh hot, 64–65
and red onion salad, 96

tomato(es) (*cont.*)
red lentil, red pepper and, soup, 66
shrimp and omelet, 80–81
stuffed with rice and mint salad, 97
zucchini and, 315
tortilla dinner, and variation, Sandra
Stewart's, 292
trout
poached, with cream sauce, 231
sautéed fillets, with lemon caper
sauce, 230–31
tuna
crepe sandwich tort, Maria
Urtubey's, 278–79
curried, salad, 104
and cheese salad, 103–4
curried, salad, 104
and green peas, crepe filling, 285
potted, 232
salad, with sauce Gribiche, 104–5
turkey breast, roast, with mushroom
and herb stuffing, 176–77

veal
birds, sautéed, herb-stuffed, 197
chop, sautéed, with mushrooms and
cream, 200
Marsala, 199
strips, sautéed, with lemon and
tarragon, 198
wiener schnitzel à la Holstein,
202
vegetables (*see also* names), 300–16
fresh crisp, with green mayonnaise,
46
marinated fresh, salad, 94–98
mixed, terrine, 51
risotto primavera, 235
stir-fried fresh, 314
storing, 29
vermicelli with anchovy, tomato, and
onion sauce, 122–23

vinaigrette
asparagus, cold, 301
beef, cold, 105
vinaigrette sauce, 107
anchovy, 107
blue cheese, 107
caper and red onion, 107
cornichon and onion, 107
garlic, 107
herb, fresh, 107
herb, with dill, 110–11
with herbs, one pint of, 111
Italian, 107
lemon, 108
mustard, 108
onion, 108
Oriental, 108
Roquefort, 108

Wiener schnitzel à la Holstein, 202

yams
baked, 329
à la St. Thomas, 329
yogurt
ayran, and variations, 375
dressing, tomato with mint, low-
calorie, 109
with golden raisins, fresh fruit, and
honey, 349
luncheon, spinach salad and
strawberry, Suzanne Evans Levi's,
92–93
meal-in-a-drink, 374
soup, cold cucumber and, 62
strawberry, 93

zabaglione, 362
ziti, baked, with sausage, 126
zucchini, 316
cake, and variation, 353–54
and red pepper sauté, 315
and tomatoes, 315